Abortion Bibliography
for 1975

Abortion Bibliography

for 1975

Compiled by

Mary K. Floyd

Whitston Publishing Company
Incorporated
Troy, New York
1976

PREFACE

ABORTION BIBLIOGRAPHY for 1975 is the fifth
annual list of books and articles surrounding the subject of abortion in the preceeding year. It appears
serially each fall as a contribution toward documenting
in one place as comprehensively as possible the literature of one of our central social issues. It is an attempt
at a comprehensive world bibliography.

Searches in compiling this material have covered the
following sources: ART INDEX; APPLIED SCIENCE AND
TECHNOLOGY INDEX; BIBLIOGRAPHIC INDEX; BIO-
LOGICAL ABSTRACTS; BOOKS IN PRINT; BRITISH
BOOKS IN PRINT; BRITISH HUMANITIES INDEX; BUS-
INESS PERIODICALS INDEX; CANADIAN PERIODICAL
INDEX; CATHOLIC PERIODICALS AND LITERATURE IN-
DEX; CUMULATIVE BOOK INDEX; CURRENT INDEX TO
JOURNALS IN EDUCATION; CURRENT LITERATURE OF
VENEREAL DISEASE; EDUCATION INDEX; GUIDE TO
SOCIAL SCIENCE AND RELIGION IN PERIODICAL LIT-
ERATURE; HOSPITAL LITERATURE INDEX; HUMANI-
TIES INDEX; INDEX TO LEGAL PERIODICALS; INDEX
MEDICUS; INDEX TO PERIODICAL ARTICLES RELATED
TO LAW; INDEX TO RELIGIOUS PERIODICAL LITERA-
TURE; INTERNATIONAL NURSING INDEX; LIBRARY OF
CONGRESS CATALOG: BOOKS: SUBJECTS; NURSING
LITERATURE INDEX; PHILOSOPHERS INDEX: PUBLIC
AFFAIRS INFORMATION SERVICE; READERS GUIDE TO
PERIODICAL LITERATURE; SOCIAL SCIENCES INDEX;
WHITAKER'S CUMULATIVE BOOK INDEX.

The bibliography is divided into two sections: a title

section in alphabetical order; and a subject section. Thus, if the researcher does not wish to observe the subject heads of the compiler, he can use the title section exclusively. The 208 subject heads have been allowed to issue from the nature of the material indexed rather than being imposed from Library of Congress subject heads of other standard lists.

Countries are listed alphabetically under subjects: "Abortion: Africa," etc.; with states listed alphabetically under "Abortion: United States:" Arkansas, California, etc.; and drugs are listed under the specific drug involved.

Mary K. Floyd
Troy, New York
June, 1976

LIST OF PERIODICALS

Acta Anaesthesiologica Scandinavica. Supplement
Acta Chirurgica Academiae Scientiarum Hungaricae
Acta Europaea Fertilitatis
Acta Obstetricia et Gynecologica Scandinavica
Acta Obstetricia et Gynecologica Scandinavica. Supplement
Acta Psychiatrica Scandinavica. Supplement
Advances in Experimental Medicine and Biology
Akron Law Review
Akusherstvo i Ginekologiia (Moscow)
Akusherstvo i Ginekologiia (Sofiia)
Albany Law Review
America
American Ecclesiastical Review
American Journal of Epidemiology
American Journal of Nursing
American Journal of Obstetrics and Gynecology
American Journal of Orthopsychiatry
American Journal of Psychiatry
American Journal of Psychoanalysis
American Journal of Public Health
American Journal of Public Health and the Nation's Health
American Journal of Veterinary Research
American Legion Magazine
American Medical Association News
American Statistical Association Journals
Anaesthesist
Analysis
Anesthesiology
Annales Chirurgiae et Gynaecologiae Fenniae
Annali di Ostetricia, Ginecologia, Medicina Perinatale
Antibiotiki
Archiv fur Gynaekologie
Archives des Maladies du Coeur et des Vaisseaux
Archives of Pathology

Archives of Surgery
Archives of Virology
Archivio di Ostetricia et Ginecologia
Archivos de la Fundacion Roux-Ocefa
Arquivos de Instituto Biologico
Ateneo Parmense; Sezione I: Acta Bio-Medica
Atlantic
Australian Veterinary Journal

Basic Life Sciences
Baylor Law Review
Berliner und Munchener Tierarztliche Wochenschrift
Bible Today
Boletin Medico del Hospital Infantil de Mexico
Bratislauske Lekarske Listy
British Journal of Anaesthesia
British Journal of Clinical Practice
British Journal of Experimental Pathology
British Journal of Obstetrics and Gynaecology
British Journal of Psychiatry
British Medical Journal
British Veterinary Journal
Broadcasting
Brooklyn Law Review
Bruxelles Medical

C.I.C.I.A.M.S. Nouvelles; Bulletin d'Information du
    Comite International Catholique des Infiamieres et
    Assistants Medico-Sociales
Les Cahiers de Droit
Cahiers de Medecine
Canadian Forum
Canadian Dimension
Canadian Journal of Comparative Medicine
Canadian Journal of Public Health
Canadian Medical Association Journal
Catholic Hospital
Catholic Lawyer
Catholic Mind
Ceskoslovenska Gynekologie

Christian Century
Christian Herald
Christian Home
Christianity Today
Chronobiologia
Clergy Review
Clinical Genetics
Columbia
Commonweal
Comptes Rendus des Seances de la Societe de Biologie
  et de ses Foliales
Congressional Quarterly Service: Weekly Report
Connecticut Medicine
Current Medical Research and Opinion
Cytogentics and Cell Genetics

Daily Telegraph
Dalhousie Law Journal
Demography
Deutsch Medizinsche Wochenschrift
Deutsche Tieraerztliche Wochenschrift
Dimensions in Health Service
La Documentation Catholique
Duodecim
Duquensne Law Review

Economist
Editor and Publisher--The Fourth Estate
Ethics
Etudes

Family Coordinator
Family Planning Perspectives
Far Eastern Economic Review
Fel'dsker i Akusherka
Fertility and Sterility
Folia Clinica Internacional
Folia Endocrinologica Japonica
Fordham Law Review
Fortschritte du Medizin

Gaceta Medica de Mexico
Gallup Opinion Index
Geburtshilfe und Frauenheilkunde
Ginekologia Polaska
Ginecologia y Obstetricia de Mexico
Godisen Zbornik na Medicinskiot Fakultet vo Skopje
Guardian
Gynaekologische Rundschau

Haematologia
Harefauh
Harvard Civil Rights - Civil Liberties Law Review
Hastings Center Report
Health Bulletin (Edinburgh)
Health Care Dimensions
Health Visitor
Herald of Holiness
Hereditas
Hippokrates
Homiletic and Pastoral Review
Hospital Formulary Management
Hospital Law
Hospital Practice
Hospital Progress
Hospitals
Human Biology
Humangenetik
Humanist

Illinois Medical Journal
Indian Journal of Experimental Biology
International Journal of Epidemiology
International Journal of Fertility
International Philosophical Quarterly
Intervirology
Irish Medical Journal

JOGN Nursing
Jamaican Nurse
Japanese Journal for the Midwife

Journal for the Scientific Study of Religion
Journal of the American Medical Association
Journal of the American Veterinary Medical Association
Journal of Biosocial Science
Journal of Counceling Psychology
Journal of Clinical and Laboratory Investigation
Journal of Endocrinology
Journal of Family Law
Journal of Family Practice
Journal of Health and Social Behavior
Journal of the Indian Medical Association
Journal of the Kentucky Medical Association
Journal of Legal Medicine
Journal of the Louisiana State Medical Society
Journal of Medical Genetics
Journal of the Mississippi State Medical Association
Journal of Nuclear Medicine
Journal of Obstetrics and Gynaecology of the British Common-
    wealth
Journal of Postgraduate Medicine
Journal of Practical Nursing
Journal of Reproductive Fertility
Journal of Reproductive Medicine
Journal of the South African Veterinary Association
Journal of Urban Law
Journal of Youth and Adolescence

Katilolehti

Laboratory Animal Science
Lakartidningen
Lancet
Linacre Quarterly
Link
Liguorian
Loyola University of Chicago Law Journal
Lutheran

Mademoiselle
Maroc Medical

Maryland State Medical Journal
McCalls
Medical Care
Medical Journal of Australia
Medical Service
Medical Times
Medical Trial Technique Quarterly
Medical World News
Medicine, Science and Law
Medicinski Arhiv
Medizinische Klinik
Medizinische Welt
Memphis State University Law Review
Midwife and Health Visitor
Minerva Ginecologia
Minerva Nefrologica
Minerva Pediatrica
Modern Law Review
Modern Veterinary Practice
Ms Magazine
Muenchener Medizinische Wochenschrift

Nation
National Catholic Reporter
National Institute of Animal Health Quarterly
National Review
Nature
Nederlands Tijdschrift voor Geneeskunde
New England Journal of Medicine
New Humanist
New Law Journal
New Republic
New Society
New Statesman
New York State Journal of Medicine
New Zealand Law Journal
New Zealand Medical Journal
New Zealand Veterinary Journal
Newsweek
Nigerian Nurse

Nordisk Medicin
Nordisk Veterinaer Medicin
North Carolina Central Law Journal
Notre Dame Lawyer
Nouvelle Presse Medicale
Nouvelle Revue Theologique
Nuclear-Medizin
Nursing
Nursing Forum
Nursing Mirror and Midwives' Journal
Nursing Times
Nursing Update

Observer
Obstetrical and Gynecological Survey
Obstetrics and Gynecology
Oeffentliche Gesundheitswesen
Orvosi Hetilap
L'Osservatore Romano
Our Sunday Visitor

Pediatrics
Pediatriia Akusherstvo i Ginekologiia
The Philosophical Forum
Philosophy and Public Affairs
Polski Tygodnik Lekarski
Population Studies
Praxis
Presbyterian Journal
Priest
Proceedings of the Royal Society of Medicine
Proceedings of the United States Animal Health Association
Prostaglandins
Psychiatria et Neurologia Japonica
Psychological Reports

RN; National Magazine for Nurses
Reproduccion
Research in Veterinary Science
Revista Chilena de Obstetricia y Ginecologia

Revista Clinica Espanola
Revista del Colegio de Abadagos de Puerto Rico
Revue d'Elevage et de Medecine Veterinaire des Pays
  Tropicaux
Revue Medicale de Liege
The Royal College of General Practitioners

Scandinavian Journal of Haematology
Scandinavin Journal of Clinical and Laboratory Investigation
School Counselor
School Press Review
Schweizer Archiv fur Tierheilkunde
Schweizerische Medizinische Wochenschrift
Schwestern Revue
Science
Scientific American
Semaine des Hopitaux de Paris
Seventeen
Social Biology
Social Justice Review
Social Theology and Practice
South African Medical Journal
South Dakota Law Review
Southern Medical Journal
Soviet Genetics
Sovetskaia Meditsina
Spectator
Srpski Arhiv za Celojupno Lekarstvo
St. Anthony Messenger
Studies in Family Planning
Suffolk University Law Review
Sunday Times
Supervisor Nurse
Supreme Court Review
Sygeplejersken
Sykepleien

Tablet
Teratology; Journal of Abnormal Development
Texas Hospitals

Texas Medicine
Texas Reports on Biology and Medicine
Texas Tech Law Review
Theological Studies
Theology Today
Therapia Hungarica
Thomist
Time
Time Canada
Times
Transplantation
Triumph
Tunisie Medicale

UMKC Law Review
Ugeskrift for Laeger
Union Medicale du Canada
University of Michigan Journal of Law Reform
Urologiia i Neferologiia
U. S. Catholic
U. S. News and World Report

Valparaiso University Law Review
Veterinariia
Veterinaro-Meditsinski
Veterinary Recard
Vital Christianity
Voprosy Okhrany Materinstva i Detstva
Voprosy Virusologii
Vrachobnoe Delo

Washington University Law Quarterly
Wayne Law Review
West Indian Medical Journal
West Virginia Medical Journal
Western Journal of Medicine
Western Ontario Law Review
Wiadomasci Lekarskie

Zeitschrift fur Geburtschilfe und Perinatologie

Zentralblatt fuer Veterinaermedizine. Journal of
   Veterinary Medicine
Zentralblatt fur Arbeitsmedizin und Arbeitsschutz
Zentralblatt fur Gynaekologie
Zhurnal Eksperimental'noi i Klinicheskoi Meditsiny

SUBJECT HEADINGS USED IN THIS BIBLIOGRAPHY

Abnormalities
Abortion (General)
Abortion Act
Abortion: Austria
Abortion: Belgium
Abortion: Canada
Abortion: Caroline Islands
Abortion: Chile
Abortion: China
Abortion: Cuba
Abortion: Czechoslovakia
Abortion: Denmark
Abortion: England
Abortion: Finland
Abortion: France
Abortion: Germany
Abortion: Hungary
Abortion: India
Abortion: Italy
Abortion: Jamaica
Abortion: Japan
Abortion: Mexico
Abortion: Netherlands
Abortion: New Zealand
Abortion: Nigeria
Abortion: Norway
Abortion: Pakistan
Abortion: Poland
Abortion: Puerto Rico
Abortion: Rhodesia
Abortion: Romania
Abortion: Singapore
Abortion: Sweden
Abortion: Thailand

Abortion: Uganda
Abortion: United Kingdom
Abortion: United States
Arkansas
California
Chicago
Cincinnati
Colorado
Connecticut
Florida
Georgia
Hawaii
Illinois
Iowa
Louisiana
Maryland
Massachusetts
Michigan
Minnesota
Mississippi
Missouri
Montana
Nebraska
New Jersey
New York
North Carolina
Oklahoma
Oregon
Pennsylvania
Rhode Island
South Dakota
Tennessee
Texas
Wisconsin

Abortion: USSR
Abortion: Yugoslavia
Adoption
Alupent
American College of Ob-
    stetricians and Gynecol-
    ogists
American Hospital Asso-
    ciation
American Public Health
    Association
Amoglandin
Amoxicillin
Anestheisa
Antibodies
Arachidonic Acid
Artificial Abortion
Aspirin

Behavior
Bibliography
Birth Control
Blood

Candidiasis
Cardiovascular System
Cephalothin
Cervical Incompetence
    and Insufficiency
Chlormadinone
Clinical Aspects
Clomiphene
College Women
Complications
Contraception
Criminal Abortion

Demography
Diagnosis
Diazepam

Diethylstilbestrol
Dinoprost Thomethamine
Doxicillin
Drug Therapy

Education
Endotoxin
Epsilon-Aminocaproic
Estradiol
Ethyl Alcohol
Euthanasia

Family Planning
Faustan
Fees and Public Assistance
Fertility
Fetus
Flavoxate
Flumethasone

Genetics
Gentamicin Garamycin
Gestanon
Gonorrhea
Gynecology
Gynesthesin

Habitual Abortion
Hemorrhage
Heparin
History
Hormones
Hospitals

Immunity
Induced Abortion
Indomethacin
Infanticide
Infection
Isoptin

Isoxsuprine

Law Enforcement
Laws and Legislation
Listeriosis

Male Attitudes
March of Dimes
Mefenamic Acid
Menstruation
Mentally Retarded
Microbiology
Miscarriages
Morbidity
Mortality
Mycoplasma

NAL
NCCB
Naphthalene
Neonatal
Neuraminidase
Nurses
Nursing Homes

Obstetrics
Orciprenaline
Outpatient Abortion
Oxytocin

Paramedics
Parsley Extract
Patient Counseling
Pentazocine
Pharmacists
Physicians
Population
Potassium Ampicillin
Pregnancy Interruption
Progesterone

Prostaglandins
Psychology
Public Health

Radiologists
Referral Agencies Services
Regitine
Religion and Ethics
Research
Respiratory System
Rifampicin
Rivanol
Rubella

Sepsis
Septic Abortion and Septic
    Shock
Sociology and Behavior
Sodium Chloride
S.P.U.C.
Spontaneous Abortion
Statistics
Sterility
Sterilization
Stilbestrol
Students
Surgical Treatment and
    Management
Surveys
Symposia
Syntocinon

Techniques of Abortion
Tetracycline
Th 1165 a
Therapeutic Abortion
Threatened Abortion
Toxoplasmas
Triploidy
Transplacental Hemorrhage

Turinal

Veterinary Abortions

Youth

TABLE OF CONTENTS

Preface.................................. i

List of Periodicals....................... iii

Subject Headings Used in this Bibliography.... xiii

Books.................................... 1

Periodical Literature:
    Title Index............................ 5
    Subject Index.......................... 102

Author Index............................. 286

BOOKS

ABORTION ACT INQUIRY: SUMMARY OF CONCLUSIONS; SOME OF ITS FINDINGS; LIST OF RECOMMENDATIONS. London: Abortion Law Reform Association, 1974.

ABORTION, PROCURED, DECLARATION BY THE SACRED CONGREGATION ON THE DOCTRINE OF THE FAITH ON: "LET ME LIVE". London: Catholic Truth Society, 1975.

Bolognese, R. J., et al. INTERRUPTION OF PREGNANCY. Baltimore, Maryland: The Williams & Wilkins Company, 1975.

Brody, Baruch A. ABORTION & THE SANCTITY OF HUMAN LIFE: A PHILOSOPHICAL VIEW. Cambridge, Massachusetts: The M. I. T. Press, 1975.

California Committee On Therapeutic Abortion. ABORTION & THE UNWANTED CHILD. New York: Springer Publishing Company, Inc., 1971.

David, H. P., editor. ABORTION RESEARCH: INTERNATIONAL EXPERIENCE. Lexington, Massachusetts: D. C. Heath & Company, 1974.

David, Henry P., et al, editors. ABORTION IN PSYCHOSOCIAL PERSPECTIVE: TRENDS IN TRANSNATIONAL RESEARCH. Lexington, Massachusetts: D. C. Heath & Company, 1975.

De Danois, Vivian. ABORTION & THE MORAL DEGENERA-

TION OF THE AMERICAN MEDICAL PROFESSION.
American Classical College Press, 1975.

Devereux, George. A STUDY OF ABORTION IN PRIMI-
TIVE SOCIETIES. New York: International Univer-
sities Press, 1975.

Eastman, L. E. ABORTIVE REVOLUTION: CHINA
UNDER NATIONALIST RULE, 1927-37. Cambridge,
Massachusetts: Harvard University Press, 1975.

Faulkner, Lloyd C., editor. ABORTION DISEASES OF
LIVESTOCK. Springfield, Illinois: Charles C. Thomas,
1968.

Finnis, John, et al. THE RIGHTS & WRONGS OF ABOR-
TION. (Philosophy & Public Affairs Reader Ser.).
Princeton, New Jersey: Princeton University Press,
1974.

Fleming, Alice. CONTRACEPTION, ABORTION, PREG-
NANCY. Chicago, Illinois: Nelson-Hall Company,
1974.

Floyd, Mary K., compiler. ABORTION BIBLIOGRAPHY
FOR 1973. Troy, New York: Whitston Publishing
Company, 1974.

--ABORTION BIBLIOGRAPHY FOR 1974. Troy, New
York: Whitston Publishing Company, 1974.

Gardner, R. F., editor. ABORTION: THE PERSONAL
DILEMMA. Grand Rapids, Michigan: William B.
Eerdmans Publishing Company, 1972.

Great Britain. Office of Population Censuses and Surveys.
THE REGISTRAR GENERAL'S STATISTICAL REVIEW
OF ENGLAND AND WALES FOR THE YEAR 1973:
SUPPLEMENT ON ABORTION. London: Pendragon
Press, 1973.

Hardin, Garrett. MANDATORY MOTHERHOOD: THE TRUE MEANING OF "RIGHT TO LIFE". Boston, Massachusetts: Beacon Press, 1974.

Harris, Harry. PRENATAL DIAGNOSIS & SELECTIVE ABORTION. Cambridge, Massachusetts: Harvard University Press, 1975.

International Planned Parenthood Federation Conference, 1971, Beirut, editor. INDUCED ABORTION: A HAZARD TO PUBLIC HEALTH? New York: International Publications Service, 1971.

Kluge, Eike-Henner W. THE PRACTICE OF DEATH. New Haven, Connecticut: Yale University Press, 1975.

Kohl, Marvin. THE MORALITY OF KILLING: EUTHANASIA, ABORTION & TRANSPLANTS. New York: Humanities Press, Inc., 1974.

Luker, Kristin. TAKING CHANCES: ABORTION & THE DECISION NOT TO CONTRACEPT. Berkeley, California: University of California Press, 1975.

Mankekar, Kamia. ABORTION: A SOCIAL DILEMMA. New York: International Scholastic Book Service, 1974.

Mauriceau, A. M. THE MARRIED WOMAN'S PRIVATE MEDICAL COMPANION. New York: Arno Press, Inc., 1974.

McCormick, E. Patricia. ATTITUDES TOWARD ABORTION. Lexington, Massachusetts: D. C. Heath & Company, 1975.

McEllhenney, John G. CUTTING THE MONKEY-ROPE: IS THE TAKING OF LIFE EVER JUSTIFIED. Valley Forge, Pennsylvania: Judson Press, 1973.

Perkins, B. B. ADOLESCENT BIRTH PLANNING AND

SEXUALITY. Child Welfare League of America, 1974.

Sloane, Bruce R., editor. ABORTION: CHANGING VIEWS & PRACTICE. New York: Grune & Stratton, Inc., 1971.

Storer, Horatio R., et al. CRIMINAL ABORTION. (Sex, Marriage & Society). New York: Arno Press, Inc., 1974.

Van Der Tak. ABORTION, FERTILITY & CHANGING LEGISLATION. Lexington, Massachusetts: D. C. Heath & Company, 1974.

PERIODICAL LITERATURE

TITLE INDEX

"Abdominal fetus following induced abortion," by E. M. Silverman, et al. AMERICAN JOURNAL OF OBSTETRICS AND GYNECOLOGY 122(6):791-792, July 15, 1975.

"Abortifacient from the land of the prostaglandins," by J. A. Owen, Jr. HOSPITAL FORMULARY MANAGEMENT 10:407 plus, August, 1975.

"Abortion." JOURNAL OF THE AMERICAN MEDICAL ASSOCATION 231(6):569-701, February 10, 1975.

"Abortion." NEW ZEALAND MEDICAL JOURNAL 81(531):31-32, January 8, 1975.

"Abortion," by H. P. Dunn. NEW ZEALAND MEDICAL JOURNAL 80(527):410, November 13, 1974.

"Abortion," by J. S. Gemming, et al. NEW ZEALAND MEDICAL JOURNAL 80(524):271, September 25, 1974.

"Abortion," by D. A. Introcaso. OBSTETRICS AND GYNECOLOGY 45(2):234-235, February, 1975.

"Abortion," by A. Wenkart. AMERICAN JOURNAL OF PSYCHOANALYSIS 34(2):161, Spring, 1974.

"Abortion ad is protected by First amendment, high court says." BROADCASTING 88:41, June 23, 1975.

"Abortion advocates using false statistics." OUR SUNDAY
   VISITOR 63:3, April 27, 1975.

"Abortion (amendment) bill." BRITISH MEDICAL JOUR-
   NAL 2(5970):558-559, June 7, 1975.

"Abortion (amendment) bill." BRITISH MEDICAL JOUR-
   NAL 2(5972):686-687, June 21, 1975.

"Abortion (amendment) bill." BRITISH MEDICAL JOUR-
   NAL 2(5973):748, June 28, 1975.

"Abortion (amendment) bill." BRITISH MEDICAL JOUR-
   NAL 3(5975):99, July 12, 1975.

"Abortion (amendment) bill." BRITISH MEDICAL JOUR-
   NAL 3(5976):160, July 19, 1975.

"Abortion (amendment) bill," by H. C. McLaren. BRITISH
   MEDICAL JOURNAL 2(5971):613, June 14, 1975.

"Abortion and the conscience clause: current status," by
   D. J. Horan. CATHOLIC LAWYER 20:289-302,
   Autumn, 1974.

"Abortion & Dr. Edelin: miscarriage of justice," by
   N. Lewin. NEW REPUBLIC 172:16-19, March 1, 1975;
   Discussion 172:30-33, April 5, 1975.

"Abortion and family planning in the Soviet Union: public
   policies and private behaviour," by H. P. David.
   JOURNAL OF BIOSOCIAL SCIENCE 6(4):417-426,
   October, 1974.

"Abortion and the golden rule," by R. M. Hare. PHIL-
   OSOPHY AND PUBLIC AFFAIRS 4:201-222, Spring,
   1975.

"Abortion and the law," by D. M. Alpern. NEWSWEEK
   85:18 plus, March 3, 1975.

"Abortion and the Law for Protection of the Mother—also discussion of the decision of the National Labor-Court of 16.2.1973," by H. Marburger. OEFFENTLICHE GESUNDHEITSWESEN 37(1):37-43, January, 1975.

"Abortion and the law; implications of K. C. Edelin's conviction for manslaughter in Boston abortion trial," by D. M. Alpern. NEWSWEEK 85:18-19 plus, March 3, 1975.

"Abortion and law on abortion," by G. Oggioni, Bp. L'OSSERUATORE ROMANO 15(367):5 plus, April 10, 1975.

"Abortion and the law on abortion; document of the Permanent Council of the Italian Episcopal Conference." L'OSSERUATORE ROMANO 9(361):4-5, February 27, 1975.

"Abortion and legislation," by T. Monreal. REVISTA CHILENA DE OBSTETRICIA Y GINECOLOGIA 38(2): 76-83, 1973.

"Abortion and manslaughter; a Boston doctor goes on trial," by B. J. Culliton. SCIENCE 187:334-335, January 31, 1975.

"Abortion and money." LANCET 2(7928):315, August 16, 1975.

"Abortion and pre-natal injury: a legal and philosophical analysis." WESTERN ONTARIO LAW REVIEW 13: 97-123, 1974.

"Abortion and promiscuity," by L. F. Eickhoff. BRITISH MEDICAL JOURNAL 3(5975):99-100, July 12, 1975.

"Abortion and promiscuity," by R. G. Wilkins. BRITISH MEDICAL JOURNAL 3(5977):233, July 26, 1975.

"Abortion and the public good," by M. Pogonowska. AMERICAN JOURNAL OF PUBLIC HEALTH 65(7): 748, July, 1975.

"Abortion and research," by M. Lappe. HASTINGS CENTER REPORT 5(3):21, June, 1975.

"Abortion and the States." LANCET 2(7934):544, September 20, 1975.

"Abortion and the techniques of neutralization," by W. C. Brennan. JOURNAL OF HEALTH AND SOCIAL BEHAVIOR 15:358-365, December, 1974.

"Abortion and the true believer," by J. Fletcher; Discussion CHRISTIAN CENTURY 92:69-70, January 22, 1975.

"Abortion and a woman's right to decide," by A. Jaggar. THE PHILOSOPHICAL FORUM 5:347-360, Fall-Winter, 1973.

"Abortion, animation, and biological hominization," by J. Diamond. THEOLOGICAL STUDIES 36:305-324, June, 1975.

"Abortion: the battle's not over," by E. B. Stengel. MS MAGAZINE 3:98-100, February, 1975.

"Abortion bill; against the act." ECONOMIST 254:24, February 8, 1975.

"Abortion bill; the debate continues." ECONOMIST 254:31, February 15, 1975.

"Abortion bothers young males." NATIONAL CATHOLIC REPORTER 11:4, July 4, 1975.

"Abortion--the breath of life," by R. J. Joling, MEDICAL TRIAL TECHNIQUE QUARTERLY 21:199-232,

Fall, 1974.

"Abortion calls for public and private reparation effort; Program of Reparation and Apology and Spiritual Adoption to Save the Unborn Baby," by C. Lenta. OUR SUNDAY VISITOR 64:1 plus, July 20, 1975.

"Abortion cannula should not be reused," by W. L. Sim, et al. CANADIAN MEDICAL ASSOCIATION JOURNAL 113(2):92, July 26, 1975.

"Abortion: community trends," (letter), by K. Hume. MEDICAL JOURNAL OF AUSTRALIA 2(14):542, October 5, 1974.

"Abortion: community trends," by I. D. Truskett, et al. MEDICAL JOURNAL OF AUSTRALIA 2(8):288-291, August 24, 1974.

"Abortion: community trends. Comment 1," by C. Wood. MEDICAL JOURNAL OF AUSTRALIA 2(8):291-293, August 24, 1974.

"Abortion: community trends. Comment 2," by A. F. Connon. MEDICAL JOURNAL OF AUSTRALIA 2(8): 293-295, August 24, 1974.

"Abortion: Congress can't duck difficulties," by D. Loomis. NATIONAL CATHOLIC REPORTER 11:1 plus, May 16, 1975.

"Abortion controversy: what's it all about?" by J. Wax. SEVENTEEN 34:118-119 plus, November, 1975.

"Abortion counselling: focus on adolescent pregnancy," by C. Nadelson. PEDIATRICS 54(6):765-769, December, 1974.

"Abortion counselling; what we need to know and why," by C. Davis. JOURNAL OF PRACTICAL NURSING

9

25(6):16-17, 34, June, 1975.

"Abortion: the court decides a non-case," by J. O'Meara. SUPREME COURT REVIEW 1974:337-360, 1974.

"Abortion creates problems for nurses," by A. L. Salling. SYGEPLEJERSKEN 74(44):9, November 6, 1974.

"Abortion: the dangerous pressure on doctors," by R. Butt. TIMES p. 16, January 30, 1975.

"Abortion debate," by J. O'Hare. AMERICA 132:[inside front cover], March 1, 1975.

"Abortion: the debate continues," by F. Sherman. LUTHERAN p. 10, January 22, 1975.

"The abortion decision: two years later; symposium: More Christian than its critics," by R. Decker, et al. COMMONWEAL 101:384-392, February 14, 1975.

"Abortion: the Eldin shock wave." TIME 105:54-55, March 3, 1975.

"Abortion: an emotional issue rejoined." TIME CANADA 105:6-7, April 14, 1975.

"Abortion: an end to the taboo," by A. Josey. FAR EASTERN ECONOMIC REVIEW 86:28 plus, November 22, 1974.

"Abortion, euthanasia, and care of defective newborns," by J. Fletcher. NEW ENGLAND JOURNAL OF MEDICINE 292(2):75-78, January 9, 1975.

"Abortion--an evil necessity." NURSING MIRROR AND MIDWIVES' JOURNAL 140(7):33, February 13, 1975.

"Abortion experience in the United States," by I. M. Cushner. NURSING FORUM 2(5):10-12, November-

December, 1974.

"Abortion--have we gone too far?" by A. Reeder.
MADEMOISELLE 81:66 plus, June, 1975.

"Abortion: the high court has ruled." FAMILY PLAN-
NING PERSPECTIVES 5(1):1, Winter, 1973.

"Abortion: the husband's consitutional rights," by W.
D. H. Teo. ETHICS 85:337-342, July, 1975.

"Abortion in Jamaica," by J. Symes. JAMAICAN
NURSE 14(2):12, 14, August, 1974.

"Abortion in perspective," by B. M. Littlewood. NEW
ZEALAND LAW JOURNAL 1974:488-493, November
5, 1974.

"Abortion in a predominantly Catholic community," by
G. T. Schneider. JOURNAL OF THE LOUISIANA
STATE MEDICAL SOCIETY 126(9):323-325, Sep-
tempber, 1974.

"Abortion information: a guidance viewpoint," by P. L.
Wolleat, SCHOOL COUNSELOR 22(5):338-341,
May, 1975.

"Abortion investigation--abortion information. Experiences of a simple method for abortion investigations
in Umea," by L. Jacobsson, et al. LAKARTIDNIN-
GEN 72(1-2):44-45, 47, January 8, 1975.

"Abortion is not a 'delivery' following paragraph 9
section 1 of the Maternal Welfare Act," by T.
Reinmoeller-Schreck. ZENTRALBLATT FUR
ARBETISMEDIZIN UND ARBEITSSCHUTZ 24(4):
120-121, April, 1974.

"Abortion is second-place operation: nationwide survey
finds tonsillectomy the only surgery more common."

MEDICAL WORLD NEWS 16:54, March 10, 1975.

"Abortion: key issue in '76 ?" by R. Rashke. NATIONAL
CATHOLIC REPORTER 11:1 plus, May 30, 1975.

"The abortion law and those who are incapable to the
law," by J. Sahlin. LAKARTIDNINGEN 72(8):673-
674, February 19, 1975.

"Abortion law; Europe is moving both ways." ECONO-
MIST 254:52-53, March 1, 1975.

"Abortion law--Friendship Medical Center, Ltd. v.
Chicago Board of Health (505 F 2d 1141), invalidating
city health regulations applicable to first trimester
abortion procedures." LOYOLA UNIVERSITY OF
CHICAGO LAW JOURNAL 6:718-737, Summer, 1975.

"Abortion law reform. Fact and fiction: replying to Leo
Abse," by M. Simms. SPECTATOR p. 114, February
1, 1975.

"Abortion law reform. Permissiveness and pretence,"
by C. B. Goodhart. SPECTATOR p. 114-115,
February 1, 1975.

"Abortion laws in Hungary (letter)," by L. Iffy.
OBSTETRICS AND GYNECOLOGY 45(1):115-116,
January, 1975.

"Abortion: liberal laws do make abortion safer for
women," by B. J. Culliton. SCIENCE 188:1091,
June 13, 1975.

"Abortion: the moral status of the unborn," by R.
Werner. SOCIAL THEORY AND PRACTICE 3:
201-222, Fall, 1974.

"The abortion movements; reprint from Seido Foundation, Catholic Position Paper published in Japan,"

by C. Burke. L'OSSERVATORE ROMANO 19(371): 8-11, May 9, 1975.

"Abortion nursing expertise needed." NURSING UPDATE 6:1 plus, May, 1975.

"Abortion, obtained and denied: research approaches," by S. H. Newman, et al. STUDIES IN FAMILY PLANNING (53):1-8, May, 1970.

"Abortion: odyssey of an attitude," by A. F. Guttmacher. FAMILY PLANNING PERSPECTIVES 4(4):5-7, October, 1972.

"Abortion on maternal demand: paternal support liability implications," by G. S. Swan. VALPARAISO UNIVERSITY LAW REVIEW 9:243-272, Winter, 1975.

"Abortions on medicaid; the Bartlett amendment," by R. Drinan. COMMONWEAL 102:102-103, May 9, 1975.

"Abortion--on the social scene," by R. Sterner. VITAL CHRISTIANITY p. 12, August 11, 1974.

"Abortion on trial." NEWSWEEK 85:55, January 27, 1975.

"Abortion: an open letter," by B. Stephenson. CANADIAN MEDICAL ASSOCIATION JOURNAL 112(4):492, 494, 497, February 22, 1975.

"Abortion; or manslaughter?" ECONOMIST 254:61, February 22, 1975.

"Abortion or the unwanted child: a choice for a humanistic society," by J. W. Prescott. HUMANIST 35:11-15, March, 1975.

"Abortion, personal freedom, and public policy," by R. J. Adamek. FAMILY COORDINATOR 23(4):411-418,

October, 1974.

"Abortion--a personal testimony," by M. Potts. JAMAI-
CAN NURSE 14:6 plus, August, 1974.

"Abortion pioneer," by S. Finkbine. NEWSWEEK 85:14,
March 17, 1975.

"Abortion quiz," by H. Rodman. NATION 221:70-71,
August 2, 1975.

"Abortion; reforms accepted [Britain]." ECONOMIST
257:36, October 25, 1975.

"Abortion: the religious debate," by M. De Bolt. LINK
p. 35, September, 1974.

"Abortion--Right? Wrong?" by N. Price. HERALD OF
HOLINESS p. 12, July 31, 1974.

"Abortion: should constitution be amended?" by D.
Loomis. CONGRESSIONAL QUARTERLY SERVICE:
WEEKLY REPORT 33:917-922, May 3, 1975.

"Abortion-the story so far," by L. Swaffield. NURSING
TIMES 71(29):1120, July 17, 1975.

"Abortion; talked out." ECONOMIST 256:18, August 9,
1975.

"Abortion: 300,000 clandestine operations per year in
France." BRUXELLES MEDICAL 54(1):26-27,
January, 1974.

"Abortion: twenty-four weeks of dependency [United
States]," by L. Goodnight, et al. BAYLOR LAW
REVIEW 27:122-140, Winter, 1975.

"Abortion under ethical indication," by H. J. Rieger.
DEUTSCH MEDIZINISCHE WOCHENSCHRIFT 99(42):

2126, October 18, 1974.

"Abortion uproar awaits returning airlift nurse."
NATIONAL CATHOLIC REPORTER 11:2, April 25,
1975.

"Abortion vs manslaughter," by P. G. Stubblefield.
ARCHIVES OF SURGERY 110(7):790-791, July, 1975.

"Abortions, chromosomal aberrations, and radiation,"
by N. Freire-Maia. SOCIAL BIOLOGY 17(2):102-
106, June, 1970.

"Abortions: legal but how available?" by D. Spalding.
MS MAGAZINE 4:103-106, September, 1975.

"Abortions on Medicaid? Bartlett amendment," by R. F.
Drinan. COMMONWEAL 102:102-103, May 9, 1975;
Discussion 102:286-287, July 18, 1975.

"Abortions: where do we stand in Louisiana?" by M. G.
Koslin. JOURNAL OF THE LOUISIANA STATE MED-
ICAL SOCIETY 126(12):429-432, December, 1974.

"Accidental haemorrhage," by B. N. Chakravarty.
JOURNAL OF THE INDIAN MEDICAL ASSOCIATION
63(9):287-289, November 1, 1974.

"Accidental haemorrhage," by N. N. Chowdhury.
JOURNAL OF THE INDIAN MEDICAL ASSOCIATION
63(9):271-276, November 1, 1974.

"The action of halothane in causing abortion," by R.
Wittmann, et al. ANAESTHESIST 23(1):30-35,
January, 1974.

"Acute hematometra with peritoneal irritation following
therapeutic abortion by the Karman method of suction
curettage," by G. Bastert, et al. MUENCHENER
MEDIZINISCHE WOCHENSCHRIFT 116(38):780-781,

September 20, 1974.

"Advances in the diagnosis of bovine abortion," by H. W. Dunne, et al. PROCEEDING OF THE UNITED STATES ANIMAL HEALTH ASSOCIATION (77):515-523, 1973.

"Advantages and disadvantages of surgical treatment in imminent abortions and premature delivery," by E. Zajacová, et al. BRATISLAVSKE LEKORSKE LISTY 63(2):189-194, February, 1975.

"Advice in the abortion decision," by S. A. Luscutoff, et al. JOURNAL OF COUNCELING PSYCHOLOGY 22:140-146, March, 1975.

"After a conviction--second thoughts about abortions." U. S. NEWS AND WORLD REPORT 78:78, March 3, 1975.

"After Edelin: the abortion debate goes on," by K. Vaux. CHRISTIAN CENTURY 92:213, March 5, 1975.

"After the Lane report," by N. Waterson. NEW LAW JOURNAL 124:761-763, August 15, 1974.

"Against the act." ECONOMIST 254:24, February 8, 1975.

"Alph2 globulin pregnancy proteins in the serum of patients with missed abortion," by T. Gabor, et al. ORVOSI HETILAP 116(17):977-979, April 27, 1975.

"Alternatives to abortion needed," by E. M. Kennedy. HOSPITAL PROGRESS 56:11, September, 1975.

"Amino acid composition of proteins of the placenta and the fetal membranes in abortion," by T. N. Pogorelova. AKUSHERSTVO I GINEKOLOGIYA (Moscow) (9):51-53, September, 1974.

"An analysis of the Edelin case," by J. F. Holzer.
HOSPITAL PROGRESS 56(4):20-21, April, 1975.

"Anglican Synod takes stand against abortion on demand."
OUR SUNDAY VISITOR 64:2, August 10, 1975.

"Anti-abortion feeling; United States." L'OSSERVATORE
ROMANO 10(362):11, March 6, 1975.

"Anti-abortion: not parochial." CHRISTIANITY TODAY
19:22, August 8, 1975.

"Antiabortion policy upheld: insufficient 'state action'--
Texas." HOSPITAL LAW 8:4, January, 1975.

"Antiabortionists challenge March of dimes," by B. J.
Culliton. SCIENCE 190:538, November 7, 1975.

"Anti-Catholicism trades fantasy for fact in the media,"
by J. Anderson. OUR SUNDAY VISITOR 63:1 plus,
April 27, 1975.

"Anti-D antibodies after spontaneous abortion," by P. F.
Bolis, et al. ARCHIVIO DI OSTETRICIA E GINECOLO-
GIA 78(1-3):12-17, January-June, 1973.

"Anti-fertility drugs; novel non-hormonal compounds that
inhabit prostaglandin metabolism," by L. J. Lerner, et
al. NATURE 256(5513):130-132, July 10, 1975.

"The anti-life movement cover-up; reformers using words
as weapons," by A. Serb. OUR SUNDAY VISITOR 64:
1 plus, August 31, 1975.

"Anti-rhesus(D) immunoprophylaxis in abortion." (letter).
NEDERLANDS TIJDSCHRIFT VOOR GENEESKUNDE
118(47):1796-1797, November 23, 1974.

"Applications for abortion at a community hospital," by
M. E. Hunter. CANADIAN MEDICAL ASSOCIATION

JOURNAL 111(10):1088-1089, 1092, November 16, 1974.

"Artificial abortion and the law." HAREFUAH 88(5):238-239, March 2, 1975.

"Artificial termination of advanced pregnancy by extra-amniotic administration of prostaglandin F2 alpha and 15-me-PGF2 alpha," by E. A. Chernukha, et al. SOVETSKAIA MEDITSINA (6):21-26, June, 1975.

"Attitude of the physician towards abortion," by J. M. Cantú, et al. GINECOLOGIA Y OBSTETRICIA DE MEXICO 37(223):275-285, May, 1975.

"Attitudes of American teenagers toward abortion," by M. Zelnik, et al. FAMILY PLANNING PERSPECTIVES 7(2):89-91, March-April, 1975.

"Attitudes of senior nursing students toward the 1973 supreme court decision on abortion," by R. G. Elder. JOGN NURSING 4:46-54, July-August, 1975.

"Attitudes to legal abortion in hospital staff," by L. Jacobsson, et al. ACTA PSYCHIATRICA SCAND-INAVICA SUPPLEMENT (255):299-307, 1974.

"Avortement et divorce en Allemagne Fédérale," by H. Menudier. ETUDES 343:57-76, July, 1975.

"L'avortement et la nouvelle loi; point de vue d'un accoucheur," by R. LeLirzin. ETUDES 343:199-209, August-September, 1975.

"L'avortement, problème politique," by M. Schooyans. NOUVELLE REVUE THEOLOGIQUE 96:1031-1053, December, 1974; 97:25-50, January, 1975.

"Bacterial and viral causes of abortion (laboratory diagno-sis)," by F. Denis. CAHIERS DE MEDECINE 15(2):

65-83, February, 1974.

"Barr bodies in cervical smears," by S. H. Jackson, et al. BRITISH MEDICAL JOURNAL 1(5959):682, March 22, 1975.

"Battle for unborn life will go on as Bayh's committee vetoes pro-life amendments." OUR SUNDAY VISITOR 64:1, September 28, 1975.

"The beginning of the human being," by J. Lejeune. MAROC MEDICAL 55(590):251-258, May, 1975.

"Beyond abortion - fetal experimentation," by J. Anderson. OUR SUNDAY VISITOR 63:1 plus, April 13, 1975.

"Beyond Roe (Roe v. Wade, 93 Sup Ct 705) and Doe (Doe v. Bolton, 93 Sup Ct 739): the rights of the father," by H. Sherain. NOTRE DAME LAWYER 50:483-495, February, 1975.

"The Biblical view of abortion," by W. Luck. PRESBYTERIAN JOURNAL p. 9, April 23, 1975.

"Biological and psychological consequences of the induced abortion. Therapeutic abortion," by C. MacGregor, et al. GACETA MEDICA DE MEXICO 108(5):318-326, November, 1974.

"Biology, abortion, and ethics," by M. Potts. LANCET 1(7912):913, April 19, 1975.

"Biology, abortion, and ethics," by M. Wilkinson. LANCET 1(7914):1029-1031, May 3, 1975.

"Birth control in a sociohistorical perspective," by R. Liljeström. LAKARTIDNINGEN 71(44):4346-4348, October 30, 1974.

"Birthright--alternative to abortion," by M. Kelly.

AMERICAN JOURNAL OF NURSING 75:76-77, January, 1975.

"Birth rights," by C. Dix, et al. GUARDIAN p. 11, February 6, 1975.

"Bishop bars sacraments to backers of abortion." NATIONAL CATHOLIC REPORTER 11:1 plus, April 18, 1975.

"Bishop Maher stands firm against abortion advocates," by R. McMunn. OUR SUNDAY VISITOR 63:1, April 27, 1975.

"Bishops draft abortion letter." NATIONAL CATHOLIC REPORTER 11:15, January 24, 1975.

"Bishops may switch plan on abortion amendments." NATIONAL CATHOLIC REPORTER 11:5, October 3, 1975.

"Bishops of Pakistan on abortion and contraception; joint pastoral letter." L'OSSERVATORE ROMANO 11(363):9-10, March 13, 1975.

"Bishops' spokesman says next step must be an amendment." OUR SUNDAY VISITOR 63:3, March 2, 1975.

"Bleeding in early pregnancy investigated by ultrasound, plasma progesterone and oestradiol," by O. Piiroinen, et al. ANNALES CHIRURGIAE ET GYNAECOLOGIAE FENNIAE 63(6):451-456, 1974.

"Blood coagulation tests in prostaglandin F-2alpha induced and a one-time mechanically induced therapeutic abortion," by W. D. Junge, et al. ZENTRALBLATT FUER GYNAEKOLOGIE 96(35):1116-1120, August 30, 1974.

"The Boston-Edelin case," by N. Kase. CONNECTICUT

MEDICINE 39(6):366-367, June, 1975.

"Bovine abortion associated with Haemophilus somnus,"
by D. W. Chladek. AMERICAN JOURNAL OF
VETERINARY RESEARCH 36(7):1041, July, 1975.

"Breast gland following artifical termination of early
pregnancy and following threatened and completed
abortion," by F. Glenc. WIADOMOSCI LEKARSKIE
28(7):549-551, April 1, 1975.

"Brucella abortus biotype 1 as a cause of abortion in a
bitch," by D. J. Taylor, et al. VETERINARY RE-
CORD 96(19):428-429, May 10, 1975.

"By what authority (refuses to accept antiabortion as
only Biblical position)," by A. Taylor. PRESBY-
TERIAN JOURNAL p. 9, July 31, 1974.

"Can God forgive abortion?" by R. Fox. OUR SUNDAY
VISITOR 63:1 plus, April 6, 1975.

"Can you change people's minds on abortion?" by S.
Lockwood. LIGUORIAN 63:13-16, February, 1975.

"Canadian newspaper on abortion document; reprint
from Le Soleil, December 4, 1974," by P. Lachance.
L'OSSERVATORE ROMANO 8(360):5, February 20,
1975.

"Care by the public health nurse of the patient with
threatened abortion," by K. Katayama, et al.
JAPANESE JOURNAL FOR THE MIDWIFE 29(2):
90-95, February, 1975.

"The case against abortion," by J. Humber. THOMIST
39:65-84, January, 1975.

"Case of abortion." JOURNAL OF URBAN LAW 52:277-

338, November, 1974.

"Case of Asherman's syndrome," by M. Lazarevski, et
al. GODISEN ZBORNIK NA MEDICINSKIOT FAKUL-
TET VO SKOPJE 20:633-637, 1974.

"Catholic Hospital Association rejects CMA abortion
stand," by M. Beaton-Mamak. DIMENSION IN
HEALTH SERVICE 52(4):36, April, 1975.

"Catholic hospitals told protect right to life," by T.
Gilsenan. NATIONAL CATHOLIC REPORTER
11:4, June 20, 1975.

"Catholic League supports right of doctors to act in
harmony with their consciences." OUR SUNDAY
VISITOR 64:1, August 3, 1975.

"Catholic member offers dissent on fetal rule," by J.
Castelli. OUR SUNDAY VISITOR 64:3, June 8, 1975.

"Catholic Peace Fellowship statement on abortion."
CATHOLIC MIND 73:7-8, February, 1975.

"Cerebral abscess following septic abortion with the use
of a Dalkon shield," by A. A. Op de Coul. NEDER-
LANDS TIJDSCHRIFT VOOR GENEESKUNDE 119(12):
470-472, March 22, 1975.

"Certain indicators of the oxidation-reduction processes
in patients with septic abortions," by A. S. Shakhbazov.
AKUSHERSTVO I GINEKOLOGIIA (Moscow) (5):47-51,
May, 1974.

"Cervical dilatation with prostaglandin analogues prior
to vaginal termination of first trimester pregnancy in
nulliparous patients," by S. M. Karim, et al. PROS-
TAGLANDINS 9(4):631-638, April, 1975.

"Cervicovaginal fistula complicating induced midtrimester

abortion despite laminaria tent insertion," by J. H. Lischke, et al. AMERICAN JOURNAL OF OBSTETRICS AND GYNECOLOGY 120(6):852-853, November 15, 1974.

"Cervix carcinoma in women undergoing induced abortion for social reasons," by R. Kaliński, et al. WIADOMASCI LEKARSKIE 28(15):1281-1284, August 1, 1975.

"Cervix pregnancy following abortion," by W. Böhm, et al. ZENTRALBLATT FUER GYNAEKOLOGIE 96(44): 1399-1402, November 1, 1974.

"Characteristics of Chlamydia isolated from domestic animals," by L. N. Abramova, et al. VOPROSY VIRUSOLOGII (6):737-739, November-December, 1974.

"Characteristics of clinical course of acute post-abortion renal insufficiency," by T. I. Gromova. VRACHEBNOE DELO (1):86-88, January, 1975.

"Characteristics of the functional state of the myometrium in threatened abortion," by E. F. Kaplun-Kryzhanovskaia, et al. VOPROSY OKHRANY MATERINSTVA I DETSTVA 19(11):64-66, November, 1974.

"Characteristics of New Zealand women seeking abortion in Melbourne, Australia," by A. F. Rogers, et al. NEW ZEALAND MEDICAL JOURNAL 81(536):282-286, March 26, 1975.

"...Chicago. Confrontations," by G. Dunea. BRITISH MEDICAL JOURNAL 3(5976):151-153, July 19, 1975.

"Children--abortion--responsibility," by M. Lysnes. SYKEPLEIEN 62(3):96, February 5, 1975.

"Children born to women denied abortion," by Z. Dytrych, et al. FAMILY PLANNING PERSPECTIVES 7(4):165-171, July-August, 1975.

"Chilling effect; indictments against fetal research
scientists in Boston." SCIENTIFIC AMERICAN
232:40-41, February, 1975.

"Chorionic gonadotropin titer and anti-hormone antibodies in the blood in uterine and extrauterine
pregnancy," by IuG. Fedorov. AKUSHERSTVO I
GINEKOLOGIYA (Moscow) (9):53-56, September,
1974.

"Chromosome aberrations in the parents in the case
of repeated spontaneous abortions," by V. P. Kulazhenko, et al. SOVIET GENETICS 8(7):921-928,
July 15, 1974.

"Chromosome abnormalities and abortion," by A. Boué,
et al. BASIC LIFE SCIENCES 4(PT. B):317-339,
1974.

"Chromosome anomalies in three successive abortuses
due to paternal translocation, t(13q-18q+)," by T.
Kajii, et al. CYTOGENETICS AND CELL GENETICS
13(5):426-436, 1974.

"Chromosome 6/17 translocation as a cause of repeated
abortions," by F. Pasquali, et al. ANNALI DI
OSTETRICIA, GINECOLOGIA, MEDICINA PERINATALE
94(9-10):553-559, September-October, 1973.

"Church in the world: abortion and divorce: a change in
attitudes?" by J. Deedy. THEOLOGY TODAY 32:86-
88, April, 1975.

"Church leaders believe real reason to hope for a pro-life
constitutional amendment." OUR SUNDAY VISITOR
64:1, June 8, 1975.

"Church leaders see pro-life setback as only temporary."
OUR SUNDAY VISITOR 64:1, October 5, 1975.

"Cincinnati paper says need for new look at abortion."
OUR SUNDAY VISITOR 63:3, April 13, 1975.

"Circadian aspects of prostaglandin F2alpha-induced
termination of pregnancy," by I. D. Smith, et al.
JOURNAL OF OBSTETRICS AND GYNAECOLOGY OF
THE BRITISH COMMONWEALTH 81(11):841-848,
November, 1974.

"Circadian rhythms and abortion." BRITISH MEDICAL
JOURNAL 2(5961):3, April 5, 1975.

"Circadian timing, duration, dose and cost of prostaglandin F2alpha - induced termination of middle
trimester pregnancy," by I. D. Smith. CHRONO-
BIOLOGIA 1(1):41-53, January-March, 1974.

"Civil Rights Commission against rights of unborn."
OUR SUNDAY VISITOR 63:1, April 27, 1975.

"Clandestine abortion. Sketches of a numerical study,"
by R. Bourg. BRUXELLES MEDICAL 54(1):19-25,
January, 1974.

"Clarify the abortion law," edited by B. L. P. Brosseau.
DIMENSIONS IN HEALTH SERVICE 52:4, May, 1975.

"Clear answer to a political dilemma; the Church's
teaching on abortion," by E. von Feldt. COLUMBIA
55:4, February, 1975.

"Clinical aspects of abortion due to genetic causes
studies in fifty-two cases," by J. Cohen, et al.
ACTA EUROPAEA FERTILITATIS 2(3):405-424,
September, 1970.

"Clinical-epidemiological studies on legal abortion in
the WHO research program," by K. Edström.
LAKARTIDNINGEN 71(35):3175, August 28, 1974.

"Clinical results of therapeutic induction of abortion by extraamniotic application of prostaglandin F2 alpha," by H. Lahmann, et al. ZEITSCHRIFT FUR GEBURT-SHILFE UND PERINATOLOGIE 178(6):423-428, December, 1974.

"Clinical studies of psychotic disorders appearing during pregnancy, puerperal period and following induced abortion," by J. Ichikawa. PSYCHIATRIA ET NEU-ROLOGIA JAPONICA 76(8):457-483, August 25, 1974.

"Clinical use of a beta-mimetic drug in the control of uterine dynamics," by G. Casati, et al. ANNALI DI OSTETRICIA, GINECOLOGIA, MEDICINA PERINATALE 94(9-10):587-594, September-October, 1973.

"Clinics: run for women, not profit," by E. Krauss. MS MAGAZINE 4:106, September, 1975.

"CMA policy on abortion." (letter). CANADIAN MEDICAL ASSOCIATION JOURNAL 111(9):900, 902, 905, November 2, 1974.

"Coagulation changes during intraamniotic prostaglandin-induced abortion," by G. J. Kleiner, et al. OBSTE-TRICS AND GYNECOLOGY 44(5):757-761, November, 1974.

"Combined laparoscopic sterilization and pregnancy termination: II. Further experiences with a larger series of patients," by R. G. Cunanan, Jr., et al. JOURNAL OF REPRODUCTIVE MEDICINE 13(5):204-205, November, 1974.

"Comment and controversy," by R. Lincoln. FAMILY PLANNING PERSPECTIVES 7:185-188, July-August, 1975.

"Commonwealth v. Edelin," by R. F. Gibbs. JOURNAL OF LEGAL MEDICINE 3(3):6, March, 1975.

"Comparative assays on chorionic gonadotropin excretion and concentrations of some protein fractions in cases of threatened abortion," by J. Jakowicki, et al. GINEKOLOGIA POLASKA 46(1):17-21, January, 1975.

"Comparative evaluation of the methods of termination of advanced pregnancy," by V. I. Babukhadiia, et al. SOVETSHAIA MEDITSINA (6):97-99, June, 1975.

"Comparative studies on the new legalization of legal abortion," by S. Schultz, et al. ZENTRALBLATT FUR GYNAEKOLOGIE 96(39):1217-1222, September 27, 1974.

"Comparison of abortion performed with prostaglandin F2 alpha and hysterotomy," by H. Koeffler, et al. ANNALES CHIRURGIAE ET GYNAECOLOGIAE FENNIAE 63(6):483-486, 1974.

"Comparison of antigenic structure and pathogenicity of bovine intestinal Chlamydia isolate with an agent of epizootic bovine abortion," by D. E. Reed, et al. AMERICAN JOURNAL OF VETERINARY RESEARCH 36(08):1141-1143, August, 1975.

"Comparison of extra-amniotic administration of PGF2alpha, 0.9 per cent saline, and 20 percent saline followed by oxytocin for therapeutic abortion," by A. P. Lange, et al. ACTA OBSTETRICIA ET GYNECOLOGICA SCANDINAVICA [Suppl] (37):61-66, 1974.

"Comparison of prostaglandin F2alpha and hypertonic saline for induction of midtrimester abortion," by N. H. Lauersen, et al. AMERICAN JOURNAL OF OBSTETRICS AND GYNECOLOGY 120(7):875-879, December 1, 1974.

"A comparison of termination of pregnancies in the 2nd trimester induced by intraamniotic injection of hyper-

tonic saline, prostaglandin F2alpha or both drugs," by
E. Bostofte, et al. ACTA OBSTETRICIA ET GYNE-
COLOGICA SCANDINAVICA. SUPPLEMENT (37):
47-50, 1974.

"A comparison of two abortion-related legal inquiries,"
by C. H. Wecht, et al. JOURNAL OF LEGAL MED-
ICINE 3(8):36-44, September, 1975.

"Compelling hospitals to provide abortion services," by
M. F. McKernan, Jr. CATHOLIC LAWYER 20:317-
327, Autumn, 1974.

"Competition between spontaneous and induced abortion,"
by R. G. Potter, et al. DEMOGRAPHY 12:129-141,
February, 1975.

"Complete molar abortion induced with prostaglandin
F2 alpha," by M. Herrera, et al. REVISTA CHILENA
DE OBSTETRICIA Y GINECOLOGIA 38(3):146-149,
1973.

"Complex evaluation of recent threatened pregnancy with
special reference to placental lactogen," by J. Lukasik,
et al. GINEKOLOGIA POLSKA 46(7):777-781, July,
1975.

"Complications caused by difficult removal of laminaria
tents," by J. P. Gusdon, et al. AMERICAN JOURNAL
OF OBSTETRICS AND GYNECOLOGY 121(2):286-287,
January 15, 1975.

"Complications following prostaglandin F2alpha-induced
midtrimester abortion," by J. H. Duenhoelter, et al.
OBSTETRICS AND GYNECOLOGY 46(3):247-250,
September, 1975.

"Complications of the interruption of pregnancy by the
method of intra-amnionic administration of a hypertonic sodium chloride solution and their prevention,"

by IuM. Bloshanskii. AKUSHERSTVO I GINEKOLOGIIA (Moscow) (9):65-66, September, 1974.

"Complications of prostaglandin-induced abortion." (letter). BRITISH MEDICAL JOURNAL (5941):404-405, November 16, 1974.

"Complications of prostaglandin-induced abortion," by J. J. Amy. BRITISH MEDICAL JOURNAL 4(5945): 654, December 14, 1974.

"Complications of 10,453 consecutive first-trimester abortions: a prospective study," by J. E. Hodgson, et al. AMERICAN JOURNAL OF OBSTETRICS AND GYNECOLOGY 120(6):802-807, November 15, 1974.

"Compulsory pregnancy," by E. Doerr. HUMANIST 34:30-31, May, 1974.

"Concealed accidental ante-partum haemorrhage," by J. O. Greenhalf. NURSING TIMES 71(10):382-384, March 6, 1975.

"Concentration of DDT and its metabolities in placental tissue and venous blood of women with missed abortion," by B. Trebicka-Kwiatkowska, et al. POLSKI TYGODNIK LEKARSKI 29(42):1769-1772, October 21, 1974.

"Conflicting coverage given abortion attitudes survey." OUR SUNDAY VISITOR 63:1, March 23, 1975.

"Congenital-malformation rates and spontaneous-abortion rates," by W. H. James. LANCET 1(7917):1201, May 24, 1975.

"Conjoined twins," by L. Joshi. JOURNAL OF THE INDIAN MEDICAL ASSOCIATION 63(7):222-223, October 1, 1974.

"Constitutional law--abortion--father's rights."
DUQUESNE LAW REVIEW 13:599-610, Spring,
1975.

"Constitutional law: abortion, parental consent, minors'
rights to due process, equal protection and privacy."
AKRON LAW REVIEW 9:158-165, Summer, 1975.

"Constitutional law--abortion--putative father has no
right to prevent wife from obtaining an abortion."
MEMPHIS STATE UNIVERSITY LAW REVIEW 5:
429-437, Spring, 1975.

"Constitutional law--right to privacy--spousal consent
to abortion: foreshadowing the fall of parental consent."
SUFFOLK UNIVERSITY LAW REVIEW 9:841-872,
Spring, 1975.

"Contemporary legal standpoint on induced abortion,"
by H. J. Rieger. DEUTSCHE MEDIZINISCHE
WOCHENSCHRIFT 99(37):1837-1838, September 13,
1974.

"Content of certain chloroganic pesticides in the blood
of pregnant women and embryos after miscarriage,"
by B. F. Mazorchuk, et al. PEDIATRIIA AKUSHER-
STVO I GINEKOLOGIIA (6):59-61, November-December, 1974.

"Contraception, abortion and venereal disease: teen-
agers' knowledge and the effect of education," by
P. A. Reichelt, et al. FAMILY PLANNING PER-
SPECTIVES 7(2):83-88, March-April, 1975.

"Contraception and abortion," by M. S. Rapp. CANADIAN
MEDICAL ASSOCIATION JOURNAL 112(6):682, March
22, 1975.

"Contraceptive practice in the context of a nonrestrictive
abortion law: age-specific pregnancy rates in New

York city, 1971-1973, by C. Tietze. FAMILY PLAN-
NING PERSPECTIVES 7:197-202, September-October,
1975.

"Contraceptive therapy following therapeutic abortion:
an analysis," by W. F. Peterson. OBSTETRICS AND
GYNECOLOGY 44(6):853-857, December, 1974.

"Control and prevention of induced abortion. Field
priorities and investigation," by L. Castelazo-Ayala.
GACETA MEDICA DE MEXICO 108(5):334-339,
November, 1974.

"Cost analysis of regionalized versus decentralized
abortion programs," by M. D. Mandel. MEDICAL
CARE 13(2):137-149, February, 1975.

"The course of pregnancy and labor following legal
abortion," by H. Kirchhoff. ZEITSCHRIFT FUR
GEBURTSHILFE UND PERINATOLOGIE 178(6):
407-414, December, 1974.

"Court rules Medicaid law silent on abortions." HOS-
PITALS 49:17, September 1, 1975.

"A criminal approach to abortion." BRITISH MEDICAL
JOURNAL 2(5967):352-353, May 17, 1975.

"Croatia: outcome of pregnancy in women whose requests for legal abortion have been denied," by D.
Stampar. STUDIES IN FAMILY PLANNING 4(10):
267-269, October, 1973.

"Cyclic adenosine 3',5'-monophosphate in prostaglandin-
induced abortion," by K. Raij, et al. SCANDINAVIN
JOURNAL OF CLINICAL AND LABORATORY INVES-
TIGATION 34(4):337-342, December, 1974.

"Cytochemical changes in the endometrium of women
after spontaneous abortion," by R. K. Ryzhova.

AKUSHERSTVO I GINEKOLOGIIA (Moscow) (5):63-65,
May, 1974.

"Cytogenetic studies on spontaneous abortions," by L.
Wiśniewski, et al. GYNAEKOLOGISCHE RUNDSCHAU
14(3):184-193, 1974.

"Cytogenetic study of 30 couples having had several
spontaneous abortions," by A. Broustet, et al.
SEMAINE DES HOPITAUX DE PARIS 51(5):299-
302, January 26, 1975.

"Cytological evaluation of amniotic fluid in threatened
pregnancy," by A. Cekański, et al. WIADOMOSCI
LEKARSKIE 28(16):1375-1380, August 15, 1975.

"Cytogenetical studies on couples with repeated abortions,"
by K. Rani, et al. INDIAN JOURNAL OF EXPERIMEN-
TAL BIOLOGY 12(1):98-99, January, 1974.

"Cytogenetics of habitual abortion. A review," by G.
Khudr. OBSTETRICAL AND GYNECOLOGICAL
SURVEY 29(5):290-310, May, 1974.

"Cytomegalovirus endometritis: report of a case associated with spontaneous abortion," by L. P. Dehner,
et al. OBSTETRICS AND GYNECOLOGY 45(2):211-
214, February, 1975.

"Dalkon Shield," by F. A. Clark, et al. JOURNAL OF THE
AMERICAN MEDICAL ASSOCIATION 233(3):225-226,
June 21, 1975.

"Dalkon shield and septic abortion," by M. H. Briggs.
MEDICAL JOURNAL OF AUSTRALIA 1(3):81,
January 18, 1975.

"Dalkon shield: mid-trimester septic abortion," by J.
Matthews. MEDICAL JOURNAL OF AUSTRALIA

2(23):856-857, December 7, 1974.

"The danger of threatened miscarriage and steps to
be taken," by K. Soiva. KATILOLEHTI 80(1):7-
16, January, 1975.

"Dark shadow at the door." IRISH MEDICAL JOURNAL
68(6):150, 158, March 22, 1975.

"Debate continues." ECONOMIST 254:31, February 15,
1975.

"The decision-making process and the outcome of therapeutic abortion," by C. M. Friedman, et al.
AMERICAN JOURNAL OF PSYCHIATRY 131(12):
1332-1337, December, 1974.

"Declaration on abortion." CATHOLIC MIND p. 54,
April, 1975.

"Declaration on abortion: a religious, not political act;
interview of J. Hamer, Secretary of S. Congregation
for the Doctrine of the Faith." L'OSSERVATORE
ROMANO 2(354):8, January 9, 1975.

"Decrease of utero-placental blood flow during prostaglandin F2alpha induced abortion," by M. O. Pulk-
kinen, et al. PROSTAGLANDINS 9(1):61-66, January, 1975.

"Delay in seeking induced abortion: a review and theoretical analysis," by M. B. Bracken, et al. AMERI-
CAN JOURNAL OF OBSTETRICS AND GYNECOLOGY
121(7):1008-1019, April 1, 1975.

"Demographic repercussions of legal and illegal abortion," by S. Gaslonde. GACETA MEDICA DE MEXICO
108(5):327-334, November, 1974.

"Dependent but distinct: the fetus," by M. Novak.

NATIONAL CATHOLIC REPORTER 11:11, May 9, 1975.

"Depressed lymphocyte response in mixed-wife-husband leucocyte cultures in normal and pathological pregnancies; effect of heat-inactivated serum," by L. Komlos, et al. REPRODUCTION 1(3):253-257, July-September, 1974.

"Diagnosis of acute suppurative peritonitis in patients with sepsis and acute renal insufficiency," by O. S. Shkrob, et al. AKUSHERSTVO I GINEKOLOGIIA (Moscow) (6):32-35, June, 1974.

"Diagnosis of Asherman's syndrome (intrauterine synechiae)," by I. Smid, et al. ORVOSI HETILAP 115(51):3046-3048, December 22, 1974.

"Diagnosis of death in relation to irreversably comatose artificially ventilated patients," by G. J. Kloosterman. NEDERLANDS TIJDSCHRIFT VOOR GENEES-KUNDE 119(21):843-844, May 24, 1975.

"Diagnosis of threatened abortion using electrohysterography," by A. I. Liubimova, et al. AKUSHERSTVO I GINEKOLOGIIA (Moscow) 49(4):65-66, April, 1973.

"Diagnostic and prognostic value of bidimentional echography in threatened abortion," by N. Rodríguez. REVISTA CHILENA DE OBSTETRICIA Y GINECOL-OGIA 38(5):228-239, 1973.

"Diagnostic and prognostic value of the 'spot' phenomenon and of the colpocystogram in threatened abortion," by E. B. Derankova, et al. AKUSHERSTVO I GINEKOL-OGIIA (Moscow) 49(4):46-50, April, 1973.

"Diazepam as an adjunct in propanidid anaesthesia for abortion," by M. A. Mattila, et al. BRITISH JOURNAL OF ANAESTHESIA 46(6):446-448, June,

1974.

"Diazepam as a sedative in induced abortion," by J. B. Nielsen, et al. ACTA OBSTETRICA ET GYNECOLOGICA SCANDINAVICA 54(3):237-239, 1973.

"DIC, disseminated intravascular coagulation. Nursing grand rounds." NURSING 4(11):66-71, November, 1974.

"Dicoumarol as the cause of abortion in mink," by J. Kangas, et al. NORDISK VETERINAER MEDICIN 26(7-8):444-447, July-August, 1974.

"District court orders abortions at university hospital: Nebraska." HOSPITAL LAW 8:4-5, January, 1975.

"Doe v. Wohlgemuth, 376 F Supp 173." JOURNAL OF FAMILY LAW 14:135-139, 1975.

"Le Dr Morgentaler (Sa Majesté la Reine v. Henry Morgentaler, Cour d'appel, Dist. de Montréal, no. 10-000289 -73) devant la Cour d'appel," by M. Rivet. LES CAHIERS DE DROIT 15:889-896, 1974.

"Drive to legalize abortion in Italy starts uneasily." NATIONAL CATHOLIC REPORTER 11:20, May 23, 1975.

"Early abortion in a family planning clinic," by S. Goldsmith. FAMILY PLANNING PERSPECTIVES 6(2): 119-122, Spring, 1975.

"Early antenatal care," by R. R. Macdonald. NURSING MIRROR AND MIDWIVES' JOURNAL 139(7):56-58, August 16, 1974.

"Early mid trimester abortion - by intramuscular 15 methyl prostaglandin E2," by S. D. Sharma, et al.

PROSTAGLANDINS 8(2):171-178, October 25, 1974.

"Edelin abortion verdict." NATIONAL REVIEW 27: 260-262, March 14, 1975.

"Edelin case." NATION 200:260, March 8, 1975.

"Edelin case: further comment." NEW ENGLAND JOURNAL OF MEDICINE 292(21):1129-1130, May 22, 1975.

"Edelin decision," by C. A. Berger, et al. COMMON-WEAL 102:76-78, April 25, 1975.

"The Edelin decision," by R. V. Jaynes. JOURNAL OF LEGAL MEDICINE 3(6):8, June, 1975.

"Edelin editorial protested." NEW ENGLAND JOURNAL OF MEDICINE 292(21):1129, May 22, 1975.

"Edelin says jury in Boston biased," by R. Casey. NATIONAL CATHOLIC REPORTER 11:1 plus, February 28, 1975.

"Edelin spent $10,000 to survey prospective jurors." OUR SUNDAY VISITOR 63:2, March 16, 1975.

"Edelin supported." NEW ENGLAND JOURNAL OF MEDICINE 292(13):705, March 27, 1975.

"The Edelin trial fiasco," by F. J. Ingelfinger. NEW ENGLAND JOURNAL OF MEDICINE 292(13):697, March 27, 1975.

"Edelin trial: jury not persuaded by scientists for the defense," by B. J. Culliton. SCIENCE 187:814-816, Marcy 7, 1975.

"Efficacy and acceptability of 15(S)-15-methyl-prosta-glandin E2-methyl ester for midtrimester pregnancy

termination," by J. Bieniarz, et al. AMERICAN
JOURNAL OF OBSTETRICS AND GYNECOLOGY
120(6):840-843, November 15, 1974.

"The efficacy of intramuscular 15 methyl prostaglandin
E2 in second-trimester abortion. Coagulation and
hormonal aspects," by T. F. Dillon, et al. AMERI-
CAN JOURNAL OF OBSTETRICS AND GYNECOLOGY
121(5):584-589, March 1, 1975.

"The effect of abortions on the birth weight in infants,"
by O. Pohánka, et al. ORVOSI HETILAP 116(34):
1983-1989, August 24, 1975.

"The effect of analgesic drugs on the instillation-abortion time of hypertonic saline induced mid-trimester
abortion," by R. Waltman, et al. PROSTAGLANDINS
7(5):411-424, September 10, 1974.

"The effect of anti-prostaglandin on the hypertonic saline-
induced uterine activity," by A. I. Csapo, et al.
PROSTAGLANDINS 9(4):627-629, April, 1975.

"The effect of induced abortions on perinatal mortality,"
by G. Papaevangelou, et al. ACTA EUROPAEA
FERTILITATIS 4(1):7-10, March, 1973.

"The effect of legalization of abortion on population
growth and public health," by C. Tietze. FAMILY
PLANNING PERSPECTIVES 7(3):123-127, May-June,
1975.

"The effect of legalized abortion on morbidity resulting
from criminal abortion," by R. S. Kahan, et al.
AMERICAN JOURNAL OF OBSTETRICS AND GYNE-
COLOGY 121(1):114-116, January 1, 1975.

"Effect of prostaglandin F2 alpha and hypertonic saline
on the placental function during midtrimester abortion," by S. Jayaraman, et al. AMERICAN JOURNAL

OF OBSTETRICS AND GYNECOLOGY 121(4):528–530, February 15, 1975.

"Effect of prostaglandin F2a on the contractility of the pregnant human uterus," by G. Romero-Salinas, et al. GINECOLOGIA Y OBSTETRICIA DE MEXICO 35(212):627-656, June, 1974.

"The effect of prostaglandin F2alpha on the placental progesterone level in midtrimester abortion," by F. A. Aleem, et al. AMERICAN JOURNAL OF OBSTETRICS AND GYNECOLOGY 123(2):202-205, September 15, 1975.

"Effectiveness of abortion as birth control," by S. J. Williams, et al. SOCIAL BIOLOGY 22:23-33, Spring, 1975.

"The effects of antibiotics on indices of immunity during treatment of endomyometritis following infectious abortion," by G. S. Minasova, et al. ANTIBIOTIKI 19(1):86-89, January, 1974.

"Elective termination of pregnancy. Evaluation of fetal lung maturity for lowering risk," by A. Bhakthavath-salan, et al. NEW YORK STATE JOURNAL OF MEDICINE 75(4):569-571, March, 1975.

"Electroencephalographic changes after intra-amniotic prostaglandin F2alpha and hypertonic saline," by R. P. Shearman, et al. BRITISH JOURNAL OF OBSTETRICS AND GYNAECOLOGY 82(4)314-317, April, 1975.

"Emotional responses of women following therapeutic abortion," by N. E. Adler. AMERICAN JOURNAL OF ORTHOPSYCHIATRY 45(3):446-454, April, 1975.

"Endocrinal abortion," by E. Cittadini. MINERVA GINECOLOGIA 26(4):211-220, April, 1974.

"Endometrial aspiration as a means of early abortion,"
by T. C. Wong, et al. OBSTETRICS AND GYNECOLOGY
44(6):845-852, December, 1974.

"Endometrial regeneration after voluntary abortion," by
J. V. Reyniak, et al. OBSTETRICS AND GYNECOLOGY
45(2):203-210, February, 1975.

"Enzootic (viral) abortion in sheep," by A. G. Shakhov,
et al. VETERINARIIA (3):52-53, March, 1975.

"Epidemiology of induced abortion in Mexico," by B. R.
Ordóñez. GACETA MEDICA DE MEXICO 108(5):
310-318, November, 1974.

"Epsilon-aminocaproic acid in the treatment of abortion,"
by R. Klimek, et al. GINEKOLOGIA POLSKA 46(7):
747-750, July, 1975.

"Equine herpesvirus 1: biological and biophysical comparison of two viruses from different clinical entities,"
by H. C. Borgen, et al. INTERVIROLOGY 4(3):189-
198, 1974.

"Ethical dilemmas in obstetric and newborn care," by
T. K. Hanid. MIDWIFE AND HEALTH VISITOR
11(1):9-11, January, 1975.

"Ethical issues in amniocentesis and abortion," by T. R.
McCormick. TEXAS REPORTS ON BIOLOGY AND
MEDICINE 32(1):299-309, Spring, 1974.

"Ethical standards for fetal experimentation," by M. M.
Martin. FORDHAM LAW REVIEW 43:547-570,
March, 1975.

"Ethics of selective abortion." BRITISH MEDICAL
JOURNAL 4(5946):676, December 21, 1974.

"Etiology and pathogenesis of spontaneous abortions and

elaboration of differentiated complex therapy," by E. S. Kononova, et al. VOPROSY OKHRANY MATERINSTVA I DETSTVA 20(3):62-67, March, 1975.

"Europe is moving both ways." ECONOMIST 254:52-53, March 1, 1975.

"An evaluation of abortion: techniques and protocols," by I. S. Burnett, et al. HOSPITAL PRACTICE 10: 97-105, August, 1975.

"Evaluation of the outcome of pregnancy in threatened abortion by biochemical methods," by O. Karjalainen, et al. ANNALES CHIRURGIAE ET GYNAECOLOGIAE FENNIAE 63(6):457-464, 1974.

"Evaluation of sonar in the prediction of complications after vaginal termination of pregnancy," by M. Stone, et al. AMERICAN JOURNAL OF OBSTETRICS AND GYNECOLOGY 120(7):890-894, December 1, 1974.

"The èvil of mandatory motherhood," by G. Hardin. PSYCHOLOGY TODAY p. 42, November, 1974.

"Evolution of Canadian justice: the Morgentaler case," by E. Z. Friedenberg. CANADIAN FORUM 55:28-30, June, 1975.

"Experience with the use of the preparation Faustan in obstetric and gynecologic practice." AKUSHERSTVO I GINEKOLOGIIA (Sofiia) 13(4):308-311, 1974.

"Experiences with hormonal treatment of imminent abortuses and premature deliveries," by V. Kliment, et al. BRATISLAVSKE LEKARSKE LISTY 63(2): 209-213, February, 1975.

"Extraovular prostaglandin F2alpha for early mid-trimester abortion," by A. G. Shapiro. AMERICAN JOURNAL OF OBSTETRICS AND GYNECOLOGY

121(3):333-336, February 1, 1975.

"Factors of high fetal risk in a peripheral clinic," by
R. Molina, et al. REVISTA CHILENA DE OBSTETRI-
CIA Y GINECOLOGIA 38(1):43-53, 1973.

"Factors influencing conception in women seeking termination of pregnancy. A pilot study of 100 women," by
Y. Lucire. MEDICAL JOURNAL OF AUSTRALIA
1(26):824-827, June 28, 1975.

"Facts about abortion for the teenager," by S. Greenhause.
SCHOOL COUNSELOR 22(5):334-336, May, 1975.

"Familial translocation 15-22. A possible cause for
abortions in female carriers," by K. Fried, et al.
JOURNAL OF MEDICAL GENETICS 11(3):280-282,
September, 1974.

"Far from settling issue, Supreme Court caught in
storm over legal abortion," by C. D. Davis. TEXAS
HOSPITALS 30:28-29, March, 1975.

"Fatal complications by air embolism in legal interruption
of pregnancy," by A. Du Chesne. ZENTRALBLATT
FUR GYNAEKOLOGIE 96(50):1593-1597, December 13,
1974.

"Father and the unborn child," by P. T. O'Neill, et al.
MODERN LAW REVIEW 38:174-185, March, 1975.

"Father's rights in the abortion decision." TEXAS
TECH LAW REVIEW 6:1075-1094, Spring, 1975.

"Fertility rates and abortion rates: simulations of
family limitation," by C. Tietze, et al. STUDIES
IN FAMILY PLANNING 6(5):114-120, May, 1975.

"Fetal research," by B. J. Culliton. SCIENCE 187:

237-238 plus, 411-413, 1175-1176, January 24,
February 7, March 28, 1975.

"Fetal research and antiabortion politics: holding science
hostage," by D. S. Hart. FAMILY PLANNING PER-
SPECTIVES 7:72-82, March-April, 1975.

"Fetal thymus glands obtained from prostaglandin-induced
abortions. Cellular immune function in vitro and
evidence of in vivo thymocyte activity following transplantation," by D. W. Wara, et al. TRANSPLANTA-
TION 18(5):387-390, November, 1974.

"The fetus as person: possible legal consequences of
the Hogan-Helms Amendment," by H. F. Pilpel.
FAMILY PLANNING PERSPECTIVES 6(1):6-7,
Winter, 1974.

"Fetus papyraceus: an unusual case with congenital
anomaly of the surviving fetus," by F. Saier, et al.
OBSTETRICS AND GYNECOLOGY 45(2):217-220,
February, 1975.

"Foetal cerebral leucomalacia associated with Cupressus
macrocarpa abortion in cattle," (letter), by R. W.
Mason. AUSTRALIAN VETERINARY JOURNAL 50(9):
419, September, 1974.

"The foetal risks in sickle cell anaemia," by M. F.
Anderson. WEST INDIAN MEDICAL JOURNAL 20(4):
288-295, December, 1971.

"Four indicators of humanhand: the enquiry matures,"
by J. F. Fletcher. HASTINGS CENTER REPORT
4:4-7, December, 1974.

"Four questions about sex in our society," by J. Kirk.
MEDICAL TIMES 102(11):68-80, November, 1974.

"From Comstockery through population control: the

inevitability of balancing," by E. Silverstein. NORTH
CAROLINA CENTRAL LAW JOURNAL 6:8-47, Fall,
1974.

"From the files of the KMA Maternal Mortality Study
Committee," by J. W. Greene, Jr. JOURNAL OF
THE KENTUCKY MEDICAL ASSOCIATION 73(1):33,
January, 1975.

"Fungi isolated from bovine mycotic abortion and
pneumonia with special reference to Mortierella
wolfii," by M. E. Carter, et al. RESEARCH IN
VETERINARY SCIENCE 14(2):201-206, March, 1973.

"Further in modest defence," by J. Rudinow. ANALYSIS
35:91-92, January, 1975.

"The game-plan of pro-life and anti-life," by E. Mc-
Cormack. SOCIAL JUSTICE REVIEW 68:54-55,
May, 1975.

"General practitioners and abortion." JOURNAL OF
THE ROYAL COLLEGE OF GENERAL PRACTI-
TIONERS 24(142):298, 303, May, 1974.

"Genetic epidemiology of intra-uterine mortality. Result of an analysis in a rural population in Quebec,"
by P. Philippe, et al. UNION MEDICALE DU
CANADA 104(5):763-767, May, 1975.

"German bishops urge defence at all cost of the lives
of the unborn," by H. Volk. L'OSSERVATORE
ROMANO 2(354):8, January 9, 1975.

"Gonadotrophic hormone activity in female Angora
goats exhibiting normal and aberrant reproductive
activity," by P. S. Pretorius. JOURNAL OF THE
SOUTH AFRICAN VETERINARY ASSOCIATION
43(1):35-41, March, 1972.

"Government directed family planning," by A. Braestrup. UGESKRIFT FOR LAEGER 137(30):1742-1743, July 21, 1975.

"Gynecologists do not want to be a pure service-institution, but that is what the health personnel are," by B. H. Brundtland. NORDISK MEDICIN 90(2):39-43, February, 1975.

"Haunting shadows from the rubble of Roe's (Roe v. Wade, 93 Sup Ct 705) right of privacy." SUFFOLK UNIVERSITY LAW REVIEW 9:145-184, Fall, 1974.

"Hazards of IUDs," by J. W. Records. SOUTHERN MEDICAL JOURNAL 68(9):1061-1062, September, 1975.

"Hazards of pregnancy interruption," by G. K. Döring. FORTSCHRITTE DER MEDIZIN 92(29):1156-1160, October 17, 1974.

"The hazards of vacuum aspiration in late first trimester abortions," by P. Moberg, et al. ACTA OBSTETRICIA ET GINECOLOGICA SCANDINAVICA 54(2):113-118, 1975.

"Health care issues," by Sister M. A. A. Zasowska, et al. HEALTH CARE DIMENSIONS :1-158, Fall, 1974.

"Health personnel organization for professional self-determination," by B. Brekke. SYKEPLEIEN 61(22): 1145-1147, November 20, 1974.

"Haematological changes associated with Aspergillus fumigatus infection in experimental mycotic abortion of sheep," by C. A. Day, et al. BRITISH JOURNAL OF EXPERIMENTAL PATHOLOGY 55(4):352-362, August, 1974.

"Heparin therapy for septic abortion," by U. Stosiek. GEBURTSHILFE UND FRAUENHEILKUNDE 34(12): 1045-1046, December, 1974.

"Hippokrates and the legality of abortion," by H. M. Sutermeister. PRAXIS 63(36):1101-1103, September 10, 1974.

"Histophysiology of human amnion in the normal state and in spontaneous abortion at the early periods of pregnancy," by A. V. Shurlygina, et al. AKUSH-USTVO I GINEKOLOGIIA (Moscow) 0(7):66-67, July, 1974.

"History of the medical indication of induced abortion. A historical contribution to the discussion of a current problem," by J. Gottlieb. FOLIA CLINICA INTER-NACIONAL (Barcelona) 24(10):731-732, October, 1974.

"History of medicine aspects on the problem of artificial abortion (I)," by H. Siefert. MEDIZINISCHE WELT 25(17):769-772 plus, April 26, 1974.

"History of the pro-life movement in Quebec," by A. Morais. CATHOLIC HOSPITAL 3:8-9, January-February, 1975.

"Homo sapienism: critique of Roe v. Wade (93 Sup Ct 705) and abortion." ALBANY LAW REVIEW 39:856-893, 1975.

"Hormonal determinism of the embryolethality of Triton W. R. 1339 in mice," by C. Roussel, et al. COMP-TES RENDUS DES SEANCES DE LA SOCIETE DE BIOLOGIE ET DE SES FOLIALES 167(12):1713-1717, 1973.

"Hormonal parameters following termination of pregnancy: a guide to the management of threatened abortion," by D. M. Saunders, et al. AMERICAN JOURNAL OF

OBSTETRICS AND GYNECOLOGY 120(8):1118-1119, December 15, 1974.

"Hormone changes occurring during second trimester abortion induced with 15 (S)-15-methyl prostaglandin F2alpha," by S. L. Corson, et al. PROSTAGLANDINS 9(6):975-983, June, 1975.

"House avoids abortion issue despite pressure; reprint from Congressional Quarterly, April 30, 1975," by D. Loomis. NATIONAL CATHOLIC REPORTER 11:1 plus, May 23, 1975.

"How many abortions?" BRUXELLES MEDICAL 54(1): 26, January, 1974.

"How shall we solve the problems of many abortions?" by A. L. Salling. SYGEPLEJERSKEN 75(23):9, June 11, 1975.

"Human life is sacred; pastoral letter of the archbishops and bishops of Ireland." L'OSSERVATORE ROMANO 21(373):6-8 plus, May 22, 1975; 24(376):6-8, June 12, 1975; 25(377):6-9, June 19, 1975.

"Humans and persons: a reply to Tuistram Englehardt," by L. Newton. ETHICS 85:332-336, July, 1975.

"Hydrocallantois in the bitch," (letter), by P. E. Holt, et al. VETERINARY RECORD 95(5):112, August 3, 1974.

"Hygiene for a woman following surgical abortion," by S. L. Polchanova. FEL'DSHER I AKUSHERKA 40(1): 43-46, January, 1975.

"Hypertonic saline induced abortion as pathophysiologic model of low grade intravascular coagulation," by E. A. Van Royen, et al. SCANDINAVIAN JOURNAL OF HAEMATOLOGY 13(3):166-174, 1974.

"Hysterographic studies in complex treatment of pregnant
women with threatened abortion," by T. A. Aivazian.
VOPROSY OKHRANY MATERINSTVA I DETSTVA
19(11):67-70, November, 1974.

"Identification of the equine rhinopneumonitis virus
isolated from aborted fetuses," by K. Kharalambiev,
et al. VETERINARNO MEDITSINSKI 10(5):95-101,
1973.

"Ideal family size as an intervening variable between
religion and attitudes towards abortion," by M. Rerzi.
JOURNAL FOR THE SCIENTIFIC STUDY OF RE-
LIGION 14:23-27, March, 1975.

"Immunization of RhO(D)-negative secundigravidae whose
first pregnancy was terminated by induced abortion,"
by I. Simonovits, et al. HAEMATOLOGIA 8(1-4):
291-298, 1974.

"Immunological disruption of implantation in monkeys
with antibodies to human pregnancy specific beta
1-glycoprotein (SP1)," by H. Bohn, et al. ARCHIV
FUR GYNAEKOLOGIE 217(2):209-218, 1974.

"The immunological identification of foetal haemoglobin
in bloodstains in infanticide and associated crimes,"
by S. J. Baxter, et al. MEDICINE, SCIENCE AND
LAW 14(3):163-167, July, 1974.

"Immunological problems connected with pregnancy and
therapeutic deductions in case of threatened abortion,"
by M. Goisis, et al. MINERVA GINECOLOGICA
27(4):319-328, April, 1975.

"The impact of the New York State abortion law on black
and white fertility in Upstate New York," by K. J.
Roghmann. INTERNATIONAL JOURNAL OF EPI-
DEMIOLOGY 4(1):45-49, March, 1975.

"Las implicaciones legales para Puerto Rico de los casos Roe v. Wade (93 Sup Ct 705) 41 L.W. 4214 (1973) y Doe v. Bolton (93 Sup Ct 739) 41 L.W. 4233 (1973)," by C. T. Jiménez. REVISTA DEL COLEGIO DE ABOGADOS DE PUERTO RICO 35:581-610, November, 1974.

"The implications of abortion." TABLET 229:51, January 18, 1975.

"Importance of determining chorionic gonadotropin excretion in the obstetrical and gynecological clinic," by A. A. Galochkina. VOPROSY OKHRANY MATERIN-STAV I DETSTVA 18(4):77-80, 1973.

"Importance of hormone assays and high dose HCG, estrogen and 17-alpha-hydroxyprogesterone treatment in the prevention of threatened abortion due to endocrine causes," by G. Cubesi, et al. ACTA EURO-PAEA FERTILITATIS 2(3):355-358, September, 1970.

"The impossible dream," by M. Lawrence. TRIUMPH 10:9-11, March, 1975.

"Incidence of unwanted pregnancy in Australia," by E. L. Synder. MEDICAL JOURNAL OF AUSTRALIA 2(6): 233-234, August 9, 1975.

"Incomplete pregnancies in workers of the metallurgical industry," by O. S. Badyva, et al. PEDIATRIIA AKUSHERSTVO I GINEKOLOGIIA (5):36-39, September-October, 1974.

"An inconvenient fetus." NURSING MIRROR AND MID-WIVES JOURNAL 141:76, July 17, 1975.

"Induced abortion," by A. L. Castelazo. GINECOLOGIA Y OBSTETRICIA DE MEXICO 37(219):1-12, January, 1975.

"Induced abortion and its sequelae: prematurity and spontaneous abortion," by L. H. Roht, et al. AMERICAN JOURNAL OF OBSTETRICS AND GYNECOLOGY 120(7):868-874, December 1, 1974.

"Induced abortion and subsequent outcome of pregnancy. A matched cohort study," by J. R. Daling, et al. LANCET 2(7926):170-173, July 26, 1975.

"Induced abortion--a historical outline," by F. Glenc. POLSKI TYGODNIK LEKARSKI 29(45):1957-1958, November 11, 1974.

"Induced abortion using prostaglandin E2 and F2alpha gel," by T. H. Lippert, et al. GYNAEKOLOGISCHE RUNDSCHAU 14(3):234-235, 1974.

"Induced mid-trimester abortion," by D. T. Liu, et al. NURSING TIMES 70(40):1543, October 3, 1974.

"Inducing abortion in cattle." MODERN VETERINARY PRACTICE 56(9):659-661, September, 1975.

"Induction of abortion by different prostaglandin analogues," by M. Bygdeman, et al. ACTA OBSTETRICIA ET GYNECOLOGICA SCANDINAVIEA. SUPPLEMENT (37):67-72, 1974.

"Induction of abortion by oestrogens in animals. A review," by W. Velle. NORDISH VETERINAER MEDICIN 26(10):563-571, October, 1974.

"Induction of abortion in rhesus monkeys with urea," by B. Malaviya, et al. INDIAN JOURNAL OF EXPERIMENTAL BIOLOGY 12(4):372-373, July, 1974.

"Induction of abortion in the 2nd trimester by intraamniotic instillation of hypertonic sodium chloride solution," by D. Mladenović, et al. SRPSKI ARHIV ZA CELOJUPNO LEKARSTVO 102(3-4):

199-208, March-April, 1974.

"Induction of abortion with prostaglandins: clinical and metabolic aspects," by M. Bygdeman, et al. SOUTH AFRICAN MEDICAL JOURNAL 0(0):Suppl:3-8, October 16, 1974.

"Induction of labour and abortion by intravenous prostaglandins in pregnancies complicated by intra-uterine foetal death and hydatidiform mole," by G. Roberts. CURRENT MEDICAL RESEARCH AND OPINION 2(6):342-350, 1974.

"Induction of labour and perinatal mortality," by A. Singer, et al. BRITISH MEDICAL JOURNAL 2(5961): 35, April 5, 1975.

"Induction of middle trimester abortion by intra-amniotic instillation of hypertonic solution," by M. Blum, et al. HAREFUAH 88(4):167-169, February 16, 1975.

"Infections with mycoplasma and bacteria in induced midtrimester abortion and fetal loss," by D. Sompolinsky, et al. AMERICAN JOURNAL OF OBSTETRICS AND GYNECOLOGY 121(5):610-616, March 1, 1975.

"Infectious bovine rhinotracheitis virus and its role in bovine abortion," by P. J. Durham. NEW ZELAND VETERINARY JOURNAL 22(10):175-180, October, 1974.

"Infective complications of the IUD." MEDICAL JOURNAL OF AUSTRALIA 2(7):241-242, August 16, 1975.

"Information meeting about hormonal contraception and the abortion situation," by J. Wiese. UGESKRIFT FOR LAEGER 137(23):1279-1282, June 2, 1975.

"Inherited (13; 14) translocation and reproduction. Report on three families," by H. von Koskull, et al. HUMAN-

GENETIK 24(2):85-91, 1974.

"Inhibition of labour. Symposium by letter," by J.
Hütter, et al. MUENCHENER MEDIZINISCHE
WOCHENSCHRIFT 116(38):689-698, September 20,
1974.

"Initiation of human parturition. I. Mechanism of
action of arachidonic acid," by P. C. MacDonald,
et al. OBSTETRICS AND GYNECOLOGY 44(5):
629-636, November, 1974.

"Insect hormones as tsetse abortifacients," by D. L.
Denlinger. NATURE 253(5490):347-348, January 31,
1975.

"The Institute of Medicine reports on legalized abortion
and the public health," by R. Lincoln. FAMILY
PLANNING PERSPECTIVES 7(4):185-188, July-
August, 1975.

"Intelligent woman's guide to sex; abortion is a fact
in our society," by K. Durbin. MADEMOISELLE
81:41, March, 1975.

"Interruption of the late stages of pregnancy by means
of transcervical amniocentesis and the replacement
of the amniotic fluid," by V. I. Babukhadiia, et al.
PEDIATRIIA AKUSHERSTVO I GINEKOLOGIIA
(5):53-55, September-October, 1974.

"Interruption of pregnancy at midterm by intrauterine
application of solutions," by Y. Manabe. OBSTE-
TRICAL AND GYNECOLOGICAL SURVEY 27(10):
701-710, October, 1972.

"Interruption of pregnancy by PGF 2 alpha. II. Extraovular administration," by F. E. Szontágh, et al.
ACTA EUROPAEA FERTILITATIS 4(1):23-30, March,
1973.

"Interruption of pregnancy in Boeck's disease?" (letter), by
K. Wurm. DEUTSCH MEDIZINISCHE WOCHENSCHRIFT
99(46):2374-2375, November 15, 1974.

"Interruption of pregnancy without cervic dilatation," by
L. Lázló, et al. ORVOSI HETILAP 115(50):2967-
2969, December 15, 1974.

"Interruption using prostaglandin F2alpha and E2," by H.
Henner, et al. GYNAEKOLOGISCHE RUNDSCHAU
14(3):236-237, 1974.

"Intra-amniotic administration of prostaglandin E2 in
midtrimester abortions," (letter), by H. Neifeld.
SOUTH AFRICAN MEDICAL JOURNAL 48(63):2614,
December 28, 1974.

"Intraamniotic administration of prostaglandin F2alpha
for therapeutic abortion," by R. Nyberg. ACTA
OBSTETRICIA ET GYNECOLOGICA SCANDINAVICA
(37):41-46, 1974.

"Intra-amniotic administration of prostaglandin in
second trimester of pregnancy," by C. Galatis.
SOUTH AFRICAN MEDICAL JOURNAL 49(3):65,
January 18, 1975.

"Intra-amniotic prostaglandin F 2alpha as a midtrimester
abortifacient: effect of oxytocin and laminaria," by
S. L. Corson, et al. JOURNAL OF REPRODUCTIVE
MEDICINE 14(2):47-51, February, 1975.

"Intra-amniotic prostaglandin techniques for induction
of mid-trimester abortion and associated changes in
plasma steroid hormones," by I. Craft, et al. SOUTH
AFRICAN MEDICAL JOURNAL 0(0):Suppl:31-35,
October 16, 1974.

"Intra-amniotic urea and low-dose prostaglandin E2 for
midtrimester termination," by I. Craft. LANCET

1(7916):1115-1116, May 17, 1975.

"Intra-amniotic urea as a midtrimester abortifacient:
clinical results and serum and urinary changes,"
by L. S. Burnett, et al. AMERICAN JOURNAL OF
OBSTETRICS AND GYNECOLOGY 121(1):7-16,
January 1, 1975.

"Intraamniotic urea for induction of midtrimester pregnancy termination: a further evaluation," by P. C.
Weinberg, et al. OBSTETRICS AND GYNECOLOGY
45(3):320-324, March, 1975.

"Intramuscular administration of 15(S)-15-methylprosta-
glandin E2-methyl ester for induction of abortion,"
by W. E. Brenner, et al. AMERICAN JOURNAL OF
OBSTETRICS AND GYNECOLOGY 120(6):833-836,
November 15, 1974.

"Intramuscular administration of 15(S) 15 methyl prostaglandin E2 methyl ester for induction of abortion: a
comparison of two dose schedules," by W. E. Brenner,
et al. FERTILITY & STERILITY 26(4):369-379,
April, 1975.

"Intramuscular administration of a prostaglandin analogue
during pregnancy in the goat," by P. J. Holst, et al.
JOURNAL OF REPRODUCTIVE FERTILITY 43(2):403-
404, May, 1975.

"Intrauterine death treated with intrauterine extra-amniotic
prostaglandin E2," by H. Wagman, et al. BRITISH
JOURNAL OF CLINICAL PRACTICE 28(9):318, September, 1974.

"Intrauterine instillation of prostaglandin F2ALPHA IN
EARLY PREGNANCY," by J. R. Jones, et al.
PROSTAGLANDINS 9(6):881-892, June, 1975.

"Intravaginal insertion of a dimethylpolysiloxane-polyvinyl

pyrrolidone-prostaglandin F2alpha tube for midterm abortion in rabbits," by I. F. Lau, et al. AMERICAN JOURNAL OF OBSTETRICS AND GYNECOLOGY 120 (6):837–839, November 15, 1974.

"Intravascular hemolysis: a complication of midtrimester abortion: a report of two cases," by A. Adachi, et al. OBSTETRICS AND GYNECOLOGY 45(4):467–469, April, 1975.

"Intravenous prostaglandins and oxytocin for mid-trimester abortion," by J. M. Beazley. LANCET 1(7902): 335, February 8, 1975.

"Intravenous prostaglandins and oxytocin for mid-trimester abortion," by T. M. Coltart, et al. LANCET 1(7899):173–174, January 18, 1975.

"Iowa public hospitals cannot discharge staff for abortion views." HOSPITAL LAW 8:4, February, 1975.

"Is any change in the abortion law really needed?" by T. Smith. TIMES p. 11, January 31, 1975.

"Is the fetus a person," by A. DiIanni. AMERICAN ECCLESIASTICAL REVIEW p. 309, May, 1974.

"Is support of abortion political suicide?" by J. I. Rosoff. FAMILY PLANNING PERSPECTIVES 7(1):13–22, January-February, 1975.

"Is it advisable to interrupt pregnancy by vacuum aspiration?" by G. Janny. ORVOSI HETILAP 116(15):885–886, April 13, 1975.

"Isolation of bacteria and viruses from aborted bovine fetuses," by T. Sugimura, et al. NATIONAL INSTITUTE OF ANIMAL HEALTH QUARTERLY 14(2):42–47, Summer, 1974.

"The isolation of Leptospira hardjo from an aborting cow," by S. W. Michna, et al. RESEARCH IN VETERINARY SCIENCE 17(1):133-135, July, 1974.

"Isolation of leptospira serotype pomona and brucella suls from swines from the State of Santa Catarina, Brazil," by C. A. Santa Rosa, et al. ARQUIVOS DE INSTITUTO BIOLOGICO 40(1):29-32, January-March, 1973.

"Isolation of Mycoplasma bovigenitalium from an aborted equine foetus," by E. V. Langford. VETERINARY RECORD 94(23):528, June 8, 1974.

"Isoxsuprine chlorhydrate in the treatment of threatened abortion," by L. Ballestrin. ARCHIVIO DI OSTETRI- CIA E GINECOLOGIA 78(1-3):53-66, January-June, 1973.

"Issue they wanted to avoid." ECONOMIST 255:33, January 25, 1975

"It is time to take a stand," by D. R. Shanklin. JOURNAL OF REPRODUCTIVE MEDICINE 14(2):41-42, February, 1975.

"Italian sci-fi: too close for comfort?" by J. Harris. MS MAGAZINE 4:17, October, 1975

"Julie who walks in the sunlight," by R. DuBois. LIGUORIAN 63:26-29, July, 1975.

"Lamenting a misconception." CHRISTIANITY TODAY 19:46, February 28, 1975.

"Late sequelae of induced abortion: complications and outcome of pregnancy and labor," by S. Harlap, et al. AMERICAN JOURNAL OF EPIDEMIOLOGY 102(3):

217-224, September, 1975.

"Law for the nurse supervisor: more about abortion decisions," by H. Creighton. RN; NATIONAL MAGAZINE FOR NURSES 6(4):10-11, April 14, 1975.

"Law, morals and abortion," by D. Degnan. COMMONWEAL p. 305, May 31, 1974.

"Legal abortion among New York City residents: an analysis according to socioeconomic and demographic characteristics," by M. J. Kramer. FAMILY PLANNING PERSPECTIVES 7(3):128-137, May-June, 1975.

"Legal abortion in Bexar county hospital," by C. E. Gibbs, et al. TEXAS MEDICINE 71(2):92-95, February, 1975.

"Legal abortion in England," by H. P. Tarnesby. NOUVELLE PRESSE MEDICALE 4(19):1443-1444, 1446-1448, May 10, 1975.

"Legal abortions in the United States since the 1973 Supreme Court decisions," by E. Weinstock, et al. FAMILY PLANNING PERSPECTIVES 7(1):23-31, January-February, 1975.

"The legal aspects of abortion," by L. D. Collins. CANADIAN JOURNAL OF PUBLIC HEALTH 66(3): 234-236, May-June, 1975.

"Legal guidelines for the performance of abortions," by H. L. Hirsh. AMERICAN JOURNAL OF OBSTETRICS AND GYNECOLOGY 122(6):679-682, July 15, 1975.

"Legal interruption of pregnancy. Medical considerations," by R. Bourg. BRUXELLES MEDICAL 54(1):

13-17, January, 1974.

"Legislation--abortion--Michigan's 'conscience clause'."
WAYNE LAW REVIEW 21:175-182, November, 1974.

"The legitimacy of a diverse society," by K. J. Ryan.
JOURNAL OF THE AMERICAN MEDICAL ASSOCIATION
233(7):781, August 18, 1975.

"Leptospira pomona and reproductive failure in California
sea lions," by A. W. Smith, et al. JOURNAL OF THE
AMERICAN VETERINARY MEDICAL ASSOCIATION
165(11):996-998, December 1, 1974.

"Let live," by M. Belton. HEALTH VISITOR 47(9):278,
September, 1974.

"Let's break the law to stop abortions," by P. Riga.
U. S. CATHOLIC 40:13-14, September, 1975.

"Liberalization of legal abortion," by K. J. Rees.
C.I.C.I.A.M.S. NOUVELLES 0(4):12-21, 1974.

"Life/death decisions; interview by J. Castelli," by R. Mc-
Cormick. ST. ANTHONY MESSENGER 83:32-35,
August, 1975.

"Life-saving and life-taking: a comment," by R. Mc-
Cormick. LINACRE QUARTERLY 42:110-115, May,
1975.

"Listeria as a cause of abortion and neonatal mortality in
sheep," by K. L. Hughes. AUSTRALIAN VETERINARY
JOURNAL 51(2):97-99, February, 1975.

"Listeria monocytogenes type 5 as a cause of abortion in
sheep," by N. S. Macleod, et al. VETERINARY RE-
CORD 95(16):365-367, October 19, 1974.

"Magnesium electrophoresis by means of a sinusoid modulated current in the treatment of spontaneous abortion," by A. I. Liubimova, et al. AKUSHERSTVO I GINEKOLOGIIA (Moscow) (9):45-48, September, 1974.

"Male-induced pregnancy termination in the prairie vole, Microtus ochrogaster," by A. C. Fraser-Smith. SCIENCE 187(4182):1211-1213, March 28, 1975.

"Male parent versus female parent: separate and unequal rights." UMKC LAW REVIEW 43:392-412, Spring, 1975.

"Management of missed abortion, intrauterine death and hydatidiform mole using prostaglandin E2," by C. P. Murray, et al. IRISH MEDICAL JOURNAL 68(6):133-135, March 22, 1975.

"Management of septic abortion," by R. H. Bartlett. NEW ENGLAND JOURNAL OF MEDICINE 293(3): 152-153, July 17, 1975.

"Management of septic chemical abortion with renal failure. Use of a conservative regimen," by D. F. Hawkins, et al. NEW ENGLAND JOURNAL OF MEDICINE 292(14):722-725, April 3, 1975.

"Marker chromosomes in parents of spontaneous abortuses," by S. Holbek, et al. HUMANGENETIK 25(1): 61-64, 1974.

"Maternal influence on postimplantation survival in inbred rats," by D. V. Cramer, et al. JOURNAL OF REPRODUCTION AND FERTILITY 44(2):317-321, August, 1975.

"Materno-fetal ABO incompatibility as a cause of spontaneous abortion," by J. G. Lauritsen, et al. CLINICAL GENETICS 7(4):308-316, April, 1975.

"Matters of life and death. The manipulative society,"
by E. H. Patey. NURSING MIRROR AND MIDWIVES'
JOURNAL 139(23):40-41, December 5, 1974.

"MDs wary of abortion verdict implications." AMERICAN
MEDICAL ASSOCIATION NEWS 18:3, March 3, 1975.

"The meaning of abortion," by S. MacDonald. AMERICAN
ECCLESIASTICAL REVIEW 169:219-236, April, 1975;
291-315, May, 1975.

"Medicaid coverage of abortions in New York City: costs
and benefits," by M. Robinson, et al. FAMILY
PLANNING PERSPECTIVES 6:202-208, Fall, 1974.

"Medical and social aspects of adolescent pregnancies.
I. Adolescents applying for termination of an illegiti-
mate pregnancy," by O. Widholm, et al. ACTA
OBSTETRICIA ET GYNECOLOGICA SCANDINAVICA
53(4):347-353, 1974.

"Medical and social characteristics of Irish residents
whose pregnancies were terminated under the 1967
Abortion Act in 1971 and 1972," by D. Walsh.
IRISH MEDICAL JOURNAL 68(6):143-149, March 22,
1975.

"Medical consequences of teenage sexuality," by A. R.
Hinman, et al. NEW YORK STATE JOURNAL OF
MEDICINE 75(9):1439-1442, August, 1975.

"Medical cop-out? the physician's role in abortion
counseling," by H. Klaus. AMERICA 133:68-70,
August 16, 1975.

"Medical coverage of abortions in New York city: costs
and benefits [based on conference paper]," by M.
Robinson, et al. FAMILY PLANNING PERSPEC-
TIVES 6:202-208, Fall, 1974.

"Medical ethics in the courtroom. The role of law vs professional self-discipline," by J. A. Robertson. HASTINGS CENTER REPORT 4(4):1-3, September, 1974.

"Medical responsibility for fetal survival under Roe (Roe v. Wade, 93 Sup Ct 705) and Doe (Doe v. Bolton, 93 Sup Ct 739)." HARVARD CIVIL RIGHTS - CIVIL LIBERTIES LAW REVIEW 10:444-471, Spring, 1975.

"Medical termination of pregnancy act," by J. Minattur. MEDICAL SERVICE 31:56 plus, December, 1974.

"Medicine and the law: Attorney general clarifies status of Texas abortion laws," by S. V. Stone, Jr. TEXAS MEDICINE 70(11):107-108, November, 1974.

"Medico-legal briefs: husband may not prevent wife from having abortion." JOURNAL OF THE MISSISSIPPI STATE MEDICAL ASSOCIATION 16(1):14-15, January, 1975.

"Menstrual and obstetric sequelae of missed abortion," by W. Z. Polishuk, et al. ACTA EUROPAEA FERTILITATIS 5(4):289-293, December, 1974.

"Menstrual extraction," by M. F. Atienza, et al. AMERICAN JOURNAL OF OBSTETRICS AND GYNECOLOGY 121(4):490-495, February 15, 1975.

"Menstrual regulation in the United States: a preliminary report," by W. E. Brenner, et al. FERTILITY AND STERILITY 26(3):289-295, March, 1975.

"Mental and social stress of motherhood over 40, with a view to psychiatric indication for interruption of pregnancy," by H. Kind, et al. SCHWEIZERISCHE MEDIZINISCHE WOCHENSCHRIFT 104(35):1221-1224, August 31, 1974.

"Merchants of distress," by M. Simms. NEW HUMANIST 90:334, February, 1975.

"Methodology in premature pregnancy termination. I," by A. C. Wentz, et al. OBSTETRICS AND GYNECOLOGY 28(1):2-19, January, 1973.

"Methods for early termination of pregnancy in the cow," by F. L. Dawson. VETERINARY RECORD 94(23):542-548, June 8, 1974.

"Methods for early termination of pregnancy in the cow," by P. G. Millar. VETERINARY RECORD 94(26):626, June 29, 1974.

"Michigan abortion refusal act." UNIVERSITY OF MICHIGAN JOURNAL OF LAW REFORM 8:659-675, Spring, 1975.

"Midterm abortion in hamsters induced by silastic-PVP-PGE2 tubes," by I. F. Lau, et al. PROSTAGLANDINS 8(5):423-431, December 10, 1974.

"Midterm abortion with silastic-PVP implant containing prostaglandin F2 alpha in rabbits, rats, and hamsters," by I. F. Lau, et al. FERTILITY AND STERILITY 25(10):839-844, October, 1974.

"Mid-trimester abortion induced by intravaginal administration of prostaglandin E2 suppositories," by N. H. Lauersen, et al. AMERICAN JOURNAL OF OBSTETRICS AND GYNECOLOGY 122(8):947-954, August 15, 1975.

"Midtrimester abortion induced by serial intramuscular injections of 15-(S)-15-methyl-prostaglandin F2alpha," by N. H. Lauersen, et al. AMERICAN JOURNAL OF OBSTETRICS AND GYNECOLOGY 121(2):273-276, January 15, 1975.

"Midtrimester abortion induced by serial intravaginal administration of prostaglandin E2 suppositories in conjunction with a contraceptive diaphragm," by N. H. Lauersen, et al. PROSTAGLANDINS 10(1):139-150, July, 1975.

"Midtrimester abortion induced by single intra-amniotic instillation of two dose schedules of 15(S)-15-methyl-prostaglandin F2alpha," by N. H. Lauersen, et al. PROSTAGLANDINS 9(4):617-625, April, 1975.

"Mid-trimester abortion with intra-amniotic prostaglandin F2 alpha and intravenous oxytocin infusion," by M. Salomy, et al. PROSTAGLANDINS 9(2):271-279, February, 1975.

"Mid-trimester abortion with 15 (S) methyl prostaglandin F 2 alpha," by T. Leibman, et al. PROSTAGLANDINS 7(5):443-448, September 10, 1974.

"Midtrimester pregnancy interruption and the placental progesterone levels," by F. A. Aleem, et al. PROSTAGLANDINS 9(3):495-500, March, 1975.

"Mid-trimester termination," (letter), by S. M. Karim, et al. BRITISH MEDICAL JOURNAL 4(5937):161-162, October 19, 1974.

"Miscarriages among operating theatre staff," by P. Rosenbert, et al. ACTA ANAESTHESIOLOGICA SCANDINAVICA. SUPPLEMENT 53(0):37-42, 1973.

"A mode of action of hypertonic saline in inducing abortion," by D. Llewellyn-Jones, et al. AMERICAN JOURNAL OF OBSTETRICS AND GYNECOLOGY 121(4):568-569, February 15, 1975.

"Monitoring of the induction of labour by prostaglindin f2alpha in early pregnancy," by H. Wiechell, et al. MUNCHENER MEDIZINISCHE WOCHENSCHRIFT

116(38):767-775, September 20, 1974.

"Moral issue and resolution of the time limit," by W.
Becker. MEDIZINISCHE KLINIK 69(49):2039-2040,
December 6, 1974.

"The moral message Bucharest," by D. P. Warwick.
HASTINGS CENTER REPORT 4:8-9, December, 1974.

"Morality of abortion," by G. M. Atkinson. INTERNA-
TIONAL PHILOSOPHICAL QUARTERLY 14:347-362,
September, 1974.

"The morality of abortion," by D. Doherty. AMERICAN
ECCLESIASTICAL REVIEW 169:37-47, January, 1975.

"Morbidity in legal abortions in the Perleberg District,"
by J. Berg. ZENTRALBLATT FUR GYNAEKOLOGIE
96(35):1111-1115, August 30, 1974.

"More abortions?" by M. Simms. BRITISH MEDICAL
JOURNAL 1(5949):95, January 11, 1975.

"More about abortion decisions," by H. Creighton.
SUPERVISOR NURSE 6:10 plus, April, 1975.

"Morgentaler case." NATION 221:6, July 5, 1975.

"The Morgentaler case," by P. N. Coles. CANADIAN
MEDICAL ASSOCIATION JOURNAL 113(3):181,
August 9, 1975.

"Morgentaler case divides Supreme Court in interpreta-
tion of Criminal Code," by D. Phillipson. CANADIAN
MEDICAL ASSOCIATION JOURNAL 112(8):1003-1004,
April 19, 1975.

"Morgentaler vs. the Queen," by L. E. Rozovsky.
DIMENSIONS IN HEALTH SERVICE 52(6):8-9, June,
1975.

"Morphological changes in the aborted fetuses and placentae in cases of diplococcus abortions in cows," by A. K. Angelov. VETERINARO-MEDITSINSKI 11(8):72-77, 1974.

"Morphological changes in aborted fetuses in swine brucellosis," by L. Diakov, et al. VETERINARNO-MEDITSINSKI 11 (6):91-97, 1974.

"Morphogenetic disturbances in a spontaneous abortus with trisomy B," by V. P. Kulazenko. HUMANGENETIK 25(1):53-59, 1974.

"The mystery of the unborn," by P. Fazziola. BIBLE TODAY 78:388-390, April, 1975.

"National committee for a human life amendment, inc.: its goals and origins," by R. N. Lynch. CATHOLIC LAWYER 20:303-308, Autumn, 1974.

"New doctors' dilemma: late abortion," by M. Clark, et al. NEWSWEEK 85:24-25, March 3, 1975.

"New doubts about abortion," by J. Kagan. McCALLS 101:121-123, June, 1975.

"New legislation on pregnancy interruption," by I. Stegane. SYKEPLETEN 62(6-7):267, March 20, 1975.

"A new set of rules for the abortion fight," by M. Bunson. OUR SUNDAY VISITOR 64:1 plus, August 17, 1975.

"No final solution," by M. R. Benjamin, et al. NEWS-WEEK 85:30-31, March 10, 1975.

"No going back," by D. Gould. NEW STATESMAN p. 132, January 31, 1975.

"No Medicaid payments for abortion counseling." MEDICAL

WORLD NEWS 16:96-97, January 27, 1975.

"None but the brave?" by D. Gould. NEW STATESMAN
89:774, June 13, 1975.

"Not a fetus but a baby, jury decides in Boston." OUR
SUNDAY VISITOR 63:1, March 2, 1975.

"Not our Nancy! (a feature)." CHRISTIAN HERALD
p. 26, February, 1975.

"Not self decided abortion but liberal laws in future Norwegian family politics," by N. Grünfeld. NORDISH
MEDICIN 90(2):44-47, February, 1975.

"Nurse's attitudes to termination of pregnancy." NURSING
FORUM 2(5):6-7, November-December, 1974.

"Nursing of patients with threatened abortion who are
on forced bedrest," by F. Kuwabara, et al. JAPAN-
ESE JOURNAL FOR THE MIDWIFE 28(6/7):333-335,
June-July, 1974.

"N. Y. abortion stirs outcry." NATIONAL CATHOLIC
REPORTER 11:6, January 24, 1975.

"N. Y. Times is for the birds but not for unborn babies."
OUR SUNDAY VISITOR 63:1, March 9, 1975.

"Observations on abortions in cattle: a comparison of
pathological, microbiological and immunological
findings   in aborted foetuses and foetuses collected
at abattoirs," by R. B. Miller, et al. CANADIAN
JOURNAL OF COMPARATIVE MEDICINE 39(3):270-
290, July, 1975.

"Observations on patients two years after legal abortion,"
by P. Jouppila, et al. INTERNATIONAL JOURNAL
OF FERTILITY 19(4):223-239, 1974.

"Occupational disease among operating room personnel,"
by L. F. Walts, et al. ANESTHESIOLOGY 42:608-
611, May, 1975.

"Occurrence of viral abortion in mares (Contribution to
diagnosis)," by H. Hartmann, et al. SCHWEIZER
ARCHIV FUR TIERHEILKUNDE 117(7):393-395,
July, 1975.

"Of many things; Edelin case; victims of ambiguity."
AMERICA 132:inside cover-141, March 1, 1975.

"On abortion and neonatal mortality," by M. J. Mahoney.
AMERICAN JOURNAL OF PUBLIC HEALTH 65(7):
747-748, July, 1975.

"On the abortion front..." NATIONAL REVIEW 27:
147-148, February 14, 1975.

"On the abortive and teratogenous action of volatile
and gaseous anaesthetis agents," by V. Hempel.
ANAESTHESIST 24(6):249-252, June, 1975.

"On a constitutional amendment protecting unborn human
life." CATHOLIC MIND p. 43, October, 1974.

"On human life," by W. Reinsdorf. HOMILETIC AND
PASTORAL REVIEW 65:65-68, January, 1975.

"On life and death," by R. Sterner. VITAL CHRISTIAN-
ITY p. 15, August 25, 1974.

"On priests and abortion," by A. E. Hellegers. FAMILY
PLANNING PERSPECTIVES 6(4):194-195, Fall, 1974.

"On 'the right to choose abortion', an editorial," (letter),
by M. J. Mahoney. AMERICAN JOURNAL OF PUBLIC
HEALTH 65(7):748, July, 1975.

"On the slippery slope again," by A. Lindsay. ANALYSIS

35:32, October, 1974.

"On unbiased estimation for randomized response models,"
by P. K. Sen. AMERICAN STATISTICAL ASSOCIA-
TION JOURNAL 69:997-1001, December, 1974.

"Ontario bishops blast government on abortion." OUR
SUNDAY VISITOR 64:2, May 25, 1975.

"Opportunities for the application of the prostaglandins
in gynecology. Interruption of pregnancy in acute
leukosis. Description of a case," by P. Krieglsteiner,
et al. MUNCHENER MEDIZINISCHE WOCHEN-
SCHRIFT 117(7):245-248, February 14, 1975.

"Opposition to a constitutional amendment on abortion:
American Public Health Association resolution."
AMERICAN JOURNAL OF PUBLIC HEALTH AND
THE NATION'S HEALTH 65:203, February, 1975.

"Or manslaughter?" ECONOMIST 254:61, February 22,
1975.

"The organization and results of a pregnancy termination
service in a National Health Service hospital," by M.
G. Hull, et al. JOURNAL OF OBSTETRICS AND
GYNAECOLOGY OF THE BRITISH COMMONWEALTH
81(8):577-587, August, 1974.

"Origin of triploidy in human abortuses," by J. Jonasson,
et al. HEREDITAS 71(1):168-171, 1972.

"Our approach to interruption of pregnancy in a myomatous
uterus," by I. Knejzlíková, et al. CESKOSLOVENSKA
GYNEKOLOGIE 40(5):353-354, June, 1975.

"Outbreak of vibrio abortion in sheep in Iraq," by G. M.
Al-Khatib, et al. BERLINER UND MUNCHENER
TIERAERZTLICHE WOCHENSCHRIFT 88(5):86-88,
March 1, 1975.

"Outpatient laparoscopic sterilization with therapeutic abortion versus abortion alone," by J. I. Fishburne, et al. OBSTETRICS AND GYNECOLOGY 45(6):665-668, June, 1975.

"Outpatient pregnancy termination in an NHS hospital," by M. G. Hull, et al. NURSING TIMES 70(40):1540-1542, October 3, 1974.

"Oxytocin administration, instillation-to-abortion time, and morbidity associated with saline instillation," by G. S. Berger, et al. AMERICAN JOURNAL OF OBSTETRICS AND GYNECOLOGY 121(7):941-946, April 1, 1975.

"Pain barrier," by J. Tweedie. GUARDIAN p. 9, March 3, 1975.

"Parental preferences and selective abortion: a commentary on Roe v. Wade (93 Sup Ct 705), Doe v. Bolton (93 Sup Ct 739) and the shape of things to come," by R. Delgado. WASHINGTON UNIVERSITY LAW QUARTERLY 1974:203-226, 1974.

"The pastoral care of those confronted with abortion," by H. McHugh. CLERGY REVIEW 60:218-223, April, 1975.

"Pastoral counseling and abortion," by M. Pable. PRIEST 31:15-16 plus, October, 1975.

"Pat Goltz - pro-life feminist," by J. Anderson. OUR SUNDAY VISITOR 64:1 plus, May 18, 1975.

"Pathological changes in tetrasploid abortuses after spontaneous abortion," by V. P. Kulazhenko, et al. AKUSHERSTVO I GINEKOLOGIIA (Moscow) (3):32-37, March, 1974.

"The pathology of birth control," by J. M. Craig.
ARCHIVES OF PATHOLOGY 99(5):233-236, May, 1975.

"Pathomorphological changes in guinea pigs and their
aborted fetuses in experimental Neorickettsia infection," by A. Dzhurov, et al. VETERINARNO-MEDI-
TSINSKI 10(6):57-66, 1973.

"Perforation of a cornual pregnancy at induced first-
trimester abortion," by B. Delson. AMERICAN
JOURNAL OF OBSTETRICS AND GYNECOLOGY
121(4):581-582, February 15, 1975.

"Perforation of the uterus and injuries of the internal
organs in violent interruption of pregnancy," by
B. Veković, et al. MEDICINSKI ARHIV 28(6):585-
587, November-December, 1974.

"Perinatal lamb mortality in Western Australia. 3.
Congenital infections," by S. M. Dennis. AUSTRAL-
IAN VETERINARY JOURNAL 50(11):507-510,
November, 1974.

--5. Vibrionic infection," by S. M. Dennis. AUSTRAL-
IAN VETERINARY JOURNAL 51(1):11-13, January,
1975.

--6. Listeric infection," by S. M. Dennis. AUSTRAL-
IAN VETERINARY JOURNAL 51(2):75-79, February,
1975.

"Perinatology begins before conception," by F. Hecht,
et al. NEW ENGLAND JOURNAL OF MEDICINE
293(12):604-605, September 18, 1975.

"Persistence of lymphocytotoxic antibodies in multiparas
examined several years after their last pregnancy,"
by M. Savi, et al. ATENEO PARMENSE; SEZIONE
I: ACTA BIO-MEDICA 46(1-2):61-75, January-April,
1975.

"Persistence of Salmonella abortus ovis in soil," by H. Tadjebakhche, et al. REVUE D'ELEVAGE ET DE MEDECINE VETERINAIRE DES PAYS TROPICAUX 27(1):57-59, 1974.

"The pill and subsequent pregnancies," by D. T. Janerich. LANCET 1(7908):681-682, March 22, 1975.

"Placental energy adequacy and tissue respiration in the normal course of pregnancy and in its spontaneous interruption," by V. V. Andrashko, et al. PEDIATRIIA AKUSHERSTVO IN GINEKOLOGIIA (5):41-44, September-October, 1974.

"Placental lactogenic hormone content of the blood of women with normal pregnancies and those complicated by late toxemia or miscarriage," by N. A. Stepanova, et al. AKUSHERSTVO I GINEKOLOGIIA (Moscow) (9):15-17, September, 1974.

"Politicizing the Catholic community," by V. Blum. HOSPITAL PROGRESS 56:84-88, September, 1975.

"Population and the crisis of culture," by T. Lane. HOMILETIC AND PASTORAL REVIEW 75:61-65, April, 1975.

"Possibilities of contraception, artificial abortion and premature labor in cattle," by E. Grunert, et al. DEUTSCHE TIERAERZTLICHE WOCHENSCHRIFT 81(23):588-591, December 1, 1974.

"Postabortion disseminated intravascular coagulation with reversible acute renal failure (report of 2 cases treated with heparin)," by V. Gutiérrez Millet, et al. REVISTA CLINICA ESPANOLA 134(2):149-156, July 31, 1974.

"Postabortion true mural thromboendocarditis," by R. Drut, et al. ARCHIVOS DE LA FUNDACION ROUX-

OCEFA 8(2-4):161-166, January-December, 1974.

"Post-abortion uterine perforation. Chilean experience,"
by R. García Valenzuela, et al. REVISTA CHILENA
DE OBSTETRICIA Y GINECOLOGIA 38(3):138-145,
1973.

"Post-abortum acute renal insufficiency," by A. Amerio,
et al. MINERVA NEFROLOGICA 21(2):95-103, March-
April, 1974.

"Postpartum and postabortal insertion of intrauterine
contraceptive devices," by L. A. Martorella, et al.
JOURNAL OF REPRODUCTIVE MEDICINE 14(4):
178-181, April, 1975.

"Predicting contraceptive use in postabortion patients,"
by G. M. Selstad, et al. AMERICAN JOURNAL OF
PUBLIC HEALTH 65(7):708-713, July, 1975.

"Prediction of fetal outcome in threatened abortion by
maternal serum placental lactogen and alpha fetopro-
tein," by L. Garoff, et al. AMERICAN JOURNAL OF
OBSTETRICS AND GYNECOLOGY 121(2):257-261,
January 15, 1975.

"Pregnancy in the single adolescent girl: the role of
cognitive functions," by W. G. Cobliner. JOURNAL
OF YOUTH AND ADOLESCENCE 3(1):17-30, March,
1974.

"Pregnancy interruption in cardiac patients," by A.
Barrillon, et al. ARCHIVES DES MALADIES DER
COEUR ET DES VAISSEAUX 67(5):555-564, May,
1974.

"Pregnancy planning in Hawaii," by P. G. Steinhoff, et
al. FAMILY PLANNING PERSPECTIVES 7(3):138-
142, May-June, 1975.

"Pregnancy wastage and age of mother among the Amish," by L. J. Ressegule. HUMAN BIOLOGY 46(4):633-639, December, 1974.

"Pregnancy with an intrauterine contraceptive device." BRITISH MEDICAL JOURNAL 2(5969):458, May 31, 1975.

"Preliminary experience in the clinical use of F2alpha prostaglandins in missed abortion," by M. Herrera, et al. REVISTA CHILENA DE OBSTETRICIA Y GINECOLOGIA 38(4):187-190, 1973.

"Preliminary experience with 15 (S) 15-methyl prostaglandin F2 alpha for midtrimester abortion," by B. E. Greer, et al. AMERICAN JOURNAL OF OBSTETRICS AND GYNECOLOGY 121(4):524-527, February 15, 1975.

"Prenatal exposure to stilboestrol." MEDICAL JOURNAL OF AUSTRALIA 1(12):373-374, March 22, 1975.

"Prenatal pediatric ethics," by A. Prado-Vértiz. BOLETIN MEDICO DEL HOSPITAL INFANTIL DE MEXICO 31(2):183-197, March-April, 1974.

"Prevention of genetic diseases through prenatal diagnosis," by H. Hübner, et al. GINEKOLOGIA POLASKA 45(11): 1313-1323, November, 1974.

"Prevention of Rh haemolytic disease," by C. A. Clarke. NURSING MIRROR AND MIDWIVES' JOURNAL 139 (17):57-59, October 24, 1974.

"Preventive treatment of habitual abortion caused by internal os incompetence," by S. Krzysztoporski. ZENTRALBLATT FUER VETERINAERMEDIZINE. JOURNAL OF VETERINARY MEDICINE 3(4):215-218, November, 1974.

"Previous reproductive history in mothers presenting
with spontaneous abortions," by E. Alberman, et al.
BRITISH JOURNAL OF OBSTETRICS AND GYNAECOL-
OGY 82(5):366-373, May, 1975.

"Priests urged to pro-life leadership in new booklet:
Abortion, attitudes and the law, by NCCB and Our
Sunday Visitor." OUR SUNDAY VISITOR 64:1,
August 31, 1975.

"Private hospitals not required to perform nontherapeutic
abortions," by W. A. Regan. HOSPITAL PROGRESS
56:28 plus, April, 1975.

"The problem of abortion," by R. Spiazzi. L'OSSERVA-
TORE ROMANO 39(391):9-10, September 25, 1975.

"The problem of the medical indication for artificial
abortion," by G. Fanconi. MINERVA PEDIATRICA
27(8):455-461, March 10, 1975.

"Professional perspectives on abortion," by R. C.
Burchell. JOGN NURSING 3(6):25-27, November-
December, 1974.

"Profile of an abortion counselor," by B. Dauber.
FAMILY PLANNING PERSPECTIVES 6(3):185-187,
Summer, 1974.

"The prognosis in pregnancy after threatened abortion,"
by P. Jouppila, et al. ANNALES CHIRURGIAE ET
GYNAECOLOGIAE FENNIAE 63(6):439-444, 1974.

"Prognosis in threatened abortion and chorionic hormone
levels in the blood," by N. Medoki, et al. FOLIA
ENDOCRINOLOGICA JAPONICA 50(2):520, February
20, 1974.

"The prognostic value of chorionic-gonadotrophins in
the urine of miscarrying women," by H. Dyková,

et al. CESKOSLOVENSKA GYNEKOLOGIE 40(6): 417-420, July, 1975.

"The prognostic value of human placental lactogen (HPL) levels in threatened abortion," by M. W. Gartside, et al. BRITISH JOURNAL OF OBSTETRICS AND GYNAECOLOGY 82(4):303-309, April, 1975.

"Prolactin in the blood-serum during physiological and pathological gravidity," by F. Gzaárek, et al. CESKOSLOVENSKA GYNEKOLOGIE 40(1):39-40, February, 1975.

"Pro-lifers bring high hopes, food, to Washington march," by S. Shoemaker. NATIONAL CATHOLIC REPORTER 11:1-2, January 31, 1975.

"Prophylactic use of tetracycline for first trimester abortions," by J. E. Hodgson, et al. OBSTETRICS AND GYNECOLOGY 45(5):574-578, May, 1975.

"A propos de la nouvelle loi sur l'interruption volontaire de la grossesse; intervention du cardinal Marty," by F. Marty. LA DOCUMENTATION CATHOLIQUE 72:125, February 2, 1975.

"Proposed decree on abortion and nurses' role," by S. A. Jegede. NIGERIAN NURSE 7(1):33-34, January-March, 1975.

"Prosecution of Dr. Morgentaler," by M. Gordon, et al. CANADIAN DIMENSION 10:9-11, June, 1975.

"Prostaglandin abortions in an outpatient ward," by O. Ylikorkala, et al. DUODECIM 90(19):1308-1316, 1974.

"Prostaglandin delivery by cervical dilator," by H. Balin, et al. JOURNAL OF REPRODUCTIVE MEDI-

CINE 13(6):208-212, December, 1974.

"Prostaglandin F alpha in amniotic fluid in man," by
K. Hillier, et al. JOURNAL OF ENDOCRINOLOGY
64(1):13P, January, 1975.

"Prostaglandin F2alpha and oxytocin compared with
hypertonic saline and oxytocin for the induction of
second trimester abortion," by K. R. Nielsen, et al.
ACTA OBSTETRICIA ET GYNECOLOGICA SCAN-
DINAVICA. SUPPLEMENT. (37):57-60, 1974.

"Prostaglandin F2alpha as a method of choice for inter-
ruption of pregnancy," by V. Zahn, et al. GEBURT-
SHILFE UND FRAUENHEILKUNDE 35(3):203-210,
March, 1975.

"Prostaglandin F2-alpha for induction of midterm abortion:
a comparative study," by I. F. Lau, et al. FERTIL-
ITY AND STERILITY 26(1):74-79, January, 1975.

"Prostaglandin F2alpha given by continuous transcervical
extra-amniotic infusion combined with intravenous
oxytocin infusion for therapeutic termination of mid-
trimester pregnancies," by K. W. Waldron, et al.
MEDICAL JOURNAL OF AUSTRALIA 1(17):525-527,
April 26, 1975.

"Prostaglandin F2 alpha implant-induced abortion: effect
on progestin and luteinizing hormone concentration
and its reversal by progesterone in rabbits, rats, and
hamsters," by S. K. Saksena, et al. FERTILITY AND
STERILITY 25(10):845-850, October, 1974.

"Prostaglandin F2alpha: modification of its abortifacient
effect by depo-estradiol cypionate in rats," by S. K.
Saksena, et al. FERTILITY AND STERILITY 26(2):
126-130, February, 1975.

"Prostaglandin-induced abortion and cervical incompetence,"

by M. P. Embrey. BRITISH MEDICAL JOURNAL
2(5969):497, May 31, 1975.

"Prostaglandin-induced abortion: assessment of operative complications and early morbidity," by I. Z.
Mackenzie, et al. BRITISH MEDICAL JOURNAL
4(5946):683-686, December 21, 1974.

"Prostaglandin induction of midtrimester abortions:
three years' experience of 626 cases," by P. Kajanoja,
et al. ACTA OBSTETRICIA ET GYNECOLOGICA
SCANDINAVICA. SUPPLEMENT (37):51-56, 1974.

"The prostaglandins," by C. B. Clayman. JOURNAL OF
THE AMERICAN MEDICAL ASSOCIATION 233(8):
904-906, August 25, 1975.

"Prostaglandins and induction of abortion," by P.
Kopecky. HIPPOKRATES 46(1):117-119, February,
1975.

"Prostaglandins for termination of second trimester
pregnancy," by U. R. Krishna, et al. JOURNAL OF
POSTGRADUATE MEDICINE 20(4):176-181, October,
1974.

"Prostaglandins F2 alpha (Amoglandin, Dinoprost) for
induced abortion in the second trimester," by E. B.
Obel. UGESKRIFT FOR LAEGER 137(25):1417-1418,
June 16, 1975.

"Prostaglandins in clinical obstetrics and gynaecology."
ACTA OBSTETRICIA ET GYNECOLOGICA SCANDIN-
AVICA. SUPPLEMENT (37):1-72, 1974.

"The prostaglandins in obstetrics and gynaecology. Are
they living up to expectations?..." by A. Gillespie.
MEDICAL JOURNAL OF AUSTRALIA 1(2):38-41,
January 11, 1975.

"Protestant women mobilize forces against abortion."
OUR SUNDAY VISITOR 64:2, September 7, 1975,

"Protestants organize to speak out on abortion; the
Christian Action Council." OUR SUNDAY VISITOR
64:1, July 20, 1975.

"Psychodiagnostic factors of indication for abortion,"
by A. Blaser, et al. SCHWEIZERISCHE MEDIZIN-
ISCHE WOCHENSCHRIFT 105(14):436-438, April 5,
1975.

"Psychological antecedents to conception among abortion
seekers," by W. B. Miller. WESTERN JOURNAL OF
MEDICINE 122(1):12-19, January, 1975.

"Psychological aspects of interruption," by S. Fukalová.
CESKOSLOVENSKA GYNEKOLOGIE 39(3):204-206,
April, 1974.

"Psychological factors in contraceptive failure and
abortion request." MEDICAL JOURNAL OF AUS-
TRALIA 1(26):800, June 28, 1975.

"Psychological femininity and legal abortion," by L.
Jacobsson, et al. ACTA PSYCHIATRICA SANDIN-
AVICA. SUPPLEMENT (255):291-298, 1974.

"Psychological problems following birth and miscarriage,"
by K. L. Trick. NURSING MIRROR AND MIDWIVES'
JOURNAL 141(2):61-62, July 10, 1975.

"The psychological sequelae of abortion performed for a
genetic indication," by B. D. Blumberg, et al. AMERI-
CAN JOURNAL OF OBSTETRICS AND GYNECOLOGY
122(7):799-808, August 1, 1975.

"Psychological sequelae of elective abortion," by B. D.
Blumberg, et al. WESTERN JOURNAL OF MEDICINE
123(3):188-193, September, 1975.

"Psychosexual problems connected with artificial inter-
ruption of pregnancy," by F. Kohoutek, et al.
CESKOSLOVENSKA GYNEKOLOGIE 39(3):206-207,
April, 1974.

"Putting the clock back on abortion," by P. Ferris.
OBSERVER p. 10, February 16, 1975.

"Questions no one asked Dr. Kenneth Edelin on the witness stand: interview edited by G. Steinem," by K. C.
Edelin. MS MAGAZINE 4:76-78 plus, August, 1975.

"Radiological aspects of indications for pregnancy interruption." ORVOSI HETILAP 116(23):1351, June
8, 1975.

"Radioreceptorassay of human chorionic gonadotropin as
an aid in miniabortion," by R. Landesman, et al.
FERTILITY AND STERILITY 25(12):1022-1029,
December, 1974.

"Rapid hCG-specific radioimmunoassay for menstrual
aspiration," by T. S. Kosasa, et al. OBSTETRICS
AND GYNECOLOGY 45(5):566-568, May, 1975.

"Rare case of choriocarcinoma in ectopic pregnancy
following removal of coexisting uterine pregnancy,"
by B. Buczek, et al. WIADOMOSCI LEKARSKIE
28(10):895-897, May 15, 1975.

"Rate of fall in plasma progesterone and time to abortion
following intra-amniotic injection of prostaglandin F2-
alpha, with or without urea, in the second trimester
of human pregnancy," by S. M. Walker, et al. BRITISH
JOURNAL OF OBSTETRICS AND GYNAECOLOGY 82
(6):488-492, June, 1975.

"Reaction split to Kennedy abortion view: federal funds

for abortion," by R. Rashke. NATIONAL CATHOLIC
REPORTER 11:1 plus, May 2, 1975.

"Read the lobbying report," by P. L. Lowry. AMERICAN
JOURNAL OF PUBLIC HEALTH 65(10):1115, October,
1975.

"Reassessment of systemic administration of prostaglan-
dins for induction of midtrimester abortion," by M.
Bygdeman, et al. PROSTAGLANDINS 8(2):157-169,
October 25, 1974.

"Recent advances in the cytogenetic study of human spon-
taneous abortions," by H. D. McConnell, et al.
OBSTETRICS AND GYNECOLOGY 45(5):547-552,
May, 1975.

"Reduction of cervical resistance by prostaglandin suppositories prior to dilatation for induced abortion,"
by J. R. Dingfelder, et al. AMERICAN JOURNAL
OF OBSTETRICS AND GYNECOLOGY 122(1):25-30,
May 1, 1975.

"Refusal of assistance in abortion," by A. Hollmann.
DEUTSCHE MEDIZINISCHE WOCHENSCHRIFT
100(2):65-67, January 10, 1975.

"Relations of personality factors and student nurses'
attitudes toward abortion," by J. M. Jones.
PSYCHOLOGICAL REPORTS 35:927-931, October,
1974.

"The relationship between pregnancy indices and
problems of premature deliveries in Hungary during
the years 1934-1970," by O. Pohanka, et al.
ORVOSI HETILAP 116(5):243-248, February 2, 1975.

"Religion and legal abortion in Northern Ireland," by
P. A. Compton, et al. JOURNAL OF BIOSOCIAL
SCIENCE 6(4):493-500, October, 1974.

"Report on abortion," by M. Clark. NEWSWEEK 85:
97, February 17, 1975.

"Report on abortion activities in nearly 3,000 hospitals,
clinics and private physicians' offices," by M. Clark.
NEWSWEEK 85:97, February 17, 1975.

"Report on a case of consumption coagulopathy following
abortion in a patient with genital and peritoneal
tuberculosis," by H. F. Orth, et al. GEBURTSHILFE
UND FRAUENHEILKUNDE 34(8):623-632, August,
1974.

"Requests for abortion in general practice," by H. W.
Ashworth. JOURNAL OF THE ROYAL COLLEGE OF
GENERAL PRACTITIONERS 24(142):329-330, 335-339,
May, 1974.

"Requests for termination of pregnancy in the East Mid-
land area--Sheffield region," by C. P. Seager, et al.
JOURNAL OF THE ROYAL COLLEGE OF GENERAL
PRACTITIONERS 24(142):320-328, May, 1974.

"Response of the primate fetus to intra-amniotic saline
injection," by A. Comas-Urrutia, et al. AMERICAN
JOURNAL OF OBSTETRICS AND GYNECOLOGY 122
(5):549-554, July 1, 1975.

"Restricting legal abortion: Some maternal and child
health effects in Romania," by N. H. Wright. AMERI-
CAN JOURNAL OF OBSTETRICS AND GYNECOLOGY
121(2):246-256, January 15, 1975.

"Restriction of medical aid in abortion," by N. Chisholm.
BRITISH MEDICAL JOURNAL 1(5958):629, March 15,
1975.

"Results of HPL radioimmunoassay in normal and pathologic early pregnancy," by G. Hör, et al. NUCLEAR-
MEDIZIN 13(4):371-378, January 31, 1975.

"Results of treatment of threatened abortion with Partu-
    sisten (preparation Th 1165 A)," by A. Dzioba, et al.
    WIADOMOSCI LEKARSKIE 28(14):1193-1196, July 15,
    1975.

"Retrospective and prospective epidemiological studies
    of 1500 karyotyped spontaneous human abortions," by
    J. Boué, et al. TERATOLOGY; JOURNAL OF
    ABNORMAL DEVELOPMENT 12(1):11-26, August,
    1975.

"Reversal of abortion decisions urgent issue U. S. bishops
    say after series of meetings." OUR SUNDAY VISITOR
    64:1, August 24, 1975.

"Review of legal challenges to Catholic hospitals," by
    E. J. Schulte. HOSPITAL PROGRESS 56:10-11,
    April, 1975.

"A review of 700 hysterotomies," by B. J. Nottage, et al.
    BRITISH JOURNAL OF OBSTETRICS AND GYNAECOL-
    OGY 82(4):310-313, April, 1975.

"Rh-immunization following abortion," by J. Eklund.
    DUODECIM 90(23):1641-1643, 1974.

"Rh sensitization following abortion," (letter), by E. P.
    Reid. CANADIAN MEDICAL ASSOCIATION JOURNAL
    111(11):1182, December 7, 1974.

"Ribonucleic acid content in the endometrium of women
    suffering from habitual abortions in inadequacy of the
    luteinic phase of the menstrual cycle," by E. P.
    Maizel', et al. VOPROSY OKHRANY MATERINSTVA
    I DETSTVA 18(5):65-71, 1973.

"The right of privacy: what next?" by K. O'Rourke.
    HOSPITAL PROGRESS 56:58-63, April, 1975.

"Right to life: time for a new strategy; symposiums:

Moral credibility," by W. Carroll; "Grassroots revolution," by R. Engel; "Conditional allegiance," by W. Devlin; "The best chance," by P. Fisher; "Get tough," by T. May; "Unacceptable principle," by C. Rice; "Bear witness," by M. Schwartz; "The ethical issue," by J. Willke. TRIUMPH 10:11-16, January, 1975.

"Right-to-life--two crusaders," by J. B. Cumming, Jr. NEWSWEEK 85:29, March 3, 1975.

"Roentgenological image of the uterus after miscarriage," by E. P. Maizel', et al. AKUSHERSTVO I GINEKOLO-GIIA (Moscow) (5):65-67, May, 1974.

"Role of sensitization of the body of pregnant women with antigens of embryonal tissues and placenta in the pathogenesis of miscarriage," by N. S. Motavkina, et al. AKUSHERSTVO I GINEKOLOGIIA (Moscow) 0(7):30-34, July, 1974.

"Roma locuta, causa finita? Prevention or insensitivity?" SCHWESTERN REVUE 13(3):10, March 15, 1975.

"Rules prohibiting abortions at St. Louis city hospitals are upheld by court." HOSPITALS 49:17, February 16, 1975.

"Rupture of uterus during prostaglandin-induced abortion," by A. M. Smith. BRITISH MEDICAL JOURNAL 1(5951): 205, January 25, 1975.

"Russell Shaw criticizes news media." OUR SUNDAY VISITOR 63:1, March 2, 1975.

"Salmonella dublin abortion in cattle: incidence and epidemiology," by M. Hinton. BIRTISH VETERINARY JOURNAL 131(1):94-101, January-February, 1975.

"Salmonella dublin abortion in cattle: studies on the clinical aspects of the condition," by M. Hinton. BRITISH VETERINARY JOURNAL 130(6):556-563, November-December, 1974.

"Salting out: experience in 9,000 cases," by D. H. Sherman. JOURNAL OF REPRODUCTIVE MEDICINE 14(06):241-243, June, 1975.

"Saying no to NOW; restrictions placed on Catholic members by San Diego Bishop L. T. Maher." TIME 105:75-76, April 28, 1975.

"Says support for abortion cuts Catholic from Church; a new publication with comments on the document by the Congregation for the Doctrine of the Faith, November 18, 1974." OUR SUNDAY VISITOR 64:2, August 31, 1975.

"Scottish abortion statistics 1973." HEALTH BULLETIN (Edinburgh) 32(3):121-129, May, 1974.

"Scottish abortion statistics 1974." HEALTH BULLETIN (Edinburgh) 33(4):167-181, July, 1975.

"Second thoughts about abortions." U. S. NEWS AND WORLD REPORT 78:78, March 3, 1975.

"Second trimester abortions. Review of four procedures," by A. Risk, et al. NEW YORK STATE JOURNAL OF MEDICINE 75(7):1022-1027, June, 1975.

"Second trimester septic abortion and the Dalkon shield," by J. Vujcich, et al. MEDICAL JOURNAL OF AUSTRALIA 2(7):249-252, August 16, 1975.

"Sellout on abortion," by L. Komisar. NEWSWEEK 85:11, June 9, 1975.

"Semantics can't justify abortion, Luthern says." OUR

SUNDAY VISITOR 64:2, August 10, 1975.

"Senate rejects anti-abortion amendment [key provisions, committee action, floor action]," by E. Bowman. CONG Q W REPT 33:814-816, April 19, 1975.

"Senate unit kills pro-life amendments," by R. Rashke. NATIONAL CATHOLIC REPORTER 11:1 plus, September 26, 1975.

"Senator Kennedy explains his position on abortion in letter to Boston paper." OUR SUNDAY VISITOR 64:2, August 31, 1975.

"Septic abortion and IUD," (letter), by K. A. Carey-Smith. NEW ZEALAND MEDICAL JOURNAL 80(523):225, September 11, 1974.

"Septic abortion and IUD," (letter), by R. W. Jones. NEW ZEALAND MEDICAL JOURNAL 80(522):186, August 28, 1974.

"Septic abortion, excluding that produced by Bacillus prefringens," by M. Herrera, et al. REVISTA CHILENA DE OBSTETRICIA Y GINECOLOGIA 38 (4):176-186, 1973.

"Septic conditions following gynecologic interventions in pregnancy," by G. Bodor, et al. ORVOSI HETILAP 116(1):14-17, January 5, 1975.

"Sequential aspects of spontaneous abortion: maternal age, parity, and pregnancy compensation artifact," by A. F. Naylor. SOCIAL BIOLOGY 21(2):195-204, Summer, 1974.

"Serologic evidence for etiologic role of Akabane virus in epizootic abortion-arthrogryposis-hydranencephaly in cattle in Japan, 1972-1974," by H. Kurogi, et al. ARCHIVES OF VIROLOGY 47(1):71-83, 1975.

"Serotonin, 5-hiaa, total estrogen and pregnanediol excretion in urine during therapeutic saline abortion," by K. Fuchs, et al. ACTA OBSTETRICIA ET GYNE-COLOGICA SCANDINAVICA 54(2):157-160, 1975.

"Serum level of pregnancy associated alpha2-globulin in patients with spontaneous abortions," by G. N. Than, et al. ARCHIV FUR GYNAEKOLOGIE 218 (3):183-187, July 29, 1975.

"Serum levels of oestradiol and progresterone during administration of prostaglandin F2alpha for induction of abortion and labour," by O. Widholm, et al. ACTA OBSTETRICIA ET GINECOLOGICA SCNADINAVICA 54(2):135-139, 1975.

"Serum-transaminase activity in women after artificial interruption of gravidity," by F. Glenc. CESKOSLO-VENSKA GYNEKOLOGIE 40(5):386-387, June, 1975.

"Setback for abortion." TIME 105:67, February 24, 1975.

"A sex information program for sexually active teenagers," by P. A. Reichelt, et al. JOURNAL OF SCHOOL HEALTH 45(2):100-107, February, 1975.

"Sexual life of young women and girls following inter-ruption," by L. Kovácová, et al. CESKOSLOVENSKA GYNEKOLOGIE 39(3):218-219, April, 1974.

"Sheep placenta water-soluble proteins," by S. Georgiev. VETERINARO-MEDITSINSKI 12(2):83-89, 1975.

"Short-term psychiatric sequelae to therapeutic termina-tion of pregnancy," by B. Lask. BRITISH JOURNAL OF PSYCHIATRY 126:173-177, February, 1975.

"Should abortion laws be nullified? 'Yes,' by Robert E. Bauman; 'No,' by Ronald V. Dellums." AMERICAN LEGION MAGAZINE 98:32-33, April, 1975.

"Should your tax dollars pay for abortions and fetal research?" by W. Brennan. LIGUORIAN 63:8-12, March, 1975.

"The significance of oral contraceptives in causing chromosome anomalies in spontaneous abortions," by J. G. Lauritsen. ACTA OBSTETRIFIA ET GYNECOLOGICA SCANDINAVICA 54 (3):261-264, 1975.

"Simultaneous determination of blood and urinary HCG and observation of its daily differences and circadian rhythm for prevention of abortion," by Y. Abe, et al. FOLIA ENDOCRINOLOGICA JAPONICA 50(2):519, February 20, 1974.

"Simultaneous laparoscopic sterilization and suction curettage as an outpatient procedure," by N. Rezal. MARYLAND STATE MEDICAL JOURNAL 24(4):35-39, April, 1975.

"Single extra-amniotic injection of prostaglandin E2 in viscous gel to induce mid-trimester abortion," by I. Z. Mackenzie, et al. BRITISH MEDICAL JOURNAL 1(5952):240-242, February 1, 1975.

"A smell of burning." LANCET 1(7911):844-845, April 12, 1975.

"Social and demographic determinants of abortion in Poland," by D. P. Mazur. POPULATION STUDIES 29:21-35, March, 1975.

"Social aspects of legal abortion in Yugoslavia," by N. J. Jurukovski. GODISEN ZBORNIK NA MEDICINSKIAT FAKULTET VO SKOPJE 20:159-164, 1974.

"Social effects of abortion." NEW ENGLAND JOURNAL OF MEDICINE 292(9):484-486, February 27, 1975.

"A social-psychiatric comparison of 399 women requesting abortion and 118 pregnant women intending to deliver," by L. Jacobsson, et al. ACTA PSYCHIATRICA SCANDINAVICA. SUPPLEMENT (255):279-290, 1974.

"Some indices of the blood coagulation system in postnatal and postabortion septic diseases," by T. S. Dramplan, et al. ZHURNAL EKSPERIMENTAL'NAI I KLINICHESKOI MEDITSINY 14(3):92-95, 1974.

"Some problems in the etiology and pathogenesis of prematurity," by L. V. Sukhopol'skaia. PEDIATRIIA AKUSHERATVE I GINEKOLOGIIA (5):33-36, September-October, 1974.

"Sounding board. Deeper into abortion," by B. N. Nathanson. NEW ENGLAND JOURNAL OF MEDICINE 291(22):1188-1190, November 28, 1974.

"South Dakota's abortion experience: constitutional right or unfulfilled promise?" SOUTH DAKOTA LAW REVIEW 20:205-206, Winter, 1975.

"Spermatozoa in the abomasum of aborted bovine foetuses," by D. Jakovljevic. AUSTRALIAN VETERINARY JOURNAL 51(1):56, January, 1975.

"Spermine level in the myometrium and placenta of women with late toxemia and habitual abortion in their anamnesis," by T. G. Shorosheva, et al. AKUSHERSTVO I GINEKOLOGIIA (Moscow) (9):20-23, September, 1974.

"Spontaneous abortion." LANCET 2(7935):591-592, September 27, 1975.

"Spontaneous abortion and aging of human ova and spermatozoa," by R. Guerrero, et al. NEW ENGLAND JOURNAL OF MEDICINE 293(12):573-575, September 18, 1975.

"Spontaneous abortion and sensitization to elements of the fertilised ovum," by I. N. Odarenko. AKUSHER-STVO I GINEKOLOGIIA (Moscow) 49(4):64-65, April, 1973.

"Stage of pregnancy is key to public approval of abortion." GALLUP OPINION INDEX p. 11-13, July, 1975.

"State of the infectious foci after spontaneous abortion," by A. P. Egorova, et al. VOPRASY OKHRANY MATERINSTVA I DETSTVA 19(5):63-66, May, 1974.

"Statement concerning the discussion about the 'initiative for descriminialisation' of abortion," by P. A. Gloor, et al. PRAXIS 63(48):1423-1429, December 3, 1974.

"Statute requiring parental consent to minor's abortion unconstitutional: Massachusetts." HOSPITAL LAW 9:6, June, 1975.

"Sterilization and therapeutic abortion counseling for the mentally retarded," by C. W. Smiley. ILLINOIS MEDICAL JOURNAL 147(3):291-292, March, 1975.

"Strategy on abortion; Catholic bishops' plan." TIME 106:59, December 1, 1975.

"Studies of morbidity in anaesthetists with special reference to obstetric history," by A. A. Spence, et al. PROCEEDINGS OF THE ROYAL SOCIETY OF MEDICINE 67(10):989-990, October, 1974.

"Studies on spontaneous abortions. Fluorescence analysis of abnormal karyotypes," by J. G. Lauritsen, et al. HEREDITAS 71(1):160-163, 1972.

"Study of allylestrenol (Turinal) in pregnancy. I. Animal experiments," by G. Györy, et al. THERAPIA HUNGARICA 21(3-4):127-130, 1973.

--II. Clinical observations," by G. Győry, et al.
THERAPIA HUNGARICA 21(3-4):131-133, 1973.

"A study of reported therapeutic abortions in North
Carolina," by E. M. Howell. AMERICAN JOURNAL
OF PUBLIC HEALTH 65(5):480-483, May, 1975.

"Successive pregnancy and deliveries (gravid 14, para
12) and frequent pregnancy and repeated induced abortion (gravid 13, para 2): an observation on 2 cases,"
by A. Sasaki, et al. JAPANESE JOURNAL FOR THE
MIDWIFE 29(1):36-40, January, 1975.

"Supreme court considers Morgentaler abortion case,"
by D. Phillipson. CANADIAN MEDICAL ASSOCIA-
TION JOURNAL 111(8):872-873, October 19, 1974.

"Supreme Court rules: commercial ads protected by
First amendment," by I. W. Hill. EDITOR AND
PUBLISHER--THE FOURTH ESTATE 108:11, June
21, 1975.

"Surgical treatment of isthmocervical incompetence in
pregnant women suffering from premature delivery,"
by L. P. Zubareva. VOPROSY OKHRANY MATERINSTVA
I DETSTVA 18(5):71-75, 1973.

"Survey of Ottawa area general practitioners and obstetrician-gynecologists on abortion," by M. C. Diner.
CANADIAN JOURNAL OF PUBLIC HEALTH 65(5):
351-358, September-October, 1974.

"The synergistic activity of intra-amniotic prostaglandin
F2 alpha and urea in the midtrimester elective abor-
tion," by T. M. King, et al. AMERICAN JOURNAL
OF OBSTETRICS AND GYNECOLOGY 120(5):704-718,
November 1, 1974.

"Synthesis and use of affinity-labeling steroids for interceptive purposes," by S. W. Clark, et al. AMERICAN

JOURNAL OF OBSTETRICS AND GYNECOLOGY
121(6):864-873, March 15, 1975.

"Synthetic sex hormones," by B. Field, et al. MEDI-
CAL JOURNAL OF AUSTRALIA 2(6):232, August 9,
1975.

"Tax-exempt, bond-financed hospital can disallow abortions,"
by E. J. Schulte. HOSPITAL PROGRESS 56:18, August,
1975.

"Tax-supported abortions: the legal issues," by E. J.
Schulte. CATHOLIC LAWYER 21:1-7, Winter, 1975.

"Taxes - where the dollars go - abortions yes, private
schools no," by J. Doyle. LIGUORIAN 63:7-11,
September, 1975.

"Technics for interruption of a second-trimester pregnancy," by J. H. Ravina, et al. NOUVELLE PRESSE
MEDICALE 3(45):2733-2736, December 28, 1974.

"Techniques of pregnancy termination. Part II," by L.
S. Burnett, et al. OBSTETRICAL AND GYNECOLO-
GICAL SURVEY 29(1):6-42, January, 1974.

"Teen-age pregnancies in Denmark, 1940-71," by A.
Braestrup. JOURNAL OF BIOSOCIAL SCIENCE
6(4):741-745, October, 1974.

"10 interviews about physicians and the population
change. Abortion inevitable in developing countries.
Is forced birth control near?" by Y. Karlsson.
NORDISK MEDICIN 89(8):234-240, October, 1974.

"Termination by prostaglandin pellets in very early
pregnancy," by A. I. Csapo, et al. LANCET 2
(7883):789-790, September 28, 1974.

"Termination of first-trimester pregnancies," (letter), by S. Way. LANCET 2(7887):1017, October 26, 1974.

"Termination of mid-trimester pregnancy by transcervical extra-amniotic hypertonic saline method without in-dwelling catheter," by S. Nummi, et al. ANNALES CHIRURGIAE ET GYNAECOLOGIAE FENNIAE 63(6):479-482, 1974.

"Termination of pregnancy," by N. A. Simmons. LANCET 2(7928):281, August 9, 1975.

"Termination of pregnancy in the rat by the antiserum to the beta subunit of ovine interstitial cell stimulating hormone," by M. R. Sairam, et al. PROCEEDINGS OF THE SOCIETY FOR EXPERIMENTAL BIOLOGY AND MEDICINE 147(3):823-825, December, 1974.

"Termination of pregnancy in Wales," by B. Knight. NURSING MIRROR AND MIDWIVES' JOURNAL 140(14):69-70, April 3, 1975.

"Termination of pregnancy--the nurse's attitude," by A. B. Sclare, et al. NURSING MIRROR AND MIDWIVES' JOURNAL 140(3):59-60, January 16, 1975.

"Termination of pregnancy on psychiatric grounds," by K. Böhme, et al. DEUTSCHE MEDIZINISCHE WOCHENSCHRIFT 100(16):865-872, April 18, 1975.

"Termination of pregnancy with Utus paste: report of a fatal case," by T. A. Thomas, et al. BRITISH MEDICAL JOURNAL 1(5954):375-376, February 15, 1975.

"Termination of second trimester pregnancy with intra-amniotic 15 (S) 15 methyl prostaglandin F-2alpha - a two dose schedule study," by S. M. M. Karim, et al.

PROSTAGLANDINS 9(3):487-494, March, 1975.

"Thanatology?" WEST VIRGINIA MEDICAL JOURNAL
70(12):334-335, December, 1974.

"Therapeutic abortion," (letter). CANADIAN MEDICAL
ASSOCIATION JOURNAL 111(12):1299-1301, December 21, 1974.

"Therapeutic abortion," (letter), by H. Baunemann.
CANADIAN MEDICAL ASSOCIATION JOURNAL
112(1):27, January 11, 1975.

"Therapeutic abortion," (letter), by P. G. Coffey.
CANADIAN MEDICAL ASSOCIATION JOURNAL
112(3):283, February 8, 1975.

"Therapeutic abortion," (letter), by B. Gibbard.
CANADIAN MEDICAL ASSOCIATION JOURNAL
112(1):24, 27, January 11, 1975.

"Therapeutic abortion," (letter), by R. Halliday.
CANADIAN MEDICAL ASSOCIATION JOURNAL
113(4):276-278, August 23, 1975.

"Therapeutic abortion," (letter), by A. C. Hayes.
CANADIAN MEDICAL ASSOCIATION JOURNAL
112(10):1166, May 17, 1975.

"Therapeutic abortion," (letter), by J. J. Krayenhoff.
CANADIAN MEDICAL ASSOCIATION JOURNAL
112(1):25, January 11, 1975.

"Therapeutic abortion," (letter), by J. J. Krayenhoff.
CANADIAN MEDICAL ASSOCIATION JOURNAL
112(12):1388, June 21, 1975.

"Therapeutic abortion," (letter), by C. A. Ringrose.
CANADIAN MEDICAL ASSOCIATION JOURNAL
112(1):22, 25, January 11, 1975.

"Therapeutic abortion," (letter), by G. Schneider.
CANADIAN MEDICAL ASSOCIATION JOURNAL
112(9):1045, May 3, 1975.

"Therapeutic abortion," (letter), by W. W. Watters.
CANADIAN MEDICAL ASSOCIATION JOURNAL
112(5):558, March 8, 1975.

"Therapeutic abortion and the minor," by R. F. Gibbs.
JOURNAL OF LEGAL MEDICINE 1(1):36-42,
March-April, 1973.

"Therapeutic abortion by a single extra-amniotic instillation of prostaglandin f2alpha," by P. Fylling, et al.
ARCHIV FUR GYNAEKOLOGIE 217(2):119-125, 1974.

"Therapeutic abortion in N. Z. public hospitals. I,"
by W. A. Facer. NURSING FORUM 2(4):12-13,
September-October, 1974.

--II," by W. A. Facer. NURSING FORUM 2(5):8-10,
November-December, 1974.

"Therapeutic abortion with concurrent sterilization: comparison of methods," by M. K. Leong, et al. CANAD-
IAN MEDICAL ASSOCIATION JOURNAL 111(12):1327-
1329, December 21, 1974.

"Therapeutic policies in threatened abortion," by N.
Fujita. JAPANESE JOURNAL FOR THE MIDWIFE
28(9):444-447, September, 1974.

"They fight for life - by telephone," by F. Grones.
COLUMBIA 55:6-15, July, 1975.

"Thinking straight about abortion," by N. B. Barcus.
CHRISTIANITY TODAY 19:8-9 plus, January 17,
1975.

"This awful silence hanging over abortion on demand,"

by R. Butt. TIMES p. 16, January 23, 1975.

"Thoughts on the current situation of abortion from the clinical viewpoint," by S. Schulz, et al. ZENTRAL-BLATT FUR GYNAEKOLOGIE 96(39):1223-1226, September 27, 1974.

"Toxoplasma abortions in sheep in Switzerland," by U. Frei. SCHWEIZER ARCHIV FUR TIERHEILKUNDE 117(7):401-406, July, 1975.

"Translocation +(7p+; Bq-) associated with recurrent abortion," by H. Korner, et al. HUMANGENETIK 28(1):83-86, May 26, 1975.

"Trials: who is a person? conviction of K. C. Edelin for killing of fetus." NEWSWEEK 85:20, February 24, 1975.

"A triploid human abortus due to dispermy," by N. Niikawa, et al. HUMANGENETIK 24(3):261-264, 1974.

"The troubled anti-abortion camp," by J. Diamond. AMERICA p. 52, August 10, 1974.

"T-strain mycoplasmas and reproductive failure in monkeys," by R. B. Kundsin, et al. LABORATORY ANIMAL SCIENCE 25(2):221-227, April, 1975.

"Turning the clock back is not the way to end abortion abuses," by R. Short. TIMES p. 11, February 21, 1975.

"Ultrasonic diagnosis of miscarriage and early pregnancy complications," by B. Zsolnai, et al. ACTA CHIRURGICA ACADEMIAE SCIENTIARUM HUNGARICAE 15(4):389-407, 1974.

"Ultrasound in management of clinically diagnosed
threatened abortion," by J. E. Drumm, et al.
BRITISH MEDICAL JOURNAL 02(5968):424, May
24, 1975.

"Uneasy lies the head that wears a crown," by J. D.
Wallace. CANADIAN MEDICAL ASSOCIATION
JOURNAL 112(3):344, February 8, 1975.

"United States: therapeutic abortions, 1963 to 1968,"
by C. Tietze. STUDIES IN FAMILY PLANNING
(59):5-7, November, 1970.

"The unmet need for legal abortion services in the
U. S." FAMILY PLANNING PERSPECTIVES
7:224-230, September-October, 1975.

"Unusual protraction of oliguria in a patient with acute
renal insufficiency following a medical abortion,"
by S. A. Glants, et al. UROLOGIIA I NEFROLOGIIA
(2):54, March-April, 1974.

"Unwanted child wanted," by T. Francis. NATIONAL
CATHOLIC REPORTER 11:14, January 24, 1975.

"Unwanted pregnancies," by L. E. Mason. CANADIAN
MEDICAL ASSOCIATION JOURNAL 112(2):145-147,
January 25, 1975.

"Unwanted pregnancies," by G. W. Piper. CANADIAN
MEDICAL ASSOCIATION JOURNAL 112(2):145,
January 25, 1975.

"Unwanted pregnancy and abortion," by C. W. Kok.
CANADIAN MEDICAL ASSOCIATION JOURNAL
112(4):419-420, February 22, 1975.

"Unwanted pregnancy: background and psychological
characteristics of women who choose abortion," by
D. Clayson, et al. PRAXIS 63(42):1260-1264,

October 22, 1974.

"Urinary oestrone and chorionic gonadotrophin in threatened abortion," by U. Jarvilehto, et al. ANNALES CHIRURGIAE ET GYNAECOLOGIAE FENNIAE 63(6):445-450, 1974.

"The use of antiserotonin-cyproheptadine HCL in pregnancy: an experimental and clinical study," by E. Sadovsky, et al. ADVANCES IN EXPERIMENTAL MEDICINE AND BIOLOGY 27:399-405, 1972.

"The use of F2 alpha prostaglandin for induction of therapeutic abortion and labor in the 2d trimester of pregnancy," by G. Scarselli, et al. MINERVA GINECOLOGICA 26(12):711-716, December, 1974.

"Use of high doses of oxytocin in non-developing pregnancy," by B. L. Gurtovi, et al. VOPROSY OKHRANY MATERINSTVA I DETSTVA 19(12):45-49, December, 1974.

"Use of inductothermy of the perirenal region in the complex treatment of threatened interruption of pregnancy," by N. M. Suvorova, et al. AKUSHERSTVO I GINEKOLOGIIA (Moscow) (9):48-51, September, 1974.

"Use of intrapelvic novocaine blocks in the overall treatment of threatened and beginning late abortions and premature labor," by R. I. Il'ina. VOPROSY OKHRANY MATERINSTVA I DETSTVA 19(5):73-76, May, 1974.

"Use of prostaglandin E2 vaginal suppositories in intra-uterine fetal death and missed abortion," by C. D. Bailey, et al. OBSTETRICS AND GYNECOLOGY 45(1):110-113, January, 1975.

"Use of prostaglandins for induced abortion," by E. A. Chernukha. FEL'DSKER I AKUSHERKA 39(7):35-37,

July, 1974.

"Useful methods of contraception," by W. L. Whitehouse. NURSING MIRROR AND MIDWIVES' JOURNAL 139 (18):77-78, October 31, 1974.

"Uterine injuries complicating hypertonic saline abortion," by J. J. Willems. CANADIAN MEDICAL ASSOCIATION JOURNAL 111(11):1223, 1226, December 7, 1974.

"Vaccination against Vibrio (Campylobacter) fetus infection in sheep in late pregnancy," by N. J. Gilmour, et al. VETERINARY RECORD 96(6):129-131, February 8, 1975.

"Vacurette--a new disposable suction apparatus in induced legal abortion," by O. Als, et al. UGESKRIFT FOR LAEGER 137(8):447-450, February 17, 1975.

"Vaginal adenomatesis and adenocarcinoma in young women after diethylstilbestrol treatment," by G. Vooijs. REVUE MEDICALE DE LIEGE 29(22):682-687, November 15, 1974.

"Vaginal ligation in first trimester of pregnancy," by B. Ghosh. JOURNAL OF THE INDIAN MEDICAL ASSOCIATION 62(11):380-383, June 1, 1974.

"Vaginally administered prostaglandin E2 as a first and second trimester abortifacient," by S. L. Corson, et al. JOURNAL OF REPRODUCTIVE MEDICINE 14(2):43-46, February, 1975.

"Value of endometrial biopsy in the diagnosis of hormonal abortion," by I. Penev, et al. AKUSTERSTVO I GINEKOLOGIIA (Sofiia) 13(5):374-378, 1974.

"Various current aspects of induced abortion. I. Introduction," by L. Castelazo-Ayala. GACETA MEDICA

DE MEXICO 108(5):309-310, November, 1974.

--V. Conclusions," by L. Castelazo-Ayala. GACETA
MEDICA DE MEXICO 108(5):338-339, November,
1974.

"Various technics of interruption of pregnancy used
in our statistical service. Incidents and accidents,"
by S. Boudjemaa, et al. TUNISIE MEDICALE
52(2):83-87, March-April, 1974.

"Verdict of the Federal Constitutional Court on term
regulation," by H. J. Rieger. DEUTSCHE MED-
IZINISCHE WOCHENSCHRIFT 100(12):637-639,
March 21, 1975.

"Very early termination of pregnancy (menstrual extraction)," by J. Stringer, et al. BRITISH MEDICAL
JOURNAL 3(5974):7-9, July 5, 1975.

"Visualization of placental abruption by blood pool
scanning," by P. H. Weiss, et al. JOURNAL OF
NUCLEAR MEDICINE 15(10):900-901, October,
1974.

"Volume and sodium concentration studies in 300 saline-
induced abortions," by T. D. Kerenyi, et al. AMERI-
CAN JOURNAL OF OBSTETRICS AND GYNECOLOGY
121(5):590-596, March 1, 1975.

"Voluntary versus compulsory sterilization in sweden then
and now," byH. Sjövall. LAKARTIDNINGEN 72(4):241-
245, January 22, 1975.

"Vox populi," by G. L. Fite. JOURNAL OF THE AMERI-
CAN MEDICAL ASSOCIATION 232(6):595, May 12,
1975.

"Water intoxication associated with oxytocin administra-

tion during saline-induced abortion," by N. H.
Lauersen, et al. AMERICAN JOURNAL OF OB-
STETRICS AND GYNECOLOGY 121(1):2-6, January
1, 1975.

"West German high court denies right of abortion."
OUR SUNDAY VISITOR 63:2, March 9, 1975.

"West Germany; what is distress?" ECONOMIST
257:42 plus, October 18, 1975.

"What the abortion argument is about," by M. Muggeridge. SUNDAY TIMES p. 19, February 2, 1975.

"What about an abortion amendment?" by F. Lee.
AMERICA 132:166-168, March 8, 1975.

"What about an abortion feature?" by J. J. Roberts.
SCHOOL PRESS REVIEW 50(6):1, 4, 12, January,
1975.

"What are your feelings about death and dying," by D.
Popoff. NURSING 5:55-62, September,
1975.

"What is life?" by R. Sterner. VITAL CHRISTIANITY
p. 1, July 28, 1974.

"What it's like to do an abortion," by T. K. Edwards.
WEST VIRGINIA MEDICAL JOURNAL 71(5):122-123,
May, 1975.

"When does human life begin?" by H. Harrod. CHRIS-
TIAN HOME p. 16, May, 1974.

"When is an abortion not an abortion? K. C. Edelin case,"
by S. Mydans. ATLANTIC 235:71-73, May, 1975.

"Where have all the conceptions gone?" LANCET 1(7907):
636-637, March 15, 1975.

"The White Bill on abortion," by M. Simms. LANCET 1(7905):523-524, March 1, 1975.

"Who is a victim?" by G. Hughes. DALHOUSIE LAW JOURNAL 1:425-440, October, 1974.

"Whose 'right to life'?" edited by D. W. Fisher. HOSPITAL PRACTICE 10:11-12, April, 1975.

"Why admit abortion patients?" (letter), by D. Kerslake. LANCET 2(7888):1078, November 2, 1974.

"Why is abortion wrong?" by J. Donceel. AMERICA 133:65-67, August 16, 1975.

"Will abortion go back underground?" by D. Loshak. DAILY TELEGRAPH p. 16, February 7, 1975.

"Will the clock go back on abortion?" by M. Russell. OBSERVER p. 26 February 2, 1975.

"Will Congress be allowed to dodge the abortion issue?" by R. Shaw. COLUMBIA 55:38, July, 1975.

"Will medicine be strangled in law?" by H. Schwartz. JOURNAL OF FAMILY PRACTICE 2(3):232, June, 1975.

"Women and the Supreme Court: anatomy is destiny," by N. S. Erickson. BROOKLYN LAW REVIEW 41:209-282, Fall, 1974.

"Women exploited unite," by J. Anderson. OUR SUNDAY VISITOR 64:1 plus, September 21, 1975.

"Women help themselves," by A. Phillips. NEW SOCIETY p. 267-268, January 30, 1975.

"Working of the abortion act." BRITISH MEDICAL JOURNAL 02(5966):337, May 10, 1975.

"Working of the abortion act," by P. J. Huntingford.
BRITISH MEDICAL JOURNAL 2(5965):278, May 3,
1975.

"Would you buy an abortion from this man? the Harvey
Karman controversy," by L. C. Wohl. MS MAGA-
ZINE 4:60-64 plus, September, 1975.

PERIODICAL LITERATURE

SUBJECT INDEX

ABNORMALTIES
see: Complications

ABORTION (GENERAL)
"Abortion--have we gone too far?" by A. Reeder.
MADEMOISELLE 81:66 plus, June, 1975.

"Abortion pioneer," by S. Finkbine. NEWSWEEK
85:14, March 17, 1975.

"Abortion quiz," by H. Rodman. NATION 221:70-71,
August 2, 1975.

"Comment and controversy," by R. Lincoln. FAMILY
PLANNING PERSPECTIVES 7:185-188, July-
August, 1975.

"Early antenatal care," by R. R. Macdonald. NURS-
ING MIRROR AND MIDWIVES' JOURNAL 139(7):
56-58, August 16, 1974.

"Health care issues," by Sister M. A. A. Zasowska,
et al. HEALTH CARE DIMENSIONS :1-158, Fall,
1974.

"The meaning of abortion," by S. MacDonald. AMERI-
CAN ECCLESIASTICAL REVIEW 169:219-236, April,
1975; 291-315, May, 1975.

ABORTION (GENERAL)

"On the abortion front..." NATIONAL REVIEW 27: 147-148, February 14, 1975.

"On the slippery slope again," by A. Lindsay. ANALYSIS 35:32, October, 1974.

"Pain barrier," by J. Tweedie. GUARDIAN p. 9, March 3, 1975.

"The problem of abortion," by R. Spiazzi. L'OSSER-VATORE ROMANO 39(391):9-10, September 25, 1975.

"Report on abortion," by M. Clark. NEWSWEEK 85:97, February 17, 1975.

"The troubled anti-abortion camp," by J. Diamond. AMERICA p. 52, August 10, 1974.

"What about an abortion feature?" by J. J. Roberts. SCHOOL PRESS REVIEW 50(6):1, 4, 12, January, 1975.

"Where have all the conceptions gone?" LANCET 1(7907):636-637, March 15, 1975.

ABORTION ACT
see: Laws and Legislation

ABORTION: AUSTRIA

ABORTION: BELGIUM

ABORTION: CANADA
"Canadian newspaper on abortion documents; reprint from Le Soleil, December 4, 1974," by P. Lachance. L'OSSERVATORE ROMANO 8(360):5, February 20, 1975.

"CMA policy on abortion." (letter). CANADIAN MEDICAL ASSOCIATION JOURNAL 111(9):900, 902, November 2, 1974.

"Le Dr. Morgentaler (Sa Majesté la Reine v. Henry Morgentaler, Cour d'appel, Dist. de Montréal, no. 10-000289 -73) devant la Cour d'appel," by M. Rivet. LES CAHIERS DE DROIT 15:889-896, 1974.

"Evolution of Canadian justice: the Morgentaler case," by E. Z. Friedenberg. CANADIAN FORUM 55:28-30, June, 1975.

"Genetic epidemiology of intra-uterine mortality. Result of an analysis in a rural population in Quebec," by P. Philippe, et al. UNION MEDICALE DU CANADA 104(5):763-767, May, 1975.

"History of the pro-life movement in Quebec," by A. Morais. CATHOLIC HOSPITAL 3:8-9, January-February, 1975.

"Lamenting a misconception." CHRISTIANITY TODAY 19:46, February 28, 1975.

"Morgentaler case." NATION 221:6, July 5, 1975.

"The Morgentaler case," by P. N. Coles. CANADIAN MEDICAL ASSOCIATION JOURNAL 113(3):181, August 9, 1975.

"Morgentaler case divides Supreme Court in interpretation of Criminal Code," by D. Phillipson. CANADIAN MEDICAL ASSOCIATION JOURNAL 112(8): 1003-1004, April 19, 1975.

"Morgentaler vs. The Queen," by L. E. Rozovsky. DIMENSIONS IN HEALTH SERVICE 52(6):8-9,

ABORTION: CANADA

June, 1975.

"Ontario bishops blast government on abortion." OUR
SUNDAY VISITOR 64:2, May 25, 1975.

"Prosecution of Dr. Morgentaler," by M. Gordon, et
al. CANADIAN DIMENSION 10:9-11, June, 1975.

"Supreme court considers Morgentaler abortion case,"
by D. Phillipson. CANADIAN MEDICAL ASSOCIA-
TION JOURNAL 111(8):872-873, October 19, 1974.

"Survey of Ottawa area general practitioners and obstetrician-gynecologists on abortion," by M. C.
Diner. CANADIAN JOURNAL OF PUBLIC HEALTH
65(5):351-358, September-October, 1974.

ABORTION: CAROLINE ISLANDS

ABORTION: CHILE
"Post-abortion uterine perforation. Chilean experience," by R. García Valenzuela, et al. REVISTA
CHILENA DE OBSTETRICIA Y GINECOLOGIA
38(3):138-145, 1973.

ABORTION: CHINA
"Competition between spontaneous and induced abortion," by R. G. Potter, et al. DEMOGRAPHY
12:129-141, February, 1975.

ABORTION: CUBA

ABORTION: CZECHOSLOVAKIA

ABORTION: DENMARK
"Teen-age pregnancies in Denmark, 1940-71," by A.
Braestrup. JOURNAL OF BIOSOCIAL SCIENCE
6(4):741-745, October, 1974.

ABORTION: ENGLAND

"Legal abortion in England," by H. P. Tarnesby.
NOUVELLE PRESSE MEDICALE 4(19):1443-1444,
May 10, 1975.

ABORTION: FINLAND

ABORTION: FRANCE
"Abortion: 300,000 clandestine operations per year
in France." BRUXELLES-MEDICAL 54(1):26-27,
January, 1974.

"L'avortement et la nouvelle loi; point de vue d'un
accoucheur," by R. LeLirzin. ETUDES 343:199-
209, August-September, 1975.

"A propose de la nouvelle loi sur l'interruption volontaire
de la grossesse; intervention du cardinal Marty," by
F. Marty. LA DOCUMENTATION CATHOLIQUE
72:125, February 2, 1975.

ABORTION: GERMANY
"Avortement et divorce on Allemagne Fédéral," by H.
Menudier. ETUDES 343:57-76, July, 1975.

"German bishops urge defence at all cost of the lives
of the unborn," by H. Volk. L'OSSERVATORE
ROMANO 2(354):8, January 9, 1975.

"No final solution," by M. R. Benjamin, et al. NEWS-
WEEK 85:30-31, March 10, 1975.

"West German high court denies right of abortion."
OUR SUNDAY VISITOR 63:2, March 9, 1975.

"West Germany; what is distress?" ECONOMIST
257:42 plus, October 18, 1975.

ABORTION: HUNGARY

"Abortion laws in Hungary," (letter), by L. Iffy. OBSTETRICS AND GYNECOLOGY 45(1):115-116, January, 1975.

"The relationship between pregnancy indices and problems of premature deliveries in Hungary during the years 1934-1970," by O. Pohanka, et al. ORVOSI HETILAP 116(5):243-248, February 2, 1975.

ABORTION: INDIA

ABORTION: ITALY

"Abortion advocates using false statistics." OUR SUNDAY VISITOR 63:3, April 27, 1975.

"Abortion and the law on abortion; document of the Permanent Council of the Italian Episcopal Conference." L'OSSERVATORE ROMANO 9(361): 4-5, February 27, 1975.

"Drive to legalize abortion in Italy starts uneasily." NATIONAL CATHOLIC REPORTER 11:20, May 23, 1975.

"Italian sci-fi: too close for comfort?" by J. Harris. MS MAGAZINE 4:17, October, 1975.

"Italy; the issue they wanted to avoid." ECONOMIST 255(254):33, January 25, 1975.

"Women help themselves," by A. Phillips. NEW SOCIETY p. 267-268, January 30, 1975.

ABORTION: JAMAICA

"Abortion in Jamaica," by J. Symes. JAMAICAN NURSE 14(2):12, 14, August, 1974.

ABORTION: JAPAN

"The abortion movement; reprint from Seido Foundation, Catholic Position Paper published in Japan," by C. Burke. L'OSSERVATORE ROMANO 19(371): 8-11, May 9, 1975.

ABORTION: MEXICO
"Epidemiology of induced abortion in Mexico," by B. R. Ordónez. GACETA MEDICA DE MEXICO 108(5): 310-318, November, 1974.

ABORTION: NETHERLANDS

ABORTION: NEW ZEALAND
"Characteristics of New Zealand women seeking abortion in Melbourne, Australia," by A. F. Rogers, et al. NEW ZEALAND MEDICAL JOURNAL 81(536):282-286, March 26, 1975.

"Therapeutic abortion in N. Z. public hospitals. I," by W. A. Facer. NURSING FORUM 2(4):12-13, September-October, 1974.

--II," by W. A. Facer. NURSING FORUM 2(5):8-10, November-December, 1974.

ABORTION: NIGERIA
"Proposed decree on abortion and nurses' role," by S. A. Jegede. NIGERIAN NURSE 7(1):33-34, January-March, 1975.

ABORTION: NORWAY
"Not self decided abortion but liberal laws in future Norwegian family politics," by B. Grünfeld. NORDISH MEDICIN 90(2):44-47, February, 1975.

ABORTION: PAKISTAN
"Bishops of Pakistan on abortion and contraception; joint pastoral letter." L'OSSERVATORE ROMANO

ABORTION: PAKISTAN

11(363):9-10, March 13, 1975.

ABORTION: POLAND
"Social and demographic determinants of abortion in
Poland," by D. P. Mazur. POPULATION STUDIES
29:21-35, March, 1975.

ABORTION: PUERTO RICO
"Las implicaciones legales para Puerto Rico de los
casos Roe v. Wade (93 Sup Ct 705) 41 L. W. 4214
(1973) y Doe v. Bolton (93 Sup Ct 739) 41 L. W.
4233 (1973)," by C. T. Jiménez. REVISTA DEL
COLEGIO DE ABOGADOS DE PUERTO RICO
35:581-610, November, 1974.

ABORTION: RHODESIA

ABORTION: ROMANIA
"Restricting legal abortion: Some maternal and child
health effects in Romania," by N. H. Wright.
AMERICAN JOURNAL OF OBSTETRICS AND
GYNECOLOGY 121(2):246-256, January 15, 1975.

ABORTION: SINGAPORE
"Abortion: an end to the taboo," by A. Josey. FAR
EASTERN ECONOMIC REVIEW 86:28 plus,
November 22, 1974.

ABORTION: SWEDEN
"Voluntary versus compulsory sterilization in Sweden
then and now," by H. Sjövall. LAKARTIDNINGEN
72(4):241-245, January 22, 1975.

ABORTION: THAILAND

ABORTION: UGANDA

"Abortion law reform. Fact and fiction: replying to
Leo Abse," by M. Simms. SPECTATOR p. 114,
February 1, 1975.

"Abortion law reform. Permissiveness and pretence,"
by C. B. Goodhart. SPECTATOR p. 114-115,
February 1, 1975.

"Abortion; reforms accepted [Britain]." ECONOMIST
257:36, October 25, 1975.

"Against the act." ECONOMIST 254:24, February 8,
1975.

"Anglican Synod takes stand against abortion on demand."
OUR SUNDAY VISITOR 64:2, August 10, 1975.

"Debate continues." ECONOMIST 254:31, February 15,
1975.

"Human life is sacred; pastoral letter of the archbishops and bishops of Ireland." L'OSSERVATORE
ROMANO 21(373):6-8 plus, May 22, 1975; 24(376):
6-8, June 12, 1975; 25(377):6-9, June 19, 1975.

"Is any change in the abortion law really needed?" by
T. Smith. TIMES p. 11, January 31, 1975.

"Medical and social characteristics of Irish residents
whose pregnancies were terminated under the 1967
Abortion Act in 1971 and 1972," by D. Walsh. IRISH
MEDICAL JOURNAL 68(6):143-149, March 22, 1975.

"Merchants of distress," by M. Simms. NEW HUMANIST
90:334, February, 1975.

"No going back," by D. Gould. NEW STATESMAN
p. 132, January 31, 1975.

"None but the brave?" by D. Gould. NEW STATESMAN
89:774, June 13, 1975.

"Outpatient pregnancy termination in an NHS hospital,"
by M. G. Hull, et al. NURSING TIMES 70(40):
1540-1542, October 3, 1974.

"Putting the clock back on abortion," by P. Ferris.
OBSERVER p. 10, February 16, 1975.

"Religion and legal abortion in Northern Ireland," by
P. A. Compton, et al. JOURNAL OF BIOSOCIAL
SCIENCE 6(4):493-500, October, 1974.

"Requests for termination of pregnancy in the East
Midland area--Sheffield region," by C. P. Seager,
et al. JOURNAL OF THE ROYAL COLLEGE OF
GENERAL PRACTITIONERS 24(142):320-328,
May, 1974.

"Scottish abortion statistics 1973." HEALTH BULLE-
TIN (Edinburgh) 32(3):121-129, May, 1974.

"Scottish abortion statistics 1974." HEALTH BULLE-
TIN (Edinburgh) 33(4):167-181, July, 1975.

"Termination of pregnancy in Wales," by B. Knight.
NURSING MIRROR AND MIDWIVES' JOURNAL
140(14):69-70, April 3, 1975.

"Termination of pregnancy--the nurse's attitude," by
A. B. Sclare, et al. NURSING MIRROR AND MID-
WIVES' JOURNAL 140(3):59-60, January 16, 1975.

"Turning the clock back is not the way to end abortion abuses," by R. Short. TIMES p. 11, February
21, 1975.

ABORTION: UNITED KINGDOM

"Will abortion go back underground?" by D. Loshak.
DAILY TELEGRAPH p. 16, February 7, 1975.

"Will the clock go back on abortion?" by M. Russell.
OBSERVER p. 26, February 2, 1975.

ABORTION: UNITED STATES
ARKANSAS

CALIFORNIA
"Saying no to NOW; restrictions placed on Catholic
members by San Diego Bishop L. T. Maher."
TIME 105:75-76, April 28, 1975.

CHICAGO
"Abortion law--Friendship Medical Center, Ltd.
v. Chicago Board of Health (505 F 2d 1141),
invalidating city health regulations applicable
to first trimester abortion procedures."
LOYOLA UNIVERSITY OF CHICAGO LAW
JOURNAL 6:718-737, Summer, 1975.

"...Chicago. Confrontations," by G. Dunea.
BRITISH MEDICAL JOURNAL 3(5976):151-
153, July 19, 1975.

CINCINNATI
"Cincinnati pa per says need for new look at abortion." OUR SUNDAY VISITOR 63:3, April 13,
1975.

COLORADO

CONNECTICUT

FLORIDA

GEORGIA

112

ABORTION: UNITED STATES

HAWAII
"Pregnancy planning in Hawaii," by P. G. Steinhoff,
et al. FAMILY PLANNING PERSPECTIVES
7(3):138-142, May-June, 1975.

ILLINOIS

IOWA
"Iowa public hospitals cannot discharge staff for
abortion views." HOSPITAL LAW 8:4, February,
1975.

LOUISIANA
"Abortions: where do we stand in Louisiana?" by
M. G. Koslin. JOURNAL OF THE LOUISIANA
STATE MEDICAL SOCIETY 126(12):429-432,
December, 1974.

MARYLAND

MASSACHUSETTS
"Statute requiring parental consent to minor's abor-
tion unconstitutional: Massachusetts." HOSPITAL
LAW 8:6, June, 1975.

MICHIGAN
"Legislation--abortion--Michigan's 'conscience
clause'." WAYNE LAW REVIEW 21:175-182,
November, 1974.

"Michigan abortion refusal act." UNIVERSITY OF
MICHIGAN JOURNAL OF LAW REFORM 8:659-
675, Spring, 1975.

MINNESOTA

MISSISSIPPI

MISSOURI
"Rules prohibiting abortion at St. Louis city hospitals are upheld by court." HOSPITALS 49: 17, February 16, 1975.

MONTANA

NEBRASKA

NEW JERSEY

NEW YORK
"Contraceptive practice in the context of a non-restrictive abortion law: age-specific pregnancy rates in New York City, 1971-1973," by C. Tietze. FAMILY PLANNING PERSPECTIVES 7:197-202, September-October, 1975.

"The impact of the New York State abortion law on black and white fertility in Upstate New York," by K. J. Roghmann. INTERNATIONAL JOURNAL OF EPIDEMIOLOGY 4(1):45-49, March, 1975.

"Legal abortion among New York City residents: an analysis according to socioeconomic and demographic characteristics," by M. J. Kramer. FAMILY PLANNING PERSPECTIVES 7(3):128-137, May-June, 1975.

"Medicaid coverage of abortions in New York City: costs and benefits," by M. Robinson, et al. FAMILY PLANNING PERSPECTIVES 6:202-208, Fall, 1974.

"Medical coverage of abortions in New York City: costs and benefits [based on conference paper]," by M. Robinson, et al. FAMILY PLANNING PERSPECTIVES 6:202-208, Fall, 1974.

ABORTION: UNITED STATES

"N. Y. abortion stirs outcry." NATIONAL CATHOLIC
REPORTER 11:6, January 24, 1975.

NORTH CAROLINA
"A study of reported therapeutic abortions in North
Carolina," by E. M. Howell. AMERICAN
JOURNAL OF PUBLIC HEALTH 65(5):480-483,
May, 1975.

OKLAHOMA

OREGON

PENNSYLVANIA

RHODE ISLAND

SOUTH DAKOTA
"South Dakota's abortion experience: constitutional
right or unfulfilled promise?" SOUTH DAKOTA
LAW REVIEW 20:205-226, Winter, 1975.

TENNESSEE

TEXAS
"Medicine and the law: Attorney general clarifies
status of Texas abortion laws," by S. V. Stone,
Jr. TEXAS MEDICINE 70(11):107-108, November, 1974.

WISCONSIN

ABORTION: USSR
"Abortion and family planning in the Soviet Union:
public policies and private behaviour," by H. P.
David. JOURNAL OF BIOSOCIAL SCIENCE 6(4):
417-426, October, 1974.

ABORTION: YUGOSLAVIA

"Croatia: outcome of pregnancy in women whose requests for legal abortion have been denied," by D.
Stamper. STUDIES IN FAMILY PLANNING 4(10):
267-269, October, 1973.

"Social aspects of legal abortion in Yugoslavia," by
N. J. Jurukovski. GODISEN ZBORNIK NA MEDI-
CINSKIAT FAKULTET VO SKOPJE 20:159-164,
1974.

ADOPTION
see: Family Planning

ALUPENT

AMERICAN COLLEGE OF OBSTETRICIANS AND GYNE-
COLOGISTS

AMERICAN HOSPITAL ASSOCIATION

AMERICAN PUBLIC HEALTH ASSOCIATON
"Opposition to a constitutional amendment on abortion:
American Public Health Association resolution."
AMERICAN JOURNAL OF PUBLIC HEALTH AND
THE NATION'S HEALTH 65:203, February, 1975.

AMOGLANDIN
"Prostaglandins F2 alpha (Amoglandin, Dinoprost)
for induced abortion in the second trimester," by
E. B. Obel. UGESKRIFT FOR LAEGER 137(25):
1417-1418, June 16, 1975.

AMOXICILLIN

ANESTHESIA
see also: Induced Abortion
Therapeutic Abortion

ANESTHESIA

"The action of halothane in causing abortion," by
R. Wittmann, et al. ANAESTHESIST 23(1):
30-35, January, 1974.

"Diazepam as an adjunct in propanidid anaesthesia
for abortion," by M. A. Mattila, et al. BRITISH
JOURNAL OF ANAESTHESIA 46(6):446-448,
June, 1974.

"On the abortive and teratogenous action of volatile
and gaseous anaesthetis agents," by V. Hempel.
ANAESTHESIST 24(6):249-252, June, 1975.

"Studies of morbidity in anaesthetists with special
reference to obstetric history," by A. A. Spence,
et al. PROCEEDINGS OF THE ROYAL SOCIETY
OF MEDICINE 67(10):989-990, October, 1974.

ANTIBODIES

ARACHIDONIC ACID
"Initiation of human parturition. I. Mechanism of
action of arachidonic acid," by P. C. MacDonald,
et al. OBSTETRICS AND GYNECOLOGY 44(5):
629-636, November, 1974.

ARTIFICIAL ABORTION
see: Induced Abortion

ASPIRIN

BEHAVIOR
see: Sociology and Behavior

BIBLIOGRAPHY

BIRTH CONTROL
see also: Family Planning

"Birth control in a sociohistorical perspective," by
R. Liljeström. LAKARTIDNINGEN 71(44):4346-
4348, October 30, 1974.

"Effectiveness of abortion as birth control," by S. J.
Williams, et al. SOCIAL BIOLOGY 22:23-33,
Spring, 1975.

"The pathology of birth control," by J. M. Craig.
ARCHIVES OF PATHOLOGY 99(5):233-236,
May, 1975.

"10 interviews about physicians and the population
change. Abortion inevitable in developing countries. Is forced birth control near?" by Y.
Karlsson. NORDISK MEDICIN 89(8):234-240,
October, 1974.

BLOOD
"Chorionic gonadotropin titer and anti-hormone antibodies in the blood in uterine and extrauterine pregnancy," by IuG Fedorov. AKUSHERSTVO I
GINEKOLOGIIA (Moscow) (9):53-56, September,
1974.

"Content of certain chloroganic pesticides in the
blood of pregnant women and embryos after miscarriage," by B. F. Mazorchuk, et al. PEDIATRIIA
AKUSHERSTVO I GINEKOLOGIIA (6):59-61, November-December, 1974.

"Placental lactogenic hormone content of the blood of
women with normal pregnancies and those complicated by late toxemia or miscarriage," by N. A.
Stepanova, et al. AKUSHERSTVO I GINEKOLOGIIA
(Moscow) (9):15-17, September, 1974.

"Prolactin in the blood-serum during physiological and

BLOOD

pathological gravidity," by F. Gzaárek, et al. CESKOSLOVENSKA GYNEKOLOGIE 40(1):39-40, February, 1975.

"Serum level of pregnancy associated alpha2-globulin in patients with spontaneous abortions," by G. N. Than, et al. ARCHIV FUR GYNAEKOLOGIE 218(3):183-187, July 29, 1975.

"Some indices of the blood coagulation system in post-natal and postabortion septic diseases," by T. S. Drampian, et al. ZHURNAL EKSPERIMENTAL'NOI I KLINICHESKOI MEDITSINY 14(3):92-95, 1974.

CANDIDIASIS
see: Complications

CARDIOVASCULAR SYSTEM
see: Complications

CEPHALOTHIN

CERVICAL INCOMPETENCE AND INSUFFICIENCY
"Prostaglandin-induced abortion and cervical incom-petence," by M. P. Embrey. BRITISH MEDICAL JOURNAL 2(5969):497, May 31, 1975.

"Surgical treatment of isthmocervical incompetence in pregnant women suffering from premature delivery," by L. P. Zubareva. VOPROSY AKHRANY MATER-INSTVA I DETSTVA 18(5):71-75, 1973.

CHLORMADINONE

CLINICAL ASPECTS
"Clinical aspects of abortion due to genetic causes studies in fifty-two cases," by J. Cohen, et al. ACTA EUROPAEA FERTILITATIS 2(3):405-425,

September, 1970.

"Clinical-epidemiological studies of legal abortion in
the WHO research program," by K. Edström.
LAKARTIDNINGEN 71(35):3175, August 28, 1974.

"Clinical use of a beta-mimetic drug in the control of
uterine dynamics," by G. Casati, et al. ANNALI
DI OSTETRICIA, GINECOLOGIA, MEDICINA
PERINATALE 94(9-10):587-594, September-October,
1973.

"Clinical results of therapeutic induction of abortion
by extraamniotic application of prostaglandin F2
alpha," by H. Lahmann, et al. ZEITSCHRIFT
FUR GEBURTSHILFE UND PERINATOLOGIE
178(6):423-428, December, 1974.

"Clinical studies of psychotic disorders appearing
during pregnancy, puerperal period and following
induced abortion," by J. Ichikawa. PSYCHIATRIA
ET NEUROLOGIA JAPONICA 76(8):457-425, August
25, 1974.

"Clinics: run for women," by E. Krauss. MS MAGA-
ZINE 4:106, September, 1975.

"Factors of high fetal risk in a peripheral clinic," by
R. Molina, et al. REVISTA CHILENA DE OBSTE-
TRICIA Y GINECOLOGIA 38(1):43-53, 1973.

"Induction of abortion with prostaglandins: clinical
and metabolic aspects," by M. Bygdeman, et al.
SOUTH AFRICAN MEDICAL JOURNAL 0(0):Suppl:
3-8, October 16, 1974.

"Intra-amniotic urea as a midtrimester abortifacient:
clinical results and serum and urinary changes," by

CLINICAL ASPECTS

L. S. Burnett, et al. AMERICAN JOURNAL OF
OBSTETRICS AND GYNECOLOGY 121(1):7-16,
January 1, 1975.

"Thoughts on the current situation of abortion from
the clinical viewpoint," by S. Schulz, et al.
ZENTRALBLATT FUR GYNAEKOLOGIE 96(39):
1223-1226, September 27, 1974.

"The use of antiserotonin-cyproheptadine HCL in
pregnancy: an experimental and clinical study,"
by E. Sadovsky, et al. ADVANCES IN EXPERI-
MENTAL MEDICINE AND BIOLOGY 27:399-405,
1972.

CLOMIPHENE

COLLEGE WOMEN
see: Youth

COMPLICATIONS
see also: Hemorrhage

"Abdominal fetus following induced abortion," by E. M.
Silverman, et al. AMERICAN JOURNAL OF OB-
STETRICS AND GYNECOLOGY 122(6):791-792,
July 15, 1975.

"Acute hematometra with peritoneal irritation following
therapeutic abortion by the Karman method of suction
curettage," by G. Bastert, et al. MUENCHENER
MEDIZINISCHE WOCHENSCHRIFT 116(38):780-781,
September 20, 1974.

"Breast gland following artifical termination of early
pregnancy and following threatened and completed
abortion," by F. Glenc. WIADOMASCI LEKARSKIE
28(7):549-551, April 1, 1975.

"Cerebral abscess following septic abortion with the
use of a Dalkon shield," by A. A. Op de Coul.
NEDERLANDS TIJDSCHRIFT VOOR GENEESKUNDE
119(12):470-472, March 22, 1975.

"Cervicovaginal fistula complicating induced midtrimes-
ter abortion despite laminaria tent insertion," by
J. H. Lischke, et al. AMERICAN JOURNAL OF OB-
STETRICS AND GYNECOLOGY 120(6):852-853,
November 15, 1974.

"Cervix carcinoma in women undergoing induced abor-
tion for social reasons," by R. Kaliński, et al.
WIADOMASCI LEKARSKIE 28(15):1281-1284,
August 1, 1975.

"Cervix pregnancy following abortion," by W. Böhm,
et al. ZENTRALBLATT FUER GYNAEKOLOGIE
96(44):1399-1402, November 1, 1974.

"Characteristics of clinical course of acute postabortion renal insufficiency," by T. I. Gromova.
VRACHEBNOE DELO (1):86-88, January, 1975.

"Chromosome abnormalities and abortion," by A.
Boué, et al. BASIC LIFE SCIENCES 4(PT. B):
317-339, 1974.

"Clinical studies of psychotic disorders appearing
during pregnancy, puerperal period and following
induced abortion," by J. Ichikawa. PSYCHIATRIA
ET NEUROLOGIA JAPONICA 76(8):457-483,
August 25, 1974.

"Complications caused by difficult removal of laminaria
tents," by J. P. Gusdon, Jr., et al. AMERICAN
JOURNAL OF OBSTETRICS AND GYNECOLOGY
121(2):286-287, January 15, 1975.

"Complications following prostaglandin F2alpha-induced midtrimester abortion," by J. H. Duenhoelter, et al. OBSTETRICS AND GYNECOLOGY 46(3):247-250, September, 1975.

"Complications of the interruption of pregnancy by the method of intra-amnionic administration of a hypertonic sodium chloride solution and their prevention," by Iu. M. Bloshanskii. AKUSHERSTVO I GINEKOLO-GIIA (Moscow) (9):65-66, September, 1974.

"Complications of prostaglandin-induced abortion." (letter). BRITISH MEDICAL JOURNAL 4(5941): 404-405, November 16, 1974.

"Complications of prostaglandin-induced abortion," (letter), by J. J. Amy. BRITISH MEDICAL JOURNAL 4(5945):654, December 14, 1974.

"Complications of 10,453 consecutive first-trimester abortions: a prospective study," by J. E. Hodgson, et al. AMERICAN JOURNAL OF OBSTETRICS AND GYNECOLOGY 120(6):802-807, November 15, 1974.

"Conjoined twins," by L. Joshi. JOURNAL OF THE INDIAN MEDICAL ASSOCIATION 63(7):222-223, October 1, 1974.

"The course of pregnancy and labor following legal abortion," by H. Kirchhoff. ZEITSCHRIFT FUR GE-BURTSHILFE UND PERINATOLOGIE 178(6):407-414, December, 1974.

"Diagnosis of acute suppurative peritonitis in patients with sepsis and acute renal insufficiency," by O. S. Shkrob, et al. AKUSHERSTVO I GINEKOLOGIIA (Moscow) (6):32-35, June, 1974.

"DIC, disseminated intravascular coagulation. Nursing grand rounds." NURSING 4(11):66-71, November, 1974.

"The effects of anitbiotics on indices of immunity during treatment of endomyometritis following infectious abortion," by G. S. Minasova, et al. ANTIBIOTIKI 19(1):86-89, January, 1974.

"Electroencephalographic changes after intra-amniotic prostaglandin F2alpha and hypertonic saline," by R. P. Shearman, et al. BRITISH JOURNAL OF OBSTETRICS AND GYNAECOLOGY 82(4):314-317, April, 1975.

"Evaluation of sonar in the prediction of complications after vaginal termination of pregnancy," by M. Stone, et al. AMERICAN JOURNAL OF OBSTETRICS AND GYNECOLOGY 120(7):890-894, December 1, 1974.

"Fatal complications by air embolism in legal interruption of pregnancy," by A. Du Chesne. ZENTRAL-BLATT FUR GYNAEKOLOGIE 96(50):1593-1597, December 13, 1974.

"The foetal risks in sickle cell anaemia," by M. F. Anderson. WEST INDIAN MEDICAL JOURNAL 20(4):288-295, December, 1971.

"From the files of the KMA Maternal Mortality Study Committee," by J. W. Greene, Jr. JOURNAL OF THE KENTUCKY MEDICAL ASSOCIATION 73(1): 33, January, 1975.

"Hazards of IUDs," by J. W. Records. SOUTHERN MEDICAL JOURNAL 68(9):1061-1062, September, 1975.

"Hazards of pregnancy interruption," by G. K. Döring. FORTSCHRITTE DER MEDIZIN 92(29):1156-1160, October 17, 1974.

"Induced abortion and its sequelae: prematurity and spontaneous abortion," by L. H. Roht, et al. AMERICAN JOURNAL OF OBSTETRICS AND GYNECOLOGY 120(7):868-874, December 1, 1974.

"Induction of labour and abortion by intravenous prostaglandins in pregnancies complicated by intrauterine foetal death and hydatidiform mole," by G. Roberts. CURRENT MEDICAL RESEARCH AND OPINION 2(6):342-350, 1974.

"Infective complications of the IUD," MEDICAL JOURNAL OF AUSTRALIA 2(7):241-242, August 16, 1975.

"Intravascular hemolysis: a complication of midtrimester abortion: a report of two cases," by A. Adachi, et al. OBSTETRICS AND GYNECOLOGY 45(4):467-469, April, 1975.

"Late sequelae of induced abortion: complications and outcome of pregnancy and labor," by S. Harlap, et al. AMERICAN JOURNAL OF EPIDEMIOLOGY 102(3):217-224, September, 1975.

"Menstrual and obstetric sequelae of missed abortion," by W. Z. Polishuk, et al. ACTA EUROPAEA FERTILITATIS 5(4):289-293, December, 1974.

"Morbidity in legal abortions in the Perleberg District," by J. Berg. ZENTRALBLATT FUR GYNAEKOLOGIE 96(35):1111-1115, August 30, 1974.

"The pathology of birth control," by J. M. Craig.

ARCHIVES OF PATHOLOGY 99(5):233-236, May, 1975.

"Perforation of the uterus and injuries of the internal organs in violent interruption of pregnancy," by B. Veković, et al. MEDICINSKI ARHIV 28(6): 585-587, November-December, 1974.

"Persistence of lymphocytotoxic antibodies in multi-paras examined several years after their last pregnancy," by M. Savi, et al. ATENEO PAR-MENSE; SEZIONE I: ACTA BIO-MEDICA 46(1-2): 61-75, January-April, 1975.

"Placental lactogenic hormone content of the blood of women with normal pregnancies and those compli-cated by late toxemia or miscarriage," by N. A. Stepanova, et al. AKUSHERSTVO I GINEKOLOGIIA (Moscow) (9):15-17, September, 1974.

"Postabortion disseminated intravascular coagulation with reversible acute renal failure (report of 2 cases treated with heparin)," by V. Gutiérrez Millet, et al. REVISTA CLINICA ESPANOLA 134(2):149-156, July 31, 1974.

"Postabortion true mural thromboendocarditis," by R. Drut, et al. ARCHIVOS DE LA FUNDACION ROUX-OCEFA 8(1-4):161-166, January-December, 1974.

"Post-abortion uterine perforation. Chilean experience," by R. García Valenzuela, et al. REVISTA CHILENA DE OBSTETRICIA Y GINECOLOGIA 38(3):138-145, 1973.

"Post-Abortum acute renal insufficiency," by A. Amerio, et al. MINERVA NEFROLOGICA 21(2):95-103,

March-April, 1974.

"Pregnancy interruption in cardiac patients," by A. Barrillon, et al. ARCHIVES DES MALADIES DU COEUR ET DES VAISSEAUX 67(5):555-564, May, 1974.

"Prostaglandin-induced abortion: assessment of operative complications and early morbidity," by I. Z. Mackenzie, et al. BRITISH MEDICAL JOURNAL 4(5946):683-686, December 21, 1974.

"Psychological problems following birth and miscarriage," by K. L. Trick. NURSING MIRROR AND MIDWIVES' JOURNAL 141(2):61-62, July 10, 1975.

"The psychological sequelae of abortion performed for a genetic indication," by B. D. Blumberg, et al. AMERICAN JOURNAL OF OBSTETRICS AND GYNECOLOGY 122(7):799-808, August 1, 1975.

"Psychological sequelae of elective abortion," by B. D. Blumberg, et al. WESTERN JOURNAL OF MEDICINE 123(3):188-193, September, 1975.

"Psychosexual problems connected with artificial interruption of pregnancy," by F. Kohoutek, et al. CESKOSLOVENSKA GYNEKOLOGIE 39(3):206-207, April, 1974.

"Rare case of choriocarcinoma in ectopic pregnancy following removal of coexisting uterine pregnancy," by B. Buczek, et al. WIADOMASCI LEKARSKIE 28(10):895-897, May 15, 1975.

"Report on a case of consumption coagulopathy following abortion in a patient with genital and peritoneal tuberculosis," by H. F. Orth, et al. GEBURT-

SHILFE UND FRAUENHEILKUNDE 34(8):623–632, August, 1974.

"Rh sensitization following abortion," (letter), by E. P. Reid, CANADIAN MEDICAL ASSOCIATION JOURNAL 111(11):1182, December 7, 1974.

"Rupture of uterus during prostaglandin-induced abortion," by A. M. Smith. BRITISH MEDICAL JOURNAL 1(5951):205, January 25, 1975.

"Ultrasonic diagnosis of miscarriage and early pregnancy complications," by B. Zsolnai, et al. ACTA CHIRURGICA ACADEMIAE SCIENTIARUM HUNGARICAE 15(4):389–407, 1974.

"Unusual protraction of oliguria in a patient with acute renal insufficiency following a medical abortion," by S. A. Glants, et al. UROLOGIIA I NEFROLOGIIA (2):54, March–April, 1974.

"Uterine injuries complicating hypertonic saline abortion," by J. J. Willems. CANADIAN MEDICAL ASSOCIATION JOURNAL 111(11):1223, 1226, December 7, 1974.

"Visualization of placental abruption by blood pool scanning," by P. H. Weiss, et al. JOURNAL OF NUCLEAR MEDICINE 15(10):900–901, October, 1974.

"Water intoxication associated with oxytocin administration during saline-induced abortion," by N. H. Lauersen, et al. AMERICAN JOURNAL OF OBSTETRICS AND GYNECOLOGY 121(1):2–6, January 1, 1975.

CONTRACEPTION

"Bishops of Pakistan on abortion and contraception;
joint pastoral letter." L'OSSERVATORE ROMANO
11(363):9-10, March 13, 1975.

"Contraception, abortion and veneral disease: teen-
agers' knowledge and the effect of education," by
P. A. Reichelt, et al. FAMILY PLANNING PER-
SPECTIVES 7(2):83-88, March-April, 1975.

"Contraception and abortion," by M. S. Rapp. CAN-
ADIAN MEDICAL ASSOCIATION JOURNAL 112(6):
682, March 22, 1975.

"Contraceptive practice in the context of a nonrestric-
tive abortion law: age-specific pregnancy rates in
New York City, 1971-1973," by C. Tietze. FAMILY
PLANNING PERSPECTIVES 7:197-202, September-
October, 1975.

"Contraceptive therapy following therapeutic abortion:
an analysis," by W. F. Peterson. OBSTETRICS
AND GYNECOLOGY 44(6):853-857, December, 1974.

"Information meeting about hormonal contraception
and the abortion situation," by J. Wiese. UGESKRIFT
FOR LAEGER 137(23):1279-1282, June 2, 1975.

"Midtrimester abortion induced by serial intravaginal
administration of prostaglandin E2 suppositories in
conjunction with a contraceptive diaphragm," by N.
H. Lauersen, et al. PROSTAGLANDINS 10(1):139-
150, July, 1975.

"The pill and subsequent pregnancies," by D. T. Janerich.
LANCET 1(7908):681-682, March 22, 1975.

"Postpartum and postabortal insertion of intrauterine
contraceptive devices," by L. A. Martorella, et al.

CONTRACEPTION

JOURNAL OF REPRODUCTIVE MEDICINE 14(4):
178-181, April, 1975.

"Predicting contraceptive use in postabortion patients,"
by G. M. Selstad, et al. AMERICAN JOURNAL OF
PUBLIC HEALTH 65(7):708-713, July, 1975.

"Pregnancy with an intrauterine contraceptive device."
BRITISH MEDICAL JOURNAL 2(5969):458, May
31, 1975.

"Psychological factors in contraceptive failure and abortion request." MEDICAL JOURNAL OF AUSTRALIA
1(26):800, June 28, 1975.

"The significance of oral contraceptives in causing
chromosome anomalies in spontaneous abortions,"
by J. G. Lauritsen. ACTA OBSTETRICIA ET
GYNECOLOGICA SCANDINAVICA 54(3):261-264,
1975.

"Useful methods of contraception," by W. L. Whitehouse.
NURSING MIRROR AND MIDWIVES' JOURNAL 139
(18):77-78, October 31, 1974.

CRIMINAL ABORTION
see: Laws and Legislation

DEMOGRAPHY
see also: Population

"Demographic repercussions of legal and illegal abortion," by S. Gaslonde. GACETA MEDICA DE
MEXICO 108(5):327-334, November, 1974.

"Legal abortion among New York City residents: an
analysis according to socioeconomic and demographic
characteristics," by M. J. Kramer. FAMILY PLAN-

NING PERSPECTIVES 7(3):128-137, May-June,
1975.

"Social and demographic determinants of abortion in
Poland," by D. P. Mazur. POPULATION STUDIES
29:21-35, March, 1975.

DIAGNOSIS

"Bacterial and viral causes of abortion (laboratory
diagnosis)," by F. Denis. CAHIERS DE MEDE-
CINE 15(2):65-83, February, 1974.

"Bleeding in early pregnancy investigated by ultra-
sound, plasma progesterone and oestradiol," by
O. Piiroinen, et al. ANNALES CHIRURGIAE ET
GYNAECOLOGIAE FENNIAE 63(6):451-456, 1974.

"Case of Asherman's syndrome," by M. Lazarevski,
et al. GODISEN ZBORNIK NA MEDICINSKIOT
FAKULTET VO SKOPJE 20:633-637, 1974.

"Cytological evaluation of amniotic fluid in threatened
pregnancy," by A. Cekański, et al. WIADOMASCI
LEKARSKIE 28(16):1375-1380, August 15, 1975.

"Diagnosis of acute suppurative peritonitis in patients
with sepsis and acute renal insufficiency," by O.
S. Shkrob, et al. AKUSHERSTVO I GINEKOLEGIIA
(Moscow) (6):32-35, June, 1974.

"Diagnosis of Asherman's syndrome (intrauterine
synechiae)," by I. Smid, et al. ORVOSI HETILAP
115(51):3046-3048, December 22, 1974.

"Diagnosis of death in relation to irreversably coma-
tose artificially ventilated patients," by G. J.
Kloosterman. NEDERLANDS TIJDSCHRIFT VOOR
GENEESKUNDE 119(21):843-844, May 24, 1975.

"Diagnostic and prognostic value of bidimentional echography in threatened abortion," by N. Rodrĭguez. REVISTA CHILENA DE OBSTETRICIA Y GINECOLOGIA 38(5):228-239, 1973.

"Diagnostic and prognostic value of the 'spot' phenomenon and of the colpocystogram in threatened abortion," by E. B. Derankova, et al. AKUSHERSTVO I GINEKOLOGIIA (Moscow) 49(4):46-50, April, 1973.

"Evaluation of the outcome of pregnancy in threatened abortion by biochemical methods," by O. Karjalainen, et al. ANNALES CHIRURGIAE ET GYNAECOLOGIAE FENNIAE 63(6):457-464, 1974.

"Prevention of genetic diseases through prenatal diagnosis," by H. Hübner, et al. GINEKOLOGIA POLASKA 45(11):1313-1323, November, 1974.

"The prognosis in pregnancy after threatened abortion," by P. Jouppila, et al. ANNALES CHIRURGIAE ET GYNAECOLOGIAE FENNIAE 63(6):439-444, 1974.

"Prognosis in threatened abortion and chorionic hormone levels in the blood," by N. Medoki, et al. FOLIA ENDOCRINOLOGICA JAPONICA 50(2):520, February 20, 1974.

"The prognostic value of chorionic-gonadotrophins in the urine of miscarrying women," by H. Dyková, et al. CESKOSLOVENSKA GYNEKOLOGIE 40(6): 417-420, July, 1975.

"The prognostic value of human placental lactogen (HPL) levels in threatened abortion," by M. W. Gartside, et al. BRITISH JOURNAL OF OBSTETRICS AND GYNAECOLOGY 82(4):303-309, April,

DIAGNOSIS

1975.

"Psychodiagnostic factors of indication for abortion,"
by A. Blaser, et al. SCHWEIZERISCHE MEDIZIN-
ISCHE WOCHENSCHRIFT 105(14):436-438, April
5, 1975.

"Results of HPL radioimmunoassay in normal and
pathologic early pregnancy," by G. Hör, et al.
NUCLEAR-MEDIZIN 13(4):371-378, January 31,
1975.

"Simultaneous determination of blood and urinary HCG
and observation of its daily differences and circadian
rhythm for prevention of abortion," by Y. Abe, et
al. FOLIA ENDOCRINOLOGICA JAPONICA 50(2):
519, February 20, 1974.

"Ultrasonic diagnosis of miscarriage and early preg-
nancy complications," by B. Zsolnai, et al. ACTA
CHIRURGICA ACADEMIAE SCIENTIARUM HUNGAR-
ICAE 15(4):389-407, 1974.

"Ultrasound in management of clinically diagnosed
threatened abortion," by J. E. Drumm, et al.
BRITISH MEDICAL JOURNAL 02(5968):424, May
24, 1975.

"Value of endometrial biopsy in the diagnosis of hormonal
abortion," by I. Penev, et al. AKUSTERSTVO I
GINEKOLOGIIA (Sofiia) 13(5):374-378, 1974.

"Visualization of placental abruption by blood pool
scanning," by P. H. Weiss, et al. JOURNAL OF
NUCLEAR MEDICINE 15(10):900-901, October, 1974.

DIAZEPAM
"Diazepam as an adjunct in propanidid anaesthesia for

DIAZEPAM

abortion," by M. A. Mattila, et al. BRITISH
JOURNAL OF ANAESTHESIA 46(6):446-448, June,
1974.

"Diazepam as a sedative in induced abortion," by
J. B. Nielsen, et al. ACTA OBSTETRICA ET
GYNECOLOGICA SCANDINAVICA 54(3):237-239,
1975.

DIETHYLSTILBESTROL
"Vaginal adenomatesis and adenocarcinoma in young
women after diethylstilbestrol treatment," by G.
Vooijs. REVUE MEDICALE DE LIEGE 29(22):
682-687, November 15, 1974.

DINOPROST THOMETHAMINE
"Prostaglandins F2 alpha (Amoglandin, Dinoprost) for
induced abortion in the second trimester," by E. B.
Obel. UGESKRIFT FOR LAEGER 137(25):1417-
1418, June 16, 1975.

DOXICILLIN

DRUG THERAPY
see: Induced Abortion
Surgical Treatment and Management
Techniques of Abortion
Under Specific Drugs

EDUCATION
"Contraception, abortion and veneral disease: teen-
agers' knowledge and the effect of education," by
P. A. Reichelt, et al. FAMILY PLANNING PER-
SPECTIVES 7(2):83-88, March-April, 1975.

ENDOTOXIN

EPSILON-AMINOCAPROIC

"Epsilon-aminocaproic acid in the treatment of
abortion," by R. Klimek, et al. GINEKOLOGIA
POLSKA 46(7):747-750, July, 1975.

ESTRADIOL
"Bleeding in early pregnancy investiaged by ultrasound,
plasma progesterone and oestradiol," by O. Piiroinen,
et al. ANNALES CHIRURGIAE ET GYNAECOLOGIAE
FENNIAE 63(6):451-456, 1974.

"Serum levels of oestradiol and progesterone during
administration of prostaglandin F2alpha for induction of abortion and labour," by O. Widholm, et
al. ACAT OBSTETRICIA ET GINECOLOGICA
SCANDINAVICA 54(2):135-139, 1975.

ETHYL ALCOHOL

EUTHANASIA
"Abortion, euthanasia, and care of defective newborns,"
by J. Fletcher. NEW ENGLAND JOURNAL OF
MEDICINE 292(2):75-78, January 9, 1975.

FAMILY PLANNING
see also: Sociology and Behavior

"Abortion and family planning in the Soviet Union: pub-
lic policies and private behaviour," by H. P. David.
JOURNAL OF BIOSOCIAL SCIENCE 6(4):417-426,
October, 1974.

"Abortion, obtained and denied: research approaches,"
by S. H. Newman, et al. STUDIES IN FAMILY
PLANNING (53):1-8, May, 1970.

"Abortion: odyssey of an attitude," by A. F. Guttmacher.
FAMILY PLANNING PERSPECTIVES 4(4):5-7,
October, 1972.

FAMILY PLANNING

"Early abortion in a family planning clinic," by S.
Goldsmith. FAMILY PLANNING PERSPECTIVES
6(2):119-122, Spring, 1975.

"Fertility rates and abortion rates: simulations of
family limitation," by C. Tietze, et al. STUDIES
IN FAMILY PLANNING 6(5):114-120, May, 1975.

"Government directed family planning," by A. Braestrup.
UGESKRIFT FOR LAEGER 137(30):1742-1743, July
21, 1975.

"Ideal family size as an intervening variable between
religion and attitudes towards abortion," by M. Rerzi.
JOURNAL FOR THE SCIENTIFIC STUDY OF RELI-
GION 14:23-27, March, 1975.

"Pregnancy planning in Hawaii," by P. G. Steinhoff,
et al. FAMILY PLANNING PERSPECTIVES 7(3):
138-142, May-June, 1975.

FAUSTAN
"Experience with the use of the preparation Faustan
in obstetric and gynecologic practice." AKUSHER-
STVO IN GINEKOLOGIIA (Sofiia) 13(4):308-311,
1974.

FEES AND PUBLIC ASSISTANCE
see also: Sociology and Behavior

"Abortion and money." LANCET 2(7928):315, August
16, 1975.

"Cost analysis of regionalized versus decentralized
abortion programs," by M. D. Mandel. MEDICAL
CARE 13(2):137-149, February, 1975.

"Medicaid coverage of abortions in New York City: costs

and benefits," by M. Robinson, et al. FAMILY
PLANNING PERSPECTIVES 6(4):202-208, Fall,
1974.

"Medical coverage of abortions in New York City:
costs and benefits [based on conference paper],"
by M. Robinson, et al. FAMILY PLANNING PER-
SPECTIVES 6:202-208, Fall, 1974.

"Reaction split to Kennedy abortion view; federal
funds for abortion," by R. Rashke. NATIONAL
CATHOLIC REPORTER 11:1 plus, May 2, 1975.

"Restriction of medical aid in abortion," by N.
Chisholm. BRITISH MEDICAL JOURNAL 1(5958):
629, March 15, 1975.

"Should your tax dollars pay for abortions and fetal research?" by W. Brennan. LIGUORIAN 63:8-12,
March, 1975.

"Tax-exempt, bond-financed hospital can disallow abortions," by E. J. Schulte. HOSPITAL PROGRESS
56:18, August, 1975.

"Tax-supported abortions: the legal issues," by E. J.
Schulte. CATHOLIC LAWYER 21:1-7, Winter, 1975.

"Taxes - where the dollars go - abortions yes, private
schools no," by J. Doyle. LIGUORIAN 63:7-11,
September, 1975.

FERTILITY
see: Sterility

FETUS
"Beyond abortion - fetal experimentation," by J. Anderson. OUR SUNDAY VISITOR 63:1 plus, April 13, 1975.

"Dependent but distinct; the fetus," by M. Novak.
NATIONAL CATHOLIC REPORTER 11:11, May
9, 1975.

"Ethical standards for fetal experimentation," by
M. M. Martin. FORDHAM LAW REVIEW 43:
547-570, March, 1975.

"Fetal research," by B. J. Culliton. SCIENCE
187:237-238 plus, 411-413, 1175-1176, January
24, February 7, March 28, 1975.

"Fetal research and antiabortion politics: holding
science hostage," by D. S. Hart. FAMILY PLAN-
NING PERSPECTIVES 7:72-82, March-April, 1975.

"Fetal thymus glands obtained from prostaglandin-
induced abortions. Cellular immune function in vitro
and evidence of in vivo thymocyte activity following
transplantation," by D. W. Wara, et al. TRANS-
PLANTATION 18(5):387-390, November, 1974.

"The fetus as person: possible legal consequences of
the Hogan-Helms Amendment," by H. F. Pilpel.
FAMILY PLANNING PERSPECTIVES 6(1):6-7,
Winter, 1974.

"Fetus papyraceus: an unusual case with congenital
anomaly of the surviving fetus," by F. Saler, et
al. OBSTETRICS AND GYNECOLOGY 45(2):217-
220, February, 1975.

"An inconvenient fetus." NURSING MIRROR AND MID-
WIVES' JOURNAL 141:76, July 17, 1975.

"Is the fetus a person?" by A. DiIanni. AMERICAN
ECCLESIASTICAL REVIEW p. 309, May, 1974.

FETUS

"Not a fetus but a baby, jury decides in Boston." OUR
SUNDAY VISITOR 63:1, March 2, 1975.

FLAVOXATE

FLUMETHASONE

GENETICS

"Abortions, chromosomal aberrations, and radiation,"
by N. Freire-Maia. SOCIAL BIOLOGY 17(2):102-
106, June, 1970.

"Barr bodies in cervical smears," by S. H. Jackson,
et al. BRITISH MEDICAL JOURNAL 1(5959):682,
March 22, 1975.

"Chromosome aberrations in the parents in the case
of repeated spontaneous abortions," by V. P.
Kulazhenko, et al. SOVIET GENETICS 8(7):921-
928, July 15, 1974.

"Chromosome abnormalities and abortion," by A. Boué,
et al. BASIC LIFE SCIENCES 4(PT. B):317-339,
1974.

"Chromosome anomalies in three successive abortuses
due to paternal translocation, t(13q-18q+)," by T.
Kajii, et al. CYTOGENTICS AND CELL GENETICS
13(5):426-436, 1974.

"Chromosome 6/17 translocation as a cause of repeated abortions," by F. Pasquali, et al. ANNALI
DI OSTETRICIA, GINECOLOGIA, MEDICINA
PERINATALE 94(9-10):553-559, September-October,
1973.

"Clinical aspects of abortion due to genetic causes
studies in fifty-two cases," by J. Cohen, et al.

ACTA EUROPAEA FERTILITATIS 2(3):405-425,
September, 1970.

"Cytogenetical studies on couples with repeated abortions," by K. Rani, et al. INDIAN JOURNAL OF
EXPERIMENTAL BIOLOGY 12(1):98-99, January,
1974.

"Cytogenetic studies on spontaneous abortions," by
L. Wiśniewski,.et al. GYNAEKOLOGISCHE
RUNDSCHAU 14(3):184-193, 1974.

"Cytogenetic study of 30 couples having had several
spontaneous abortions," by A. Broustet, et al.
SEMAINE DES HOPITAUX DE PARIS 51(5):299-
302, January 26, 1975.

"Cytogenetics of habitual abortion. A review," by
G. Khudr. OBSTETRICAL AND GYNECOLOGICAL
SURVEY 29(5):290-310, May, 1974.

"Familial translocation 15-22. A possible cause for
abortions in female carriers," by K. Fried, et al.
JOURNAL OF MEDICAL GENETICS 11(3):280-282,
September, 1974.

"Genetic epidemiology of intra-uterine mortality.
Result of an analysis in a rural population in Que-
bec," by P. Philippee, et al. UNION MEDICALE
DU CANADA 104(5):763-767, May, 1975.

"Inherited (13; 14) translocation and reproduction. Report on three families," by H. von Koskull, et al.
HUMANGENETIK 24(2):85-91, 1974.

"Marker chromosomes in parents of spontaneous
abortuses," by S. Holbek, et al. HUMANGENETIK
25(1):61-64, 1974.

"Morphogenetic disturbances in a spontaneous abortus with trisomy B," by V. P. Kulazenko. HUMAN-GENETIK 25(1):53-59, 1974.

"Origin of triploidy in human abortuses," by J. Jonasson, et al. HEREDITAS 71(1):168-171, 1972.

"Prevention of genetic diseases through prenatal diagnosis," by H. Hübner, et al. GINEKOLOGIA POLASKA 45(11):1313-1323, November, 1974.

"Previous reproductive history in mothers presenting with spontaneous abortions," by E. Alberman, et al. BRITISH JOURNAL OF OBSTETRICS AND GYNAECOLOGY 82(5):366-373, May, 1975.

"The psychological sequelae of abortion performed for a genetic indication," by B. D. Blumberg, et al. AMERICAN JOURNAL OF OBSTETRICS AND GYNECOLOGY 122(7):799-808, August 1, 1975.

"Recent advances in the cytogenetic study of human spontaneous abortions," by H. D. McConnell, et al. OBSTETRICS AND GYNECOLOGY 45(5):547-552, May, 1975.

"The significance of oral contraceptives in causing chromosome anomalies in spontaneous abortions," by J. G. Lauritsen. ACTA OBSTETRICIA ET GYNECOLOGICA SCANDINAVICA 54(3):261-264, 1975.

"Studies on spontaneous abortions. Fluorescence analysis of abnormal karyotypes," by J. G. Lauritsen, et al. HEREDITAS 71(1):160-163, 1972.

"Translocation +(7p+;Bq-) associated with recurrent

abortion," by H. Körner, et al. HUMANGENETIK
28(1):83-86, May 26, 1975.

"A triploid human abortus due to dispermy," by N.
Niikawa, et al. HUMANGENETIK 24(3):261-264,
1974.

GENTAMICIN GARAMYCIN

GESTANON

GONORRHEA
see: Complications

GYNECOLOGY
"Experience with the use of the preparation Faustan
in obstetric and gynecologic practice." AKUSHER-
STVO I GINEKOLOGIIA (Sofiia) 13(4):308-311,
1974.

"Gynecologists do not want to be a pure service-institu-
tion, but that is what the health personnel are," by
G. H. Brundtland. NORDISK MEDICIN 90(2):39-43,
February, 1975.

"Importance of determining chorionic gonadotropin
excretion in the obstetrical and gynecological
clinic," by A. A. Galochkina. VOPROSY OKHRANY
MATERINSTVA I DETSTVA 18(4):77-80, 1973.

"Opportunities for the application of the prostaglandins
in gynecology. Interruption of pregnancy in acute
leukosis. Description of a case," by P. Krieglsteiner,
et al. MUNCHENER MEDIZINISCHE WOCHENSCHRIFT
117(7):245-248, February 14, 1975.

"Prostaglandins in clinical obstetrics and gynaecology."
ACTA OBSTETRICIA ET GYNECOLOGICA SCANDIN-

GYNECOLOGY

AVICA. SUPPLEMENT (37):1-72, 1974.

"The prostaglandins in obstetrics and gynaecology.
Are they living up to expectations?..." by A.
Gillespie. MEDICAL JOURNAL OF AUSTRALIA
1(2):38-41, January 11, 1975.

"Survey of Ottawa area general practitioners and
obstetrician-gynecologists on abortion," by M. C.
Diner. CANADIAN JOURNAL OF PUBLIC HEALTH
65(5):351-358, September-October, 1974.

GYNESTHESIN

HABITUAL ABORTION
"Alph2 globulin pregnancy proteins in the serum of
patients with missed abortion," by T. Gabor, et
al. ORVOSI HETILAP 116(17):977-979, April 27,
1975.

"Barr bodies in cervical smears," by S. H. Jackson,
et al. BRITISH MEDICAL JOURNAL 1(5959):682,
March 22, 1975.

"Case of Asherman's syndrome," by M. Lazarevski,
et al. GODISEN ZBORNIK NA MEDICINSKIAT
FOKULTET VO SKOPJE 20:633-637, 1974.

"Chromosome aberrations in the parents in the case of
repeated spontaneous abortions," by V. P. Kulazhenko,
et al. SOVIET GENETICS 8(7):921-928, July 15, 1974.

"Chromosome 6/17 translocation as a cause of repeated
abortions," by F. Pasquali, et al. ANNALI DI
OSTETRICIA, GINECOLOGIA, MEDICINA PERINA-
TALE 94(9-10):553-559, September-October, 1973.

"Cytogenetic study of 30 couples having had several spon-

taneous abortions," by A. Broustet, et al.
SEMAINE DES HOPITAUX DE PARIS 51(5):
299-302, January 26, 1975.

"Cytogenetical studies on couples with repeated
abortions," by K. Rani, et al. INDIAN JOURNAL
OF EXPERIMENTAL BIOLOGY 12(1):98-99,
January, 1974.

"Cytogenetics of habitual abortion. A review," by G.
Khudr. OBSTETRICAL AND GYNECOLOGICAL
SURVEY 29(5):290-310, May, 1974.

"Diagnosis of Asherman's syndrome (intrauterine
synechiae)," by I. Smid, et al. ORVOSI HETILAP
115(51):3046-3048, December 22, 1974.

"Endocrinal abortion," by E. Cittadini. MINERVA
GINECOLOGIA 26(4):211-220, April, 1974.

"Inherited (13;14) translocation and reproduction. Report on three families," by H. von Koskull, et al.
HUMANGENETIK 24(2):85-91, 1974.

"Preventive treatment of habitual abortion caused by
internal os incompetence," by S. Krzysztoporski.
ZENTRALBLATT FUER VETERINAERMEDIZINE.
JOURNAL OF VETERINARY MEDICINE 3(4):215-
218, November, 1974.

"Ribonucleic acid content in the endometrium of women
suffering from habitual abortions in inadequacy of the
luteinic phase of the menstrual cycle," by E. P.
Maizel', et al. VOPROSY OKHRANY MATERINSTVA
I DETSTVA 18(5):65-71, 1973.

"Spermine level in the myometrium and placenta of
women with late toxemia and habitual abortion in

their anamnesis," by T. G. Shorosheva, et al.
AKUSHERSTVO I GINEKOLOGIIA (Moscow) (9):
20-23, September, 1974.

"Synthetic sex hormones," by B. Field, et al. MEDI-
CAL JOURNAL OF AUSTRALIA 2(6):232, August 9,
1975.

"Translocation +(7p+; Bq-) associated with recurrent
abortion," by H. Körner, et al. HUMANGENETIK
28(1):83-86, May 26, 1975.

"The use of antiserotonin-cyproheptadine HCL in
pregnancy: an experimental and clinical study," by
E. Sadovsky, et al. ADVANCES IN EXPERIMENTAL
MEDICINE AND BIOLOGY 27:399-405, 1972.

"Value of endometrial biopsy in the diagnosis of hormonal
abortion," by I. Penev, et al. AKUSHERSTVO I
GINEKOLOGIIA (Sofiia) 13(5):374-378, 1974.

HEMORRHAGE
see also: Complications

"Accidental haemorrhage," by B. N. Chakravarty.
JOURNAL OF THE INDIAN MEDICAL ASSOCIATION
63(9):287-289, November 1, 1974.

"Accidental haemorrhage," by N. N. Chowdhury.
JOURNAL OF THE INDIAN MEDICAL ASSOCIATION
63(9):271-276, November 1, 1974.

"Concealed accidental ante-partum haemorrhage," by
J. O. Greenhalf. NURSING TIMES 71(10):382-384,
March 6, 1975.

HEPARIN
"Heparin therapy for septic abortion," by U. Stosiek.

HEPARIN

GEBURTSHILFE UND FRAUENHEILKUNDE 34(12): 1045-1046, December, 1974.

"Postabortion disseminated intravascular coagulation with reversible acute renal failure (report of 2 cases treated with heparin)," by V. Gutiérrez Millet, et al. REVISTA CLINICA ESPANOLA 134(2):149-156, July 31, 1974.

HISTORY

"Birth control in a sociohistorical perspective," by R. Liljeström. LAKARTIDNINGEN 71(44):4346-4348, October 30, 1974.

"History of the medical indication of induced abortion. A historical contribution to the discussion of a current problem," by J. Gottlieb. FOLIA CLINICA INTERNACIONAL (Barcelona) 24(10):731-732, October, 1974.

"History of medicine aspects on the problem of artifical abortion (I)," by H. Siefert. MEDIZINISCHE WELT 25(17):769-772 plus, April 26, 1974.

"History of the pro-life movement in Quebec," by A. Morais. CATHOLIC HOSPITAL 3:8-9, January-February, 1975.

"Induced abortion--a historical outline," by Flenc. POLSKI TYGODNIK LEKARSKI 29(45):1957-1958, November 11, 1974.

HORMONES

"The efficacy of intramuscular 15 methyl prostaglandin E2 in second-trimester abortion. Coagulation and hormonal aspects," by T. F. Dillon, et al. AMERICAN JOURNAL OF OBSTETRICS AND GYNECOLOGY 121(5):584-589, March 1, 1975.

"Experiences with hormonal treatment of imminent
abortuses and premature deliveries," by V. Kliment,
et al. BRATISLAVSKE LEKARSKE LISTY 63(2):
209-213, February, 1975.

"Hormonal parameters following termination of pregnancy: a guide to the management of threatened
abortion," by D. M. Saunders, et al. AMERICAN
JOURNAL OF OBSTETRICS AND GYNECOLOGY
120(8):1118-1119, December 15, 1974.

"Hormone changes occurring during second trimester
abortion induced with 15 (S)-15-methyl prostaglandin F2alpha," by S. L. Corson, et al. PROSTA-
GLANDINS 9 (6):975-983, June, 1975.

"Importance of hormone assays and high dose HCG,
estrogen and 17-alpha-hydroxyprogesterone treatment in the prevention of threatened abortion due to
endocrine causes," by G. Cubesi, et al. ACTA
EUROPAEA FERTILITATIS 2(3):355-358, September, 1970.

"Information meeting about hormonal contraception
and the abortion situation," by J. Wiese. UGE-
SHRIFT FOR LAEGER 137(23):1279-1282, June 2,
1975.

"Insect hormones as tsetse abortifacients," by D. L.
Denlinger. NATURE 253(5490):347-348, January 31,
1975.

"Intra-amniotic prostaglandin techniques for induction
of mid-trimester abortion and associated changes
in plasma steroid hormones," by I. Craft, et al.
SOUTH AFRICAN MEDICAL JOURNAL 0(0):Suppl:
31-35, October 16, 1974.

HORMONES

"Prognosis in threatened abortion and chorionic hormone levels in the blood," by N. Medoki, et al. FOLIA ENDOCRINOLOGICA JAPONICA 50(2):520, February 20, 1974.

"Synthetic sex hormones," by B. Field, et al. MEDICAL JOURNAL OF AUSTRALIA 2(6):232, August 9, 1975.

"Value of endometrial biopsy in the diagnosis of hormonal abortion," by I. Penev, et al. AKUSHERSTVO I GINEKOLOGIIA (Sofiia) 13(5):374-378, 1974.

HOSPITALS

"Applications for abortion at a community hospital," by M. E. Hunter. CANADIAN MEDICAL ASSOCIATION JOURNAL 111(10):1088-1089, 1092, November 16, 1974.

"Attitudes to legal abortion in hospital staff," by L. Jacobsson, et al. ACTA PSYCHIATRICA SCANDINAVICA. SUPPLEMENT (255):299-307, 1974.

"Catholic hospitals told protect right to life," by T. Gilsenan. NATIONAL CATHOLIC REPORTER 11:4, June 20, 1975.

"Clinics: run for women, not profit," by E. Krauss. MS MAGAZINE 4:106, September, 1975.

"Compelling hospitals to provide abortion services," by M. F. McKernan, Jr., CATHOLIC LAWYER 20:317-327, Autumn, 1974.

"Iowa public hospitals cannot discharge staff for abortion views." HOSPITAL LAW 8:4, February, 1975.

"Legal abortion in Bexar county hospital," by C. E.

Gibbs, et al. TEXAS MEDICINE 71(2):92-95, February, 1975.

"The organization and results of a pregnancy termination service in a National Health Service hospital," by M. G. Hull, et al. JOURNAL OF OBSTETRICS AND GYNAECOLOGY OF THE BRITISH COMMONWEALTH 81(8):577-587, August, 1974.

"Outpatient laparoscopic sterilization with therapeutic abortion versus abortion alone," by J. I. Fishburne, et al. OBSTETRICS AND GYNECOLOGY 45(6):665-668, June, 1975.

"Outpatient pregnancy termination in an NHS hospital," by M. G. Hull, et al. NURSING TIMES 70(40):1540-1542, October 3, 1974.

"Private hospitals not required to perform nontherapeutic abortions," by W. A. Regan. HOSPITAL PROGRESS 56:28 plus, April, 1975.

"Prostaglandin abortions in an outpatient ward," by O. Ylikorkala, et al. DUODECIM 90(19):1308-1316, 1974.

"Report on abortion activities in nearly 3,000 hospitals, clinics and private physicians' offices," by M. Clark. NEWSWEEK 85:97, February 17, 1975.

"Rules prohibiting abortions at St. Louis City hospitals are upheld by court." HOSPITALS 49:17, February 16, 1975.

"Simultaneous laparoscopic sterilization and suction curettage as an outpatient procedure," by N. Rezai. MARYLAND STATE MEDICAL JOURNAL 24(4):35-39, April, 1975.

"Tax-exempt, bond-financed hospital can disallow abortions," by E. J. Schulte. HOSPITAL PROGRESS 56:18, August, 1975.

"Therapeutic abortion in N. Z. public hospitals. I," by W. A. Facer. NURSING FORUM 2(4):12-13, September-October, 1974.

--II," by W. A. Facer. NURSING FORUM 2(5):8-10, November-December, 1974.

IMMUNITY

"Alph2 globulin pregnancy proteins in the serum of patients with missed abortion," by T. Gabor, et al. ORVOSI HETILAP 116(17):977-979, April 27, 1975.

"Anti-D antibodies after spontaneous abortion," by P. F. Bolis, et al. ARCHIVIO DI OSTETRICIA E GINECOLOGIA 78(1-3):12-17, January-June, 1973.

"Anti-rhesus(D) immunoprophylaxis in abortion." (letter). NEDERLANDS TIJDSCHRIFT VOOR GENEESKUNDE 118(47):1796-1797, November 23, 1974.

"Depressed lymphocyte response in mixed-wife-husband leucocyte cultures in normal and pathological pregnancies; effect of heat-inactivated serum," by L. Komlos, et al. REPRODUCCION 1(3):253-257, July-September, 1974.

"Immunization of RhO(D)-negative secundigravidae whose first pregnancy was terminated by induced abortion," by I. Simonovits, et al. HAEMATOLOGIA 8(1-4):291-298, 1974.

IMMUNITY

"Immunological problems connected with pregnancy
and therapeutic deductions in case of threatened
abortion," by M. Goisis, et al. MINERVA GINE-
COLOGICA 27(4):319-328, April, 1975.

"Rh-immunization following abortion," by J. Eklund.
DUODECIM 90(23):1641-1643, 1974.

"Spontaneous abortion and sensitization to elements of
the fertilised ovum," by I. N. Odarenko. AKUSH-
ERSTVO I GINEKOLOGIIA (Moscow) 49(4):64-65,
April, 1973.

INDUCED ABORTION
see also: Techniques of Abortion

"Abdominal fetus following induced abortion," by E. M.
Silverman, et al. AMERICAN JOURNAL OF OB-
STETRICS AND GYNECOLOGY 122(6):791-792,
July 15, 1975.

"Abortion," by J. S. Gemming, et al. NEW ZEALAND
MEDICAL JOURNAL 80(524):271, September 25,
1974.

"Abortion and legislation," by T. Monreal. REVISTA
CHILENA DE OBSTETRICIA Y GINECOLOGIA 38(2):
76-83, 1973.

"Abortion and research," by M. Lappe. HASTINGS
CENTER REPORT 5(3):21, June, 1975.

"Abortion creates problems for nurses," by A. L.
Salling. SYGEPLEJERSKEN 74(44):9, November 6,
1974.

"Abortion, euthanasia, and care of defective newborns,"
by J. Fletcher. NEW ENGLAND JOURNAL OF MED-

ICINE 292(2):75-78, January 9, 1975.

"Abortion experience in the United States," by
I. M. Cushner. NURSING FORUM 2(5):10-12,
November-December, 1974.

"Abortion in a predominantly Catholic community,"
by G. T. Schneider. JOURNAL OF THE LOUI-
SIANA STATE MEDICAL SOCIETY 126(9):323-
325, September, 1974.

"Abortion obtained and denied: research approached,"
by S. H. Newman, et al. STUDIES IN FAMILY
PLANNING (53):1-8, May, 1970.

"Abortion: odyssey of an attitude," by A. F. Guttmacher. FAMILY PLANNING PERSPECTIVES
4(4):5-7, October, 1972.

"Abortion-the story so far," by L. Swaffield. NURSING
TIMES 71(29):1120, July 17, 1975.

"Abortion under ethical indication," by H. J. Rieger.
DEUTSCH MEDIZINISCHE WOCHENSCHRIFT
99(42):2126, October 18, 1974.

"Abortions, chromosomal aberrations, and radiation,"
by N. Freire-Maia. SOCIAL BIOLOGY 17(2):102-
108, June, 1970.

"Amino acid composition of proteins of the placenta
and the fetal membranes in abortion," by T. N.
Pogorelova. AKUSHERSTVO I GINEKOLOGIIA
(Moscow) (9):51-53, September, 1974.

"An analysis of the Edelin case," by J. F. Holzer.
HOSPITAL PROGRESS 56(4):20-21, April, 1975.

"Artificial abortion and the law." HAREFUAH
88(5):238-239, March 2, 1975.

"Artificial termination of advanced pregnancy by
extra-amniotic administration of prostaglandin F2
alpha and 15-me-PGF2 alpha," by E. A. Chernukha,
et al. SOVETSKAIA MEDITSINA (6):21-26, June,
1975.

"Attitude of the physician towards abortion," by J. M.
Cantú, et al. GINECOLOGIA Y OBSTETRICIA DE
MEXICO 37(223):275-285, May, 1975.

"Attitudes of American teenagers toward abortion,"
by M. Zelnik, et al. FAMILY PLANNING PER-
SPECTIVES 7(2):89-91, March-April, 1975.

"Biology, abortion, and ethics," by M. Potts. LAN-
CET 1(7912):913, April 19, 1975.

"Biology, abortion, and ethics," by M. Wilkinson.
LANCET 1(7914):1029-1031, May 3, 1975.

"Birthright--alternative to abortion," by M. Kelly.
AMERICAN JOURNAL OF NURSING 75:76-77,
January, 1975.

"The Boston-Edelin case," by N. Kase. CONNECTICUT
MEDICINE 39(6):366-367, June, 1975.

"Breast gland following artifical termination of early
pregnancy and following threatened and completed
abortion," by F. Glenc. WIADOMASCI LEKARSKIE
28(7):549-551, April 1, 1975.

"Catholic Hospital Association rejects CMA abortion
stand," by M. Beaton-Mamak. DIMENSIONS IN
HEALTH SERVICE 52(4):36, April, 1975.

"Cervical dilatation with prostaglandin analogues prior
to vaginal termination of first trimester pregnancy
in nulliparous patients," by S. M. Karim, et al.
PROSTAGLANDINS 9(4):631-638, April, 1975.

"Cervicovaginal fistula complicating induced midtrimester abortion despite laminaria tent insertion,"
by J. H. Lischke, et al. AMERICAN JOURNAL
OF OBSTETRICS AND GYNECOLOGY 120(6):852-
853, November 15, 1974.

"Cervix carcinoma in women undergoing induced abor-
tion for social reasons," by R. Kaliński, et al.
WIADOMASCI LEKARSKIE 28(15):1281-1284,
August 1, 1975.

"Children--abortion--responsibility," by M. Lysnes.
SYKEPLEIEN 62(3):96, February 5, 1975.

"Circadian aspects of prostaglandin F2alpha-induced
termination of pregnancy," by I. D. Smith, et al.
JOURNAL OF OBSTETRICS AND GYNAECOLOGY
OF THE BRITISH COMMONWEALTH 81(11):841-
848, November, 1974.

"Circadian rhythms and abortion." BRITISH MEDICAL
JOURNAL 2(5961):3, April 5, 1975.

"Circadian timing, duration, dose and cost of prostaglandin F2alpha - induced termination of middle
trimester pregnancy," by I. D. Smith. CHRONO-
BIOLOGIA 1(1):41-53, January-March, 1974.

"Clinical studies of psychotic disorders appearing
during pregnancy, puerperal period and following
induced abortion," by J. Ichikawa. PSYCHIATRIA
ET NEUROLOGIA JAPONICA 76(8):457-483, August
25, 1974.

"Coagulation changes during intraamniotic prostaglandin-induced abortion," by G. J. Kleiner, et
al. OBSTETRICS AND GYNECOLOGY 44(5):757-
761, November, 1974.

"Comparative evaluation of the methods of termination
of advanced pregnancy," by V. I. Babukhadiia, et
al. SOVETSKAIA MEDITSINA (6):97-99, June, 1975.

"Comparison of abortion performed with prostaglandin
F2 alpha and hysterotomy," by H. Koeffler, et al.
ANNALES CHIRURGIAE ET GYNAECOLOGIAE
FENNIAE 63(6):483-486, 1974.

"Comparison of prostaglandin F2alpha and hypertonic
saline for induction of midtrimester abortion," by
N. H. Lauersen, et al. AMERICAN JOURNAL OF
OBSTETRICS AND GYNECOLOGY 120(7):875-879,
December 1, 1974.

"A comparison of termination of pregnancies in the
2nd trimester induced by intraamniotic injection of
hypertonic saline, prostaglandin F2alpha or both
drugs," by E. Bostofte, et al. ACTA OBSTETRICIA
ET GYNECOLOGICA SCANDINAVICA. SUPPLEMENT
(37):47-50, 1974.

"A comparison of two abortion-related legal inquiries,"
by C. H. Wecht, et al. JOURNAL OF LEGAL
MEDICINE 3(8):36-44, September, 1975.

"Competition between spontaneous and induced abortion," by R. G. Potter. DEMOGRAPHY 12(1):
129-141, February, 1975.

"Complete molar abortion induced with prostaglandin
F2 alpha," by M. Herrera, et al. REVISTA
CHILENA DE OBSTETRICIA Y GINECOLOGIA

38(3):146-149, 1973.

"Complications caused by difficult removal of laminaria tents," by J. P. Gusdon, Jr., et al. AMERICAN JOURNAL OF OBSTETRICS AND GYNECOLOGY 121(2):286-287, January 15, 1975.

"Complications following prostaglandin F2alpha-induced midtrimester abortion," by J. H. Duenhoelter, et al. OBSTETRICS AND GYNECOLOGY 46(3):247-250, September, 1975.

"Complications of the interruption of pregnancy by the method of intra-amnionic administration of a hypertonic sodium chloride solution and their prevention," by Iu. M. Bloshanskii. AKUSHERSTVO I GINEKOLOGIIA (Moscow) (9):65-66, September, 1974.

"Complications of prostaglandin-induced abortion." BRITISH MEDICAL JOURNAL 4(5941):404-405, November 16, 1974.

"Complications of prostaglandin-induced abortion," by J. J. Amy. BRITISH MEDICAL JOURNAL 4(5945):654, December 14, 1974.

"Complications of 10,453 consecutive first-trimester abortions: a prospective study," by J. E. Hodgson, et al. AMERICAN JOURNAL OF OBSTETRICS AND GYNECOLOGY 120(6):802-807, November 15, 1974.

"Contemporary legal standpoint on induced abortion," by H. J. Rieger. DEUTSCHE MEDEZINISCHE WOCHENSCHRIFT 99(37):1837-1838, September 13, 1974.

"Contraception, abortion and veneral disease: teenagers'

knowledge and the effect of education," by P. A. Reichelt, et al. FAMILY PLANNING PERSPEC-TIVES 7(2):83-88, March-April, 1975.

"Control and prevention of induced abortion. Field priorities and investigation," by L. Castelazo-Ayala. GACETA MEDICA DE MEXICO 108(5):334-339, November, 1974.

"Cost analysis of regionalized versus decentralized abortion programs," by M. D. Mandel. MEDICAL CARE 13:137-149, February, 1975.

"Cyclic adenosine 3',5'-monophosphate in prostaglandin-induced abortion," by K. Raij, et al. SCAN-DINAVIN JOURNAL OF CLINICAL AND LABORA-TORY INVESTIGATION 34(4):337-342, December, 1974.

"Decrease of utero-placental blood flow during prosta-glandin F2alpha induced abortion," by M. O. Pulk-kinen, et al. PROSTAGLANDINS 9(1):61-66, January, 1975.

"Delay in seeking induced abortion: a review and theoretical analysis," by M. B. Bracken, ět al. AMERICAN JOURNAL OF OBSTETRICS AND GYNECOLOGY 121(7):1008-1019, April 1, 1975.

"Diazepam as an adjunct in propanidid anaesthesia for abortion," by M. A. Mattila, et al. BRITISH JOURNAL OF ANAESTHESIA 46(6):446-448, June, 1974.

"Diazepam as a sedative in induced abortion," by J. B. Nielsen, et al. ACTA OBSTETRICA ET GYNECOLOGICA SCANDINAVICA 54(3):237-239, 1975.

"Early mid trimester abortion - by intramuscular 15 methyl prostaglandin E2," by S. D. Sharma, et al. PROSTAGLANDINS 8(2):171-178, October 25, 1974.

"Edelin case: further comment." NEW ENGLAND JOURNAL OF MEDICINE 292(21):1129-1130, May 22, 1975.

"The Edelin decision," by R. V. Jaynes. JOURNAL OF LEGAL MEDICINE 3(6):8, June, 1975.

"Edelin editorial protested." NEW ENGLAND JOURNAL OF MEDICINE 292(21):1129, May 22, 1975.

"The effect of analgesic drugs on the instillation-abortion time of hypertonic saline induced mid-trimester abortion," by R. Waltman, et al. PROSTAGLANDINS 7(5):411-424, September 10, 1974.

"The effect of anti-prostaglandin on the hypertonic saline-induced uterine activity," by A. I. Csapo, et al. PROSTAGLANDINS 9(4):627-629, April, 1975.

"The effect of induced abortions on perinatal mortality," by G. Papaevangelou, et al. ACTA EUROPAEA FERTILITATIS 4(1):7-10, March, 1973.

"Effect of prostaglandin F2 alpha and hypertonic saline on the placental function during midtrimester abortion," by S. Jayaraman, et al. AMERICAN JOURNAL OF OBSTETRICS AND GYNECOLOGY 121(4): 528-530, February 15, 1975.

"The effect of prostaglandin F2alpha on the placental

progesterone level in midtrimester abortion," by
F. A. Aleem, et al. AMERICAN JOURNAL OF
OBSTETRICS AND GYNECOLOGY 123(2):202-205,
September 15, 1975.

"Efficacy and acceptability of 15(S)-15-methyl-prosta-
glandin E2-methyl ester for midtrimester pregnancy
termination," by J. Bieniarz, et al. AMERICAN
JOURNAL OF OBSTETRICS AND GYNECOLOGY
120(6):840-843, November 15, 1974.

"Elective termination of pregnancy. Evaluation of
fetal lung maturity for lowering risk," by A.
Bhakthavathsalan, et al. NEW YORK STATE
JOURNAL OF MEDICINE 75(4):569-571, March,
1975.

"Endometrial aspiration as a means of early abortion,"
by T. C. Wong, et al. OBSTETRICS AND GYNE-
COLOGY 44(6):845-852, December, 1974.

"Endometrial regeneration after voluntary abortion,"
by J. V. Reyniak, et al. OBSTETRICS AND GYNE-
COLOGY 45(2):203-210, February, 1975.

"Epidemiology of induced abortion in Mexico," by B. R.
Ordónez. GACETA MEDICA DE MEXICO 108(5):
310-318, November, 1974.

"Ethical dilemmas in obstetric and newborn care," by
T. K. Hanid. MIDWIFE AND HEALTH VISITOR
11(1):9-11, January, 1975.

"Ethical issues in amniocentesis and abortion," by
T. R. McCormick. TEXAS REPORTS ON BIOLOGY
AND MEDICINE 32(1):299-309, Spring, 1974.

"Evaluation of sonar in the prediction of complications

after vaginal termination of pregnancy," by M. Stone, et al. AMERICAN JOURNAL OF OBSTETRICS AND GYNECOLOGY 120(7):890-894, December 1, 1974.

"Experience with the use of the preparation Faustan in obstetric and gynecologic practice." AKUSHER-STVO I GINEKOLOGIIA (Sofiia) 13(4):308-311, 1974.

"Extraovular prostaglandin F2alpha for early mid-trimester abortion," by A. G. Shapiro. AMERICAN JOURNAL OF OBSTETRICS AND GYNECOLOGY 121(3):333-336, February 1, 1975.

"Fertility rates and abortion rates: simulations of family limitation," by C. Tietze, et al. STUDIES IN FAMILY PLANNING 6(5):114-120, May, 1975.

"Fetal thymus glands obtained from prostaglandin-induced abortions. Cellular immune function in vitro and evidence of in vivo thymocyte activity following transplantation," by D. W. Wara, et al. TRANSPLANTATION 18(5):387-390, November, 1974.

"The fetus as person: possible legal consequences of the Hogan-Helms Amendment," by H. F. Pilpel. FAMILY PLANNING PERSPECTIVES 6(1):6-7, Winter, 1974.

"The hazards of vacuum aspiration in late first tri-mester abortions," by P. Moberg, et al. ACTA OBSTETRICIA ET GINECOLOGICA SCANDINAVICA 54(2):113-118, 1975.

"Health personnel organization for professional self-determination," by B. Brekke. SYKEPLEIEN 61(22):1145-1147, November 20, 1974.

"History of the medical indication of induced abortion. A historical contribution to the discussion of a current problem," by J. Gottlieb. FOLIA CLINICA INTERNACIONAL (Barcelona) 24(10): 731-732, October, 1974.

"History of medicine aspects on the problem of artificial abortion (I)," by H. Siefert. MEDIZINISCHE WELT 25(17):769-772,plus, April 26, 1974.

"Hormone changes occurring during second trimester abortion induced with 15 (S)-15-methyl prostaglandin F2alpha," by S. L. Corson, et al. PROSTA-GLANDINS 9(6):975-983, June, 1975.

"How many abortions?" BRUXELLES-MEDICAL 54(1):26, January, 1974.

"How shall we solve the problems of many abortions?" by A. L. Salling. SYGEPLEJERSKEN 75(23):9, June 11, 1975.

"Hypertonic saline induced abortion as pathophysiologic model of low grade intravascular coagulation," by E. A. Van Royen, et al. SCANDINAVIAN JOURNAL OF HAEMATOLOGY 13(3):166-174, 1974.

"Immunization of RhO(D)-negative secundigravidae whose first pregnancy was terminated by induced abortion," by I. Simonovits, et al. HAEMATOLOGIA 8(1-4):291-298, 1974.

"Incomplete pregnancies in workers of the metallurgical industry," by O. S. Badyva, et al. PEDIATRIIA AKUSHERSTVO I GINEKOLOGIIA (5):36-39, September-October, 1974.

"Induced abortion," by A. L. Castelazo. GINECOLOGIA

Y OBSTETRICIA DE MEXICO 37(219):1-12,
January, 1975.

"Induced abortion and subsequent outcome of pregnancy.
A matched cohort study," by J. R. Daling, et al.
LANCET 2(7926):170-173, July 26, 1975.

"Induced abortion and its sequelae: prematurity and
spontaneous abortion," by L. H. Roht, et al.
AMERICAN JOURNAL OF OBSTETRICS AND
GYNECOLOGY 120(7):868-874, December 1, 1974.

"Induced abortion--a historical outline," by F. Glenc.
POLSKI TYGODNIK LEKARSKI 29(45):1957-1958,
November 11, 1974.

"Induced abortion using prostaglandin E2 and F2alpha
gel," by T. H. Lippert, et al. GYNAEKOLOGISCHE
RUNDSCHAU 14(3):234-235, 1974.

"Induced mid-trimester abortion," by D. T. Liu, et
al. NURSING TIMES 70(40):1543, October 3, 1974.

"Induction of abortion by different prostaglandin
analogues," by M. Bygdeman, et al. ACTA OB-
STETRICIA ET GYNECOLOGICA SCANDINAVICA.
SUPPLEMENT (37):67-72, 1974.

"Induction of abortion in the 2nd trimester by intra-
amniotic instillation of hypertonic sodium chloride
solution," by D. Mladenović, et al. SRPSKI
ARHIV ZA CELOJUPNO LEKARSTVO 102(3-4):
199-208, March-April, 1974.

"Induction of abortion with prostaglandins: clinical
and metabolic aspects," by M. Bygdeman, et al.
SOUTH AFRICAN MEDICAL JOURNAL 0(0):
Suppl:3-8, October 16, 1974.

"Induction of labour and abortion by intravenous prostaglandins in pregnancies complicated by intra-uterine foetal death and hydatidiform mole," by G. Roberts. CURRENT MEDICAL RESEARCH AND OPINION 2(6):342-350, 1974.

"Induction of labour and perinatal mortality," by A. Singer, et al. BRITISH MEDICAL JOURNAL 2(5961):35, April 5, 1975.

"Induction of middle trimester abortion by intra-amniotic instillation of hypertonic solution," by M. Blum, et al. HAREFUAH 88(4):167-169, February 16, 1975.

"Infections with mycoplasma and bacteria in induced midtrimester abortion and fetal loss," by D. Sompolinsky, et al. AMERICAN JOURNAL OF OBSTETRICS AND GYNECOLOGY 121(5):610-616, March 1, 1975.

"Interruption of pregnancy by PGF 2 alpha. II. Extraovular administration," by F. E. Szontágh, et al. ACTA EUROPAEA FERTILITATIS 4(1): 23-30, March, 1973.

"Interruption of pregnancy without cervic dilatation," by L. Lázló, et al. ORVOSI HETILAP 115(50): 2967-2969, December 15, 1974.

"Interruption using prostaglandin F2alpha and E2," by H. Henner, et al. GYNAEKOLOGISCHE RUNDSCHAU 14(3):236-237, 1974.

"Intra-amniotic prostaglandin F 2alpha as a mid-trimester abortifacinet: effect of oxytocin and laminaria," by S. L. Corson, et al. JOURNAL OF REPRODUCTIVE MEDICINE 14(2):47-51,

February, 1975.

"Intra-amniotic urea and low-dose prostaglandin E2 for midtrimester termination," by I. Craft. LANCET 1(7916):1115-1116, May 17, 1975.

"Intra-amniotic urea as a midtrimester abortifacient: clinical results and serum and urinary changes," by L. S. Burnett, et al. AMERICAN JOURNAL OF OBSTETRICS AND GYNECOLOGY 121(1):7-16, January 1, 1975.

"Intraamniotic urea for induction of midtrimester pregnancy termination: a further evaluation," by P. C. Weinberg, et al. OBSTETRICS AND GYNECOLOGY 45(3):320-324, March, 1975.

"Intramuscular administration of 15(S)-15-methylprostaglandin E2-methyl ester for induction of abortion," by W. E. Brenner, et al. AMERICAN JOURNAL OF OBSTETRICS AND GYNECOLOGY 120(6):833-836, November 15, 1974.

"Intramuscular administration of 15(S) 15 methyl prostaglandin E2 methyl ester for induction of abortion: a comparison of two dose schedules," by W. E. Brenner, et al. FERTILITY AND STERILITY 26(4):369-379, April, 1975.

"Intrauterine instillation of prostaglandin F2ALPHA IN EARLY PREGNANCY," by J. R. Jones, et al. PROSTAGLANDINS 9(6):881-892, June, 1975.

"Intravascular hemolysis: a complication of midtrimester abortion: a report of two cases," by A. Adachi, et al. OBSTETRICS AND GYNECOLOGY 45(4):467-469, April, 1975.

"Intravenous prostaglandins and oxytocin for mid-
trimester abortion," by J. M. Beazley. LANCET
1(7902):335, February 8, 1975.

"Intravenous prostaglandins and oxytocin for mid-
trimester abortion," by T. M. Coltart, et al.
LANCET 1(7899):173-174, January 18, 1975.

"Is it advisable to interrupt pregnancy by vacuum
aspiration?" by G. Janny. ORVOSI HETILAP
116(15):885-886, April 13, 1975.

"Late sequelae of induced abortion: complications and
outcome of pregnancy and labor," by S. Harlap, et
al. AMERICAN JOURNAL OF EPIDEMIOLOGY
102(3):217-224, September, 1975.

"Law for the nurse supervisor: more about abortion
decisions," by H. Creighton. RN; NATIONAL
MAGAZINE FOR NURSES 6(4):10-11, April 14,
1975.

"The legal aspects of abortion," by L. D. Collins.
CANADIAN JOURNAL OF PUBLIC HEALTH
66(3):234-236, May-June, 1975.

"Management of missed abortion, intrauterine death
and hydatidiform mole using prostaglandin E2," by
C. P. Murray, et al. IRISH MEDICAL JOURNAL
68(6):133-135, March 22, 1975.

"Matters of life and death. The manipulative society,"
by E. H. Patey. NURSING MIRROR AND MIDWIVES'
JOURNAL 139(23):40-41, December 5, 1974.

"Medical consequences of teenage sexuality," by A. R.
Hinman, et al. NEW YORK STATE JOURNAL OF
MEDICINE 75(9):1439-1442, August, 1975.

"Medicine and the law: Attorney general clarifies
status of Texas abortion laws," by S. V. Stone,
Jr. TEXAS MEDICINE 70(11):107-108, November,
1974.

"Medico-legal briefs: Husband may not prevent wife
from having abortion." JOURNAL OF THE
MISSISSIPPI STATE MEDICAL ASSOCIATION
16(1):14-15, January, 1975.

"Menstrual extraction," by M. F. Atienza, et al.
AMERICAN JOURNAL OF OBSTETRICS AND
GYNECOLOGY 121(4):490-495, February 15, 1975.

"Menstrual regulation in the United States: a preliminary report," by W. E. Brenner, et al. FERTIL-
ITY AND STERILITY 26(3):289-295, March, 1975.

"Methodology in premature pregnancy termination. I,"
by A. C. Wentz, et al. OBSTETRICS AND GYNE-
COLOGY 28(1):2-19, January, 1973.

"Mid-trimester abortion induced by intravaginal
administration of prostaglandin E2 suppositories,"
by N. G. Lauersen, et al. AMERICAN JOURNAL
OF OBSTETRICS AND GYNECOLOGY 122(8):947-954,
August 15, 1975.

"Midtrimester abortion induced by serial intramuscular
injections of 15(S)-15-methyl-prostaglandin F2alpha,"
by N. H. Lauersen, et al. AMERICAN JOURNAL
OF OBSTETRICS AND GYNECOLOGY 121(2):273-276,
January 15, 1975.

"Midtrimester abortion induced by serial intravaginal
administration of prostaglandin E2 supporitories
in conjunction with a contraceptive diaphragm," by
N. H. Lauersen, et al. PROSTAGLANDINS 10(1):

139-150, July, 1975.

"Midtrimester abortion induced by single intra-
amniotic instillation of two dose schedules of
15(S)-15-methyl-prostaglandin F2alpha," by
N. H. Lauersen, et al. PROSTAGLANDINS
9(4):617-625, April, 1975.

"Mid-trimester abortion with 15 (S) methyl prostaglandin F 2 alpha," by T. Leibman, et al.
PROSTAGLANDINS 7(5):443-448, September 10,
1974.

"Mid-trimester abortion with intra-amniotic prostaglandin F2 alpha and intravenous oxytocin infusion,"
by M. Salomy, et al. PROSTAGLANDINS 9(2):271-
279, February, 1975.

"Midtrimester pregnancy interruption and the placental
progesterone levels," by F. A. Aleem, et al.
PROSTAGLANDINS 9(3):495-500, March, 1975.

"Mid-trimester termination," (letter), by S. M. Karim,
et al. BRITISH MEDICAL JOURNAL 4(5937):161-
162, October 19, 1974.

"A mode of action of hypertonic saline in inducing
abortion," by D. Llewellyn-Jones, et al. AMERI-
CAN JOURNAL OF OBSTETRICS AND GYNECOLOGY
121(4):568-569, February 15, 1975.

"Monitoring of the induction of labour by prostaglandin
f2alpha in early pregnancy," by H. Wiechell, et al.
MUNCHENER MEDIZINISCHE WOCHENSCHRIFT
116(38):767-775, September 20, 1974.

"Observations on patients two years after legal abortion," by P. Jouppila, et al. INTERNATIONAL

JOURNAL OF FERTILITY 19(4):233-239, 1974.

"On priests and abortion," by A. E. Hellegers. FAMILY PLANNING PERSPECTIVES 6(4):194-195, Fall, 1974.

"Outpatient pregnancy termination in an NHS hospital," by M. G. Hull, et al. NURSING TIMES 70(40):1540-1542, October 3, 1974.

"Oxytocin administration, instillation-to-abortion time, and morbidity associated with saline instillation," by G. S. Berger, et al. AMERICAN JOURNAL OF OBSTETRICS AND GYNECOLOGY 121(7):941-946, April 1, 1975.

"The pathology of birth control," by J. M. Craig. ARCHIVES OF PATHOLOGY 99(5):233-236, May, 1975.

"Perforation of a cornual pregnancy at induced first-trimester abortion," by B. Delson. AMERICAN JOURNAL OF OBSTETRICS AND GYNECOLOGY 121(4):581-582, February 15, 1975.

"Postabortion true mural thromboendocarditis," by R. Drut, et al. ARCHIVOS DE LA FUNDACION ROUX-OCEFA 8(1-4):161-166, January-December, 1974.

"Postpartum and postabortal insertion of intrauterine contraceptive devices," by L. A. Martorella, et al. JOURNAL OF REPRODUCTIVE MEDICINE 14(4):178-181, April, 1975.

"Pregnancy planning in Hawaii," by P. G. Steinhoff, et al. FAMILY PLANNING PERSPECTIVES 7(3): 138-142, May-June, 1975.

"Pregnancy wastage and age of mother among the Amish,"
by L. J. Resseguie. HUMAN BIOLOGY 46(4):633-
639, December, 1974.

"Preliminary experience with 15 (S) 15-methyl prosta-
glandin F2 alpha for midtrimester abortion," by
B. E. Greer, et al. AMERICAN JOURNAL OF OB-
STETRICS AND GYNECOLOGY 121(4):524-527,
February 15, 1975.

"Professional perspectives on abortion," by R. C.
Burchell. JOGN NURSING 3(6):25-27, November-
December, 1974.

"Profile of an abortion counselor," by B. Dauber.
FAMILY PLANNING PERSPECTIVES 6(3):185-187,
Summer, 1974.

"Prostaglandin abortions in an outpatient ward," by O.
Ylikorkala, et al. DUODECIM 90(19):1308-1316,
1974.

"Prostaglandin delivery by cervical dilator," by H.
Balin, et al. JOURNAL OF REPRODUCTIVE MED-
ICINE 13(6):208-212, December, 1974.

"Prostaglandin F2alpha and oxytocin compared with
hypertonic saline and oxytocin for the induction of
second trimester abortion," by K. R. Nielsen, et
al. ACTA OBSTETRICIA ET GYNECOLOGICA
SCANDINAVICA. SUPPLEMENT (37):57-60, 1974.

"Prostaglandin F2alpha as a method of choice for interruption of pregnancy," by V. Zahn, et al.
GEBURTSHILFE UND FRAUENHEILKUNDE 35(3):
203-210, March, 1975.

"Prostaglandin F2-alpha for induction of midterm abor-

tion: a comparative study," by I. F. Lau, et al.
FERTILITY AND STERILITY 26(1):74-79, January,
1975.

"Prostaglandin-induced abortion and cervical incompetence," by M. P. Embrey. BRITISH MEDICAL
JOURNAL 2(5969):497, May 31, 1975.

"Prostaglandin-induced abortion: assessment of operative complications and early morbidity," by I. Z.
Mackenzie, et al. BRITISH MEDICAL JOURNAL
4(5946):683-686, December 21, 1974.

"Prostaglandin induction of midtrimester abortion:
three years' experience of 626 cases," by P.
Kajanoja, et al. ACTA OBSTETRICIA ET GYN-
ECOLOGICA SCANDINAVICA. SUPPLEMENT
(37):51-56, 1974.

"Prostaglandins and induction of abortion," by P.
Kopecky. HIPPOKRATES 46(1):117-119, February,
1975.

"Prostaglandins for termination of second trimester
pregnancy," by U. R. Krishna, et al. JOURNAL
OF POSTGRADUATE MEDICINE 20(4):176-181,
October, 1974.

"Prostaglandins F2 alpha (Amoglandin, Dinoprost)
for induced abortion in the second trimester," by
E. B. Obel. UGESKRIFT FOR LAEGER 137(25):
1417-1418, June 16, 1975.

"Prostaglandins in clinical obstetrics and gynaecology."
ACTA OBSTETRICIA ET GYNECOLOGICA SCAN-
DINAVICA. SUPPLEMENT (37):1-72, 1974.

"The prostaglandins in obstetrics and gynaecology. Are

they living up to expectations?...," by A. Gillespie. MEDICAL JOURNAL OF AUSTRALIA 1(2):38-41, January 11, 1975.

"Psychodiagnostic factors of indications for abortion," by A. Blaser, et al. SCHWEIZERISCHE MEDIZIN-ISCHE WOCHENSCHRIFT 105(14):436-438, April 5, 1975.

"Psychological antecedents to conception among abortion seekers," by W. B. Miller. WESTERN JOURNAL OF MEDICINE 122(1):12-19, January, 1975.

"Psychological aspects of interruption," by S. Fukalová. CESKOSLOVENSKA GYNEKOLOGIE 39(3):204-206, April, 1974.

"Psychological femininity and legal abortion," by L. Jacobsson, et al. ACTA PSYCHIATRICA SCANDIN-AVICA. SUPPLEMENT (255):291-298, 1974.

"The psychological sequelae of abortion performed for a genetic indication," by B. D. Blumberg, et al. AMERICAN JOURNAL OF OBSTETRICS AND GYNECOLOGY 122(7):799-808, August 1, 1975.

"Psychosexual problems connected with artificial interruption of pregnancy," by F. Kohoutek, et al. CESKOSLOVENSKA GYNEKOLOGIE 39(3):206-207, April, 1974.

"Radiological aspects of indications for pregnancy interruption." ORVOSI HETILAP 116(23):1351, June 8, 1975.

"Radioreceptorassay of human chorionic gonadotropin as an aid in miniabortion," by R. Landesman, et al. FERTILITY AND STERILITY 25(12):1022-1029,

December, 1974.

"Rapid hCG-specific radioimmunossay for menstrual aspiration," by T. S. Kosasa, et al. OBSTETRICS AND GYNECOLOGY 45(5):566-568, May, 1975.

"Rare case of choriocarcinoma in ectopic pregnancy following removal of coexisting uterine pregnancy," by B. Buczek, et al. WIADOMOSCI LEKARSKIE 28(10):895-897, May 15, 1975.

"Rate of fall in plasma progesterone and time to abortion following intra-amniotic injection of prostaglandin F2alpha, with or without urea, in the second trimester of human pregnancy," by S. M. Walker, et al. BRITISH JOURNAL OF OB-STETRICA AND GYNAECOLOGY 82(6):488-492, June, 1975.

"Read the lobbying report," by P. L. Lowry. AMERI-CAN JOURNAL OF PUBLIC HEALTH 65(10):1115, October, 1975.

"Reduction of cervical resistance by prostaglandin suppositories prior to dilatation for induced abor-tion," by J. R. Dingfelder, et al. AMERICAN JOURNAL OF OBSTETRICS AND GYNECOLOGY 122(1):25-30, May 1, 1975.

"Response of the primate fetus to intra-amniotic saline injection," by A. Comas-Urrutia, et al. AMERICAN JOURNAL OF OBSTETRICS AND GYNECOLOGY 122(5):549-554, July 1, 1975.

"Restriction of medical aid in abortion," by N. Chisholm. BRITISH MEDICAL JOURNAL 1(5958):629, March 15, 1975.

"A review of 700 hysterotomies," by B. J. Nottage, et al. BRITISH JOURNAL OF OBSTETRICS AND GYNECOLOGY 82(4):310-313, April, 1975.

"Rh-immunization following abortion," by J. Eklund. DUODECIM 90(23):1641-1643, 1974.

"Rupture of uterus during prostaglandin-induced abortion," by A. M. Smith. BRITISH MEDICAL JOURNAL 1(5951):205, January 25, 1975.

"Salting out: experience in 9,000 cases," by D. H. Sherman. JOURNAL OF REPRODUCTIVE MEDICINE 14(06):241-243, June, 1975.

"Scottish abortion statistics 1973." HEALTH BULLETIN (Edinburgh) 32(3):121-129, May, 1974.

"Second trimester abortions. Review of four procedures," by A. Risk, et al. NEW YORK STATE JOURNAL OF MEDICINE 75(7):1022-1027, June, 1975.

"Serum levels of oestradiol and progesterone during administration of prostaglandin F2alpha for induction of abortion and labour," by O. Widholm, et al. ACTA OBSTETRICIA ET GYNECOLOGICA SCANDINAVICA 54(2):135-139, 1975.

"Serum-transaminase activity in women after artificial interruption of gravidity," by F. Glenc. CESKOSLOVENSKA GYNEKOLOGIE 40(5):386-387, June, 1975.

"Sexual life of young women and girls following interruption," by L. Kovácová, et al. CESKOSLOVENSKA GYNEKOLOGIE 39(3):218-219, April, 1974.

"Simultaneous laparoscopic sterilization and suction curettage as an outpatient procedure," by N. Rezal. MARYLAND STATE MEDICAL JOURNAL 24(4):35-39, April, 1975.

"Single extra-amniotic injection of prostaglandin E2 in viscous gel to induce mid-trimester abortion," by I. Z. Mackenzie, et al. BRITISH MEDICAL JOURNAL 1(5952):240-242, February 1, 1975.

"A smell of burning." LANCET 1(7911):844-845, April 12, 1975.

"A social-psychiatric comparison of 399 women requesting abortion and 118 pregnant women intending to deliver," by L. Jacobsson, et al. ACTA PSYCHIATRICA SCANDINAVICA. SUPPLEMENT (255):279-290, 1974.

"Successive pregnancy and deliveries (gravid 14, para 12) and frequent pregnancy and repeated induced abortion (gravid 13, par 2): an observation on 2 cases," by A. Sasaki, et al. JAPANESE JOURNAL FOR THE MIDWIFE 29(1):36-40, January, 1975.

"The synergistic activity of intra-amniotic prostaglandin F2 alpha and urea in the midtrimester elective abortion," by T. M. King, et al. AMERICAN JOURNAL OF OBSTETRICS AND GYNECOLOGY 120(5): 704-718, November 1, 1974.

"Synthesis and use of affinity-labeling steroids for interceptive purposes," by S. W. Clark, et al. AMERICAN JOURNAL OF OBSTETRICS AND GYNECOLOGY 121(6):864-873, March 15, 1975.

"Techniques of pregnancy termination. Part II," by L. S. Burnett, et al. OBSTETRICAL AND GYNE-

COLOGICAL SURVEY 29(1):6-42, January, 1974.

"Termination by prostaglandin pellets in very early pregnancy," (letter), by A. I. Csapo, et al. LANCET 2(7883):789-790, September 28, 1974.

"Termination of first-trimester pregnancies," (letter), by S. Way. LANCET 2(7887):1017, October 26, 1974.

"Termination of mid-trimester pregnancy by trans-cervical extra-amniotic hypertonic saline method without in-dwelling catheter," by S. Nummi, et al. ANNALES CHIRURGIAE ET GYNAECOLOGIAE FENNIAE 63(6):479-482, 1974.

"Termination of pregnancy in Wales," by B. Knight. NURSING MIRROR AND MIDWIVES' JOURNAL 140:69-70, April 3, 1975.

"Termination of pregnancy--the nurse's attitude," by A. B. Sclare, et al. NURSING MIRROR AND MID-WIVES' JOURNAL 140:59-60, January 16, 1975.

"Termination of second trimester pregnancy with intra-amniotic 15 (S) 15 methyl prostaglandin F-2alpha - a two dose schedule study," by S. M. Karim, et al. PROSTAGLANDINS 9(3):487-494, March, 1975.

"Thanatology?" WEST VIRGINIA MEDICAL JOURNAL 70(12):334-335, December, 1974.

"Thoughts on the current situation of abortion from the clinical viewpoint," by S. Schulz, et al. ZENTRALBLATT FUR GYNAEKOLOGIE 96(39): 1223-1226, September 27, 1974.

"Unwanted pregnancy: background and psychological characteristics of women who choose abortion," by D. Clayson, et al. PRAXIS 63(42):1260-1264, October 22, 1974.

"Use of high doses of oxytocin in non-developing pregnancy," by B. L. Gurtovoi, et al. VOPROSY OKHRANY MATERINSTVA IN DETSTVA 19(12): 45-49, December, 1974.

"Use of prostaglandin E2 vaginal suppositories in intrauterine fetal death and missed abortion," by C. D. Bailey, et al. OBSTETRICS AND GYNECOLOGY 45(1):110-113, January, 1975.

"Use of prostaglandins for induced abortion," by E. A. Chernukha. FEL'DSKER I AKUSHERKA 39(7):35-37, July, 1974.

"Uterine injuries complicating hypertonic saline abortion," by J. J. Willems. CANADIAN MEDICAL ASSOCIATION JOURNAL 111(11):1223, 1226, December 7, 1974.

"Vacurette--a new disposable suction apparatus in induced legal abortion," by O. Als, et al. UGESKRIFT FOR LAEGER 137(8):447-450, February 17, 1975.

"Vaginally administered prostaglandin E2 as a first and second trimester abortifacient," by S. L. Corson, et al. JOURNAL OF REPRODUCTIVE MEDICINE 14(2):43-46, February, 1975.

"Various current aspects of induced abortion. I. Introduction," by L. Castelazo-Ayala. GACETA MEDICA DE MEXICO 108(5):309-310, November, 1974.

INDUCED ABORTION

--V. Conclusions," by L. Castelazo-Ayala. GACETA MEDICA DE MEXICO 108(5):338-339, November, 1974.

"Various technics of interruption of pregnancy used in our statistical service. Incidents and accidents," by S. Boudjemaa, et al. TUNISIE MEDICALE 52(2): 83-87, March-April, 1974.

"Very early termination of pregnancy (menstrual extraction)," by J. Stringer, et al. BRITISH MEDICAL JOURNAL 3(5974):7-9, July 5, 1975.

"Volume and sodium concentration studies in 300 saline-induced abortions," by T. D. Kerenyi, et al. AMERICAN JOURNAL OF OBSTETRICS AND GYNECOLOGY 121(5):590-596, March 1, 1975.

"Vox populi," by G. L. Fite. JOURNAL OF THE AMERICAN MEDICAL ASSOCIATION 232(6): 595, May 12, 1975.

"Water intoxication associated with oxytocin administration during saline-induced abortion," by N. H. Lauersen, et al. AMERICAN JOURNAL OF OBSTETRICS AND GYNECOLOGY 121(1):2-6, January 1, 1975.

"What it's like to do an abortion," by T. K. Edwards. WEST VIRGINIA MEDICAL JOURNAL 71(5):122-123, May, 1975.

INDOMETHACIN

INFANTICIDE

"The immunological identification of foetal haemoglobin in bloodstains in infanticide and associated crimes," by S. J. Baxter, et al. MEDICINE, SCIENCE AND

INFANTICIDE

LAW 14(3):163-167, July, 1974.

INFECTION
see: Complications

ISOPTIN

ISOXSUPRINE
"Isoxsuprine chlorhydrate in the treatment of threatened abortion," by L. Ballestrin. ARCHIVIO DI OSTETRI-CIA E GINECOLOGIA 78(1-3):53-66, January-June, 1973.

LAW ENFORCEMENT
see: Laws and Legislation

LAWS AND LEGISLATION
"Abortion." JOURNAL OF THE AMERICAN MEDICAL ASSOCIATION 231(6):569-701, February 10, 1975.

"Abortion." NEW ZEALAND MEDICAL JOURNAL 81(531):31-32, January 8, 1975.

"Abortion," by H. P. Dunn. NEW ZEALAND MEDICAL JOURNAL 80(527):410, November 13, 1974.

"Abortion," by D. A. Introcaso. OBSTETRICS AND GYNECOLOGY 45(2):234-235, February, 1975.

"Abortion," by A. Wenkart. AMERICAN JOURNAL OF PSYCHOANALYSIS 34(2):161, Spring, 1974.

"Abortion ad is protected by First amendment, high court says." BROADCASTING 88:41, June 23, 1975.

"Abortion (amendment) bill." BRITISH MEDICAL JOURNAL 2(5970):558-559, June 7, 1975.

"Abortion (amendment) bill." BRITISH MEDICAL
JOURNAL 2(5972):686-687, June 21, 1975.

"Abortion (amendment) bill." BRITISH MEDICAL
JOURNAL 2(5973):748, June 28, 1975.

"Abortion (amendment) bill." BRITISH MEDICAL
JOURNAL 3(5975):99, July 12, 1975.

"Abortion (amendment) bill." BRITISH MEDICAL
JOURNAL 3(5976):160, July 19, 1975.

"Abortion (amendment) bill," by H. C. McLaren.
BRITISH MEDICAL JOURNAL 2(5971):613, June
14, 1975.

"Abortion and the conscience clause: current status,"
by D. J. Horan. CATHOLIC LAWYER 20:289-
302, Autumn, 1974.

"Abortion & Dr. Edelin: miscarriage of justice,"
by N. Lewin. NEW REPUBLIC 172:16-19, March
1, 1975; Discussion 172:30-33, April 5, 1975.

"Abortion and the law," by D. M. Alpern. NEWS-
WEEK 85:18 plus, March 3, 1975.

"Abortion and the law; implications of K. C. Edelin's
conviction for manslaughter in Boston abortion
trial," by D. M. Alpern. NEWSWEEK 85:18-19
plus, March 3, 1975.

"Abortion and the Law for Protection of the Mother--also
discussion of the decision of the National Labor-Court
of 16.2.1973," by H. Marburger. OEFFENTLICHE
GESUNDHEITSWESEN 37(1):37-43, January, 1975.

"Abortion and law on abortion," by G. Oggioni.

L'OSSERVATORE ROMANO 15(367):5 plus, April 10, 1975.

"Abortion and the law on abortion; document of the Permanent Council of the Italian Episcopal Conference." L'OSSERVATORE ROMANO 9(361):4-5, February 27, 1975.

"Abortion and legislation," by T. Monreal. REVISTA CHILENA DE OBSTETRICIA Y GINECOLOGIA 38(2): 76-83, 1973.

"Abortion and manslaughter; a Boston doctor goes on trial," by B. J. Culliton. SCIENCE 187:334-335, January 31, 1975.

"Abortion and money." LANCET 2(7928):315, August 16, 1975.

"Abortion and pre-natal injury: a legal and philosophical analysis." WESTERN ONTARIO LAW REVIEW 13:97-123, 1974.

"Abortion and the public good," by M. Pogonowska. AMERICAN JOURNAL OF PUBLIC HEALTH 65(7): 748, July, 1975.

"Abortion and the States." LANCET 2(7934):544, September 20, 1975.

"Abortion and the techniques of neutralization," by W. C. Brennan. JOURNAL OF HEALTH AND SOCIAL BEHAVIOR 15:358-365, December, 1974.

"Abortion and a woman's right to decide," by A. Jaggar. THE PHILOSOPHICAL FORUM 5:347-360, Fall-Winter, 1973.

"Abortion: the battle's not over," by E. B. Stengel. MS MAGAZINE 3:98-100, February, 1975.

"Abortion bill; against the act." ECONOMIST 254: 24, February 8, 1975.

"Abortion bill; the debate continues." ECONOMIST 254:31, February 15, 1975.

"Abortion--the breath of life," by R. J. Joling. MEDICAL TRIAL TECHNIQUE QUARTERLY 21:199-232, Fall, 1974.

"Abortion: community trends," (letter), by K. Hume. MEDICAL JOURNAL OF AUSTRALIA 2(14):542, October 5, 1974.

"Abortion: community trends," by I. D. Truskett, et al. MEDICAL JOURNAL OF AUSTRALIA 2(8): 288-291, August 24, 1974.

"Abortion: community trends. Comment 1," by C. Wood. MEDICAL JOURNAL OF AUSTRALIA 2(8): 291-293, August 24, 1974.

"Abortion: community trends. Comment 2," by A. F. Connon. MEDICAL JOURNAL OF AUSTRALIA 2(8):293-295, August 24, 1974.

"Abortion: Congress can't duck difficulties," by D. Loomis. NATIONAL CATHOLIC REPORTER 11:1 plus, May 16, 1975.

"Abortion controversy: what's it all about?" by J. Wax. SEVENTEEN 34:118-119 plus, November, 1975.

"Abortion counselling: focus on adolescent pregnancy," by C. Nadelson. PEDIATRICS 54(6):765-769, December, 1974.

"Abortion: the court decides a non-case," by J. O'Meara. SUPREME COURT REVIEW 1974:337-360, 1974.

"Abortion: the dangerous pressure on doctors," by R. Butt. TIMES p. 16, January 30, 1975.

"Abortion debate," by J. O'Hare. AMERICA 132:[inside front cover], March 1, 1975.

"Abortion: the debate continues," by F. Sherman. LUTHERAN p. 10, January 22, 1975.

"The abortion decision: two years later; symposium: More Christian than its critics," by R. Decker, et al. COMMONWEAL 101:384-392, February 14, 1975.

"Abortion: the Eldin shock wave." TIME 105:54-55, March 3, 1975.

"Abortion--an evil necessity." NURSING MIRROR AND MIDWIVES' JOURNAL 140(7):33, February 13, 1975.

"Abortion: the high court has ruled." FAMILY PLAN-NING PERSPECTIVES 5(1):1, Winter, 1973.

"Abortion: the husband's constitutional rights," by W. D. H. Teo. ETHICS 85:337-342, July, 1975.

"Abortion in Jamaica," by J. Symes. JAMAICAN NURSE 14:12 plus, August, 1974.

"Abortion in perspective," by B. M. Littlewood. NEW ZEALAND LAW JOURNAL 1974:488-493, November 5, 1974.

"Abortion investigation--abortion information. Experiences of a simple method for abortion investigations in Umea," by L. Jacobsson, et al. LAKARTIDNIN-GEN 72(1-2):44-45, 47, January 8, 1975.

"Abortion is not a 'delivery' following paragraph 9 section 1 of the Maternal Welfare Act," by T. Reinmoeller-Schreck. ZENTRALBLATT FUR ARBEITSMEDIZIN UND ARBEITSSCHUTZ 24(4): 120-121, April, 1974.

"Abortion: key issue in '76?" by R. Rashke. NATION-AL CATHOLIC REPORTER 11:1 plus, May 30, 1975.

"The abortion law and those who are incapable to the law," by J. Sahlin. LAKARTIDNINGEN 72(8):673-674, February 19, 1975.

"Abortion law; Europe is moving both ways." ECONO-MIST 254:52-53, March 1, 1975.

"Abortion law--Friendship Medical Center, Ltd. v. Chicago Board of Health (505 F 2d 1141), invalidating city health regulations applicable to first trimester abortion procedures." LOYOLA UNIVERSITY OF CHICAGO LAW JOURNAL 6:718-737, Summer, 1975.

"Abortion law reform. Fact and fiction: replying to Leo Abse," by M. Simms. SPECTATOR p. 114, February 1, 1975.

"Abortion law reform. Permissiveness and pretence," by C. B. Goodhart. SPECTATOR p. 114-115, February 1, 1975.

"Abortion laws in Hungary," (letter), by L. Iffy. OBSTETRICS AND GYNECOLOGY 45(1):115-116, January, 1975.

"Abortion: liberal laws do make abortion safer for
women,"by B. J. Culliton. SCIENCE 188:1091,
June 13, 1975.

"Abortion on maternal demand: paternal support
liability implications," by G. S. Swan. VALPAR-
AISO UNIVERSITY LAW REVIEW 9:243-272, Winter, 1975.

"Abortion on medicaid; the Bartlett amendment," by
R. Drinan. COMMONWEAL 102:102-103, May 9,
1975.

"Abortions on medicaid? Bartlett amendment," by
R. F. Drinan. COMMONWEAL 102:102-103, May
9, 1975; Discussion 102:286-287, July 18, 1975.

"Abortion on trial." NEWSWEEK 85:55, January 27,
1975.

"Abortion; or manslaughter?" ECONOMIST 254:61,
February 22, 1975.

"Abortion; reforms accepted [Britain]." ECONOMIST
257:36, October 25, 1975.

"Abortion: should constitution be amended?" by D.
Loomis. CONGRESSIONAL QUARTERLY SERVICE:
WEEKLY REPORT 33:917-922, May 3, 1975.

"Abortion; talked out." ECONOMIST 256:18, August
9, 1975.

"Abortion: 300,000 clandestine operations per year
in France." BRUXELLES MEDICAL 54(1):26-27,
January, 1974.

"Abortion: twenty-four weeks of dependency [United

States]," by L. Goodnight, et al. BAYLOR LAW
REVIEW 27:122-140, Winter, 1975.

"Abortion vs manslaughter," by P. G. Stubblefield.
ARCHIVES OF SURGERY 110(7):790-791, July,
1975.

"Abortions: legal but how available?" by D. Spalding.
MS MAGAZINE 4:103-106, September, 1975.

"Abortions: where do we stand in Louisiana?" by
M. G. Koslin. JOURNAL OF THE LOUISIANA
STATE MEDICAL SOCIETY 126(12):429-432,
December, 1974.

"Advice in the abortion decision," by S. A. Luscutoff,
et al. JOURNAL OF COUNCELING PSYCHOLOGY
22:140-146, March, 1975.

"After a conviction--second thoughts about abortions."
U. S. NEWS AND WORLD REPORT 78:78, March
3, 1975.

"After Edelin: the abortion debate goes on," by K.
Vaux. CHRISTIAN CENTURY 92:213, March 5,
1975.

"After the Lane report," by N. Waterson. NEW LAW
JOURNAL 124:761-763, August 15, 1974.

"Against the Act." ECONOMIST 254:24, February 8,
1975.

"Analysis of the Edelin case," by J. F. Holzer. HOS-
PITAL PROGRESS 56:20-21, April, 1975.

"Anglican Synod takes stand against abortion on demand."
OUR SUNDAY VISITOR 64:2, August 10, 1975.

"Anti-abortion feeling; United States." L'OSSERVA-
TORE ROMANO 10(362):11, March 6, 1975.

"Antiabortion policy upheld: insufficient 'state action'--
Texas." HOSPITAL LAW 8:4, January, 1975.

"Artificial abortion and the law." HAREFUAH 88(5):
238-239, March 2, 1975.

"Attitudes to legal abortion in hospital staff," by L.
Jacobsson, et al. ACTA PSYCHIATRICA SCANDIN-
AVICA. SUPPLEMENT (255):299-307, 1974.

"Attitudes of senior nursing students toward the 1973
supreme court decision on abortion," by R. G.
Elder. JOGN NURSING 4:46-54, July-August,
1975.

"Avortement et divorce en Allemagne Fédérale," by H.
Menudier. ETUDES 343:57-76, July, 1975.

"L'avortement et la nouvelle loi; point de vue d'un
accoucheur," by R. LeLirzin. ETUDES 343:199-
209, August-September, 1975.

"L'avortement, problème politique," by M. Schooyans.
NOUVELLE REVUE THEOLOGIQUE 96:1031-1053,
December, 1974; 97:25-50, January, 1975.

"Battle for unborn life will go on as Bayn's committee
vetoes pro-life amendments." OUR SUNDAY VISI-
TOR 64:1, September 28, 1975.

"The beginning of the human being," by J. Lejeune.
MAROC MEDICAL 55(590):251-258, May, 1975.

"Beyond Roe (Roe v. Wade, 93 Sup Ct 705) and Doe
(Doe v. Bolton, 93 Sup Ct 739): the rights of the

father," by H. Sherain. NOTRE DAME LAWYER
50:483-495, February, 1975.

"Birth rights," by C. Dix, et al. GUARDIAN p. 11,
February 6, 1975.

"Birth control in a sociohistorical perspective," by R.
Liljeström. LAKARTIDNINGEN 71(44):4346-4348,
October 30, 1974.

"Bishops may switch plan on abortion amendments."
NATIONAL CATHOLIC REPORTER 11:5, October
3, 1975.

"Bishops' spokesman says next step must be an amendment." OUR SUNDAY VISITOR 63:3, March 2, 1975.

"The Boston-Edelin case," by N. Kase. CONNECTICUT
MEDICINE 39(6):366-367, June, 1975.

"Case of abortion." JOURNAL OF URBAN LAW 52:
277-338, November, 1974.

"Catholic League supports right of doctors to act in
harmony with their consciences." OUR SUNDAY
VISITOR 64:1, August 3, 1975.

"Catholic member offers dissent on fetal rule," by J.
Castelli. OUR SUNDAY VISITOR 64:3, June 8, 1975.

"Cervix pregnancy following abortion," by W. Böhm, et
al. ZENTRALBLATT FUER GYNAEKOLOGIE 96(44):
1399-1402, November 1, 1974.

"Characteristics of New Zealand women seeking abortion
in Melbourne, Australia," by A. F. Rogers, et al.
NEW ZEALAND MEDICAL JOURNAL 81(536):282-286,
March 26, 1975.

"...Chicago. Confrontations," by G. Dunea. BRITISH
   MEDICAL JOURNAL 3(5976):151-153, July 19, 1975.

"Chilling effect; indictments against fetal research
   scientists in Boston." SCIENTIFIC AMERICAN
   232:40-41, February, 1975.

"Church leaders believe real reason to hope for a pro-
   life constitutional amendment." OUR SUNDAY VISI-
   TOR 64:1, June 8, 1975.

"Church leaders see pro-life setback as only temporary."
   OUR SUNDAY VISITOR 64:1, October 5, 1975.

"Civil Rights Commission against rights of unborn."
   OUR SUNDAY VISITOR 63:1, April 27, 1975.

"Clandestine abortion. Sketches of a numerical study,"
   by R. Bourg. BRUXELLES-MEDICAL 54(1):19-25,
   January, 1974.

"Clarify the abortion law," by B. L. P. Brosseau.
   DIMENSIONS IN HEALTH SERVICE 52:4, May,
   1975.

"Clinical-epidemiological studies of legal abortion in
   the WHO research program," by K. Edström.
   LAKARTIDNINGEN 71(35):3175, August 28, 1974.

"Combined laparoscopic sterilization and pregnancy
   termination: II. Further experiences with a larger
   series of patients," by R. G. Cunanan, Jr., et al.
   JOURNAL OF REPRODUCTIVE MEDICINE 13(5):
   204-205, November, 1974.

"Commonwealth v. Edelin," by R. F. Gibbs. JOURNAL
   OF LEGAL MEDICINE 3(3):6, March, 1975.

"Comparative studies on the new legalization of legal abortion," by S. Schultz, et al. ZENTRALBLATT FUR GYNAEKOLOGIE 96(39):1217-1222, September 27, 1974.

"A comparison of two abortion-related legal inquiries," by C. H. Wecht, et al. JOURNAL OF LEGAL MEDICINE 3(8):36-44, September, 1975.

"Compelling hospitals to provide abortion services," by M. McKernan, Jr. CATHOLIC LAWYER 20: 317-327, Fall, 1974.

"Constitutional law--abortion--father's rights." DUQUENSNE LAW REVIEW 13:599-610, Spring, 1975.

"Constitutional law: abortion, parental consent, minors' rights to due process, equal protection and privacy." AKRON LAW REVIEW 9:158-165, Summer, 1975.

"Constitutional law--abortion--putative father has no right to prevent wife from obtaining an abortion." MEMPHIS STATE UNIVERSITY LAW REVIEW 5: 429-437, Spring, 1975.

"Constitutional law--right to privacy--spousal consent to abortion: foreshadowing the fall of parental consent." SUFFOLK UNIVERSITY LAW REVIEW 9:841-872, Spring, 1975.

"Contemporary legal standpoint on induced abortion," H. J. Rieger. DEUTSCHE MEDIZINISCHE WOCHEN-SCHRIFT 99(37):1837-1838, September 13, 1974.

"Contraception and abortion," by M. S. Rapp. CAN-ADIAN MEDICAL ASSOCIATION JOURNAL 112(6):

682, March 22, 1975.

"Contraceptive practice in the context of a nonrestrictive abortion law: age-specific pregnancy rates in New York City, 1971-1973," by C. Tietze. FAMILY PLANNING PERSPECTIVES 7:197-202, September-October, 1975.

"The course of pregnancy and labor following legal abortion," by H. Kirchhoff. ZEITSCHRIFT FUR GEBURTSHILFE UND PERINATOLOGIE 178(6): 407-414, December, 1974.

"Court rules Medicaid law silent on abortions." HOSPITALS 49:17, September 1, 1975.

"A criminal approach to abortion." BRITISH MEDICAL JOURNAL 2(5967):352-353, May 17, 1975.

"Croatia: outcome of pregnancy in women whose requests for legal abortion have been denied," by D. Stampar. STUDIES IN FAMILY PLANNING 4(10): 267-269, October, 1973.

"The debate continues." ECONOMIST 254:31, February 15, 1975.

"Demographic repercussions of legal and illegal abortion," by S. Gaslonde. GACETA MEDICA DE MEXICO 108(5):327-334, November, 1974.

"Diazepam as an adjunct in propanidid anaesthesia for abortion," by M. A. Mattila, et al. BRITISH JOURNAL OF ANAESTHESIA 46(6):446-448, June, 1974.

"District court orders abortions at university hospital: Nebraska." HOSPITAL LAW 8:4-5, January, 1975.

"Doe v. Wohlgemuth, 376 F Supp 173." JOURNAL OF
FAMILY LAW 14:135-139, 1975.

"Le Dr. Morgentaler (Sa Majesté la Reine v. Henry
Morgentaler, Cour d'appel. Dist. de Montréal, no.
10-000289 -73) devant la Cour d'appel," by M.
Rivet. LES CAHIERS DE DROIT 15:889-896, 1974.

"Drive to legalize abortion in Italy starts uneasily."
NATIONAL CATHOLIC REPORTER 11:20, May 23,
1975.

"Early abortion in a family planning clinic," by S.
Goldsmith. FAMILY PLANNING PERSPECTIVES
6(2):119-122, Spring, 1975.

"Edelin abortion verdict." NATIONAL REVIEW 27:
260, 262, March 14, 1975.

"Edelin case." NATION 220:260, March 8, 1975.

"Edelin case: further comment." NEW ENGLAND
JOURNAL OF MEDICINE 292(21):1129-1130, May
22, 1975.

"Edelin decision," by C. A. Berger, et al. COMMON-
WEAL 102:76-78, April 25, 1975.

"The Edelin decision," by R. V. Jaynes. JOURNAL OF
LEGAL MEDICINE 3(6):8, June, 1975.

"Edelin editorial protested." NEW ENGLAND JOURNAL
OF MEDICINE 292(21):1129, May 22, 1975.

"Edelin says jury in Boston biased," by R. Casey.
NATIONAL CATHOLIC REPORTER 11:1 plus,
February 28, 1975.

"Edelin supported." NEW ENGLAND JOURNAL OF
MEDICINE 292(13):705, March 27, 1975.

"The Edelin trial fiasco," by F. J. Ingelfinger. NEW
ENGLAND JOURNAL OF MEDICINE 292(13):697,
March 27, 1975.

"Edelin trial: jury not persuaded by scientists for the
defense," by B. J. Culliton. SCIENCE 187:814-
816, March 7, 1975.

"The effect of legalization of abortion on population
growth and public health," by C. Tietze. FAMILY
PLANNING PERSPECTIVES 7(3):123-127, May-
June, 1975.

"The effect of legalized abortion on morbidity resulting
from criminal abortion," by R. S. Kahan, et al.
AMERICAN JOURNAL OF OBSTETRICS AND GYN-
ECOLOGY 121(1):114-116, January 1, 1975.

"Ethics of selective abortion." BRITISH MEDICAL
JOURNAL 4(5946):676, December 21, 1974.

"Europe is moving both ways." ECONOMIST 254:52-
53, March 1, 1975.

"Evolution of Canadian justice: the Morgentaler case,"
by E. Z. Friedenberg. CANADIAN FORUM 55:28-
30, June, 1975.

"Far from settling issue, Supreme Court caught in
storm over legal abortion," by C. D. Davis.
TEXAS HOSPITALS 30:28-29, March, 1975.

"Fatal complications by air embolism in legal interruption of pregnancy," by A. Du Chesne. ZEN-
TRALBLATT FUR GYNAEKOLOGIE 96(50):1593-

1597, December 13, 1974.

"Father and the unborn child," by P. T. O'Neill, et al. MODERN LAW REVIEW 38:174-185, March, 1975.

"Father's rights in the abortion decision." TEXAS TECH LAW REVIEW 6:1075-1094, Spring, 1975.

"The fetus as person: possible legal consequences of the Hogan-Helms Amendment," by H. F. Pilpel. FAMILY PLANNING PERSPECTIVES 6(1):6-7, Winter, 1974.

"Four indicators of humanhand: the enquiry matures," by J. F. Fletcher. HASTINGS CENTER REPORT 4:4-7, December, 1974.

"Four questions about sex in our society," by J. Kirk. MEDICAL TIMES 102(11):68-80, November, 1974.

"Further in modest defence," by J. Rudinow. ANALYSIS 35:91-92, January, 1975.

"General practitioners and abortion." JOURNAL OF THE ROYAL COLLEGE OF GENERAL PRACTITIONERS 24(142):298, 303, May, 1974.

"German bishops urge defence at all cost of the lives of the unborn," by H. Volk. L'OSSERVATORE ROMANO 2(354):8, January 9, 1975.

"Government directed family planning," by A. Braestrup. UGESKRIFT FOR LAEGER 137(30):1742-1743, July 21, 1975.

"Haunting shadows from the rubble of Roe's (Roe v. Wade, 93 Sup Ct 705) right of privacy." SUFFOLK

UNIVERSITY LAW REVIEW 9:145-184, Fall, 1974.

"Hazards of pregnancy interruption," by G. K. Döring. FORTSCHRITTE DER MEDIZIN 92(29):1156-1160, October 17, 1974.

"Hippokrates and the legality of abortion," by H. M. Sutermeister. PRAXIS 63(36):1101-1103, September 10, 1974.

"Homo sapienism: critique of Roe v. Wade (93 Sup Ct 705) and abortion." ALBANY LAW REVIEW 39:856-893, 1975.

"House avoids abortion issue despite pressure; reprint from Congressional Quarterly, April 30, 1975," by D. Loomis. NATIONAL CATHOLIC REPORTER 11:1 plus, May 23, 1975.

"Human life is sacred; pastoral letter of the archbishops and bishops of Ireland." L'OSSERVATORE ROMANO 21(373):6-8 plus, May 22, 1975; 24(376): 6-8, June 12, 1975.

"Humans and persons: a reply to Tuistram Englehardt," by L. Newton. ETHICS 85:332-336, June, 1975.

"The immunological identification of foetal haemoglobin in bloodstains in infanticide and associated crimes," by S. J. Baxter, et al. MEDICINE, SCIENCE AND LAW 14(3):163-167, July, 1974.

"The impact of the New York State abortion law on black and white fertility in Upstate New York," by K. J. Roghmann. INTERNATIONAL JOURNAL OF EPIDEMIOLOGY 4(1):45-49, March, 1975.

"Las implicaciones legales para Puerto Rico de los

casos Roe v. Wade (93 Sup Ct 705) 41 L.W. 4214
(1973) y Doe v. Bolton (93 Sup Ct 739) 41 L.W. 4233
(1973)," by C. T. Jiménez. REVISTA DEL COLEGIO
DE ABOGADAS DE PUERTO RICO 35:581-610, November, 1974.

"The implications of abortion." TABLET 229:51,
January 18, 1975.

"The impossible dream," by M. Lawrence. TRIUMPH
10:9-11, March, 1975.

"Induction of labour and perinatal mortality," by A.
Singer, et al. BRITISH MEDICAL JOURNAL 2(5961):
35, April 5, 1975.

"Information meeting about hormonal contraception and
the abortion situation," by J. Wiese. UGESKRIFT
FOR LAEGER 137(23):1279-1282, June 2, 1975.

"The Institute of Medicine reports on legalized abor-
tion and the public health," by R. Lincoln. FAMILY
PLANNING PERSPECTIVES 7(4):185-188, July-
August, 1975.

"Intelligent woman's guide to sex; abortion is a fact in
our society," by K. Durbin. MADEMOISELLE 81:
41, March, 1975.

"Intra-amniotic prostaglandin techniques for induction
of mid-trimester abortion and associated changes
in plasma steroid hormones," by I. Craft, et al.
SOUTH AFRICAN MEDICAL JOURNAL 0(0):Suppl:
31-35, October 16, 1974.

"Iowa public hospitals cannot discharge staff for abortion views." HOSPITAL LAW 8:4, February, 1975.

"Is any change in the abortion law really needed?" by
T. Smith. TIMES p. 11, January 31, 1975.

"Is support of abortion political suicide?" by J. I.
Rosoff. FAMILY PLANNING PERSPECTIVES
7(1):13-22, January-February, 1975.

"It is time to take a stand," by D. R. Shanklin. JOUR-
NAL OF REPRODUCTIVE MEDICINE 14(2):41-42,
February, 1975.

"Lamenting a misconception." CHRISTIANITY TODAY
19:46, February 28, 1975.

"Law, morals and abortion," by D. Degnan. COMMON-
WEAL p. 305, May 31, 1974.

"Legal abortion among New York City residents: an
analysis according to socioeconomic and demographic
characteristics," by M. J. Kramer. FAMILY PLAN-
NING PERSPECTIVES 7(3):128-137, May-June, 1975.

"Legal abortion in Bexar County Hospital," by C. E.
Gibbs, et al. TEXAS MEDICINE 71:92-95, February,
1975.

"Legal abortion in England," by H. P. Tarnesby.
NOUVELLE PRESSE MEDICALE 4(19):1443-1444,
1446-1448, May 10, 1975.

"Legal abortions in the United States since the 1973
Supreme Court decisions," by E. Weinstock, et al.
FAMILY PLANNING PERSPECTIVES 7(1):23-31,
January-February, 1975.

"Legal aspects of abortion," by L. D. Collins. CAN-
ADIAN JOURNAL OF PUBLIC HEALTH 66:234-236,
May-June, 1975.

"Legal guidelines for the performance of abortions,"
by H. L. Hirsh. AMERICAN JOURNAL OF OBSTE-
TRICS AND GYNECOLOGY 122(6):679-682, July 15,
1975.

"Legal interruption of pregnancy. Medical considerations," by R. Bourg. BRUXELLES-MEDICAL 54(1):
13-17, January, 1974.

"Legislation--abortion--Michigan's 'conscience clause'."
WAYNE LAW REVIEW 21:175-182, November, 1974.

"The legitimacy of a diverse society," by K. J. Ryan.
JOURNAL OF THE AMERICAN MEDICAL ASSOCIA-
TION 233(7):781, August 18, 1975.

"Let's break the law to stop abortions," by P. Riga.
U. S. CATHOLIC 40:13-14, September, 1975.

"Liberalization of legal abortion," by K. J. Rees.
C.I.C.I.A.M.S. NOUVELLES 0(4):12-21, 1974.

"Male parent versus female parent: separate and unequal rights." UMKC LAW REVIEW 43:392-412,
Spring, 1975.

"MDs wary of abortion verdict implications." AMERI-
CAN MEDICAL ASSOCIATION NEWS 18:3, March 3,
1975.

"Medical and social aspects of adolescent pregnancies.
I. Adolescents applying for termination of an illegiti-
mate pregnancy," by O. Widholm, et al. ACTA OB-
STETRICIA ET GY NECOLOGICA SCANDINAVICA
53(4):347-353, 1974.

"Medical and social characteristics of Irish residents
whose pregnancies were terminated under the 1967

Abortion Act in 1971 and 1972," by D. Walsh.
IRISH MEDICAL JOURNAL 68(6):143-149, March
22, 1975.

"Medical ethics in the courtroom. The role of law vs
professional self-discipline," by J. A. Robertson.
HASTINGS CENTER REPORT 4(4):1-3, September,
1974.

"Medical responsibility for fetal survival under Roe
(Roe v. Wade, 93 Sup Ct 705) and Doe (Doe v.
Bolton, 93 Sup Ct 739)." HARVARD CIVIL RIGHTS-
CIVIL LIBERTIES LAW REVIEW 10:444-471, Spring,
1975.

"Medical termination of pregnancy act," by J. Minattur.
MEDICAL SERVICE 31:56 plus, December, 1974.

"Medicine and the law: attorney general clarifies
status of Texas abortion laws," by S. V. Stone, Jr.
TEXAS MEDICINE 70(11):107-108, November, 1974.

"Medico-legal briefs: husband may not prevent wife
from having abortion." JOURNAL OF THE MISSISSI-
PPI STATE MEDICAL ASSOCIATION 16(1):14-15,
January, 1975.

"Michigan abortion refusal act." UNIVERSITY OF
MICHIGAN JOURNAL OF LAW REFORM 8:659-
675, Spring, 1975.

"Moral issue and resolution of the time limit," by W.
Becker. MEDIZINISCHE KLINIK 69(49):2039-2040,
December 6, 1974.

"Morbidity in legal abortions in the Perleberg District,"
by J. Berg. ZENTRALBLATT FUR GYNAEKOLOGIE
96(35):1111-1115, August 30, 1974.

"More abortions?" by M. Simms. BRITISH MEDICAL JOURNAL 1(5949):95, January 11, 1975.

"More about abortion decisions," by H. Creighton. SUPERVISOR NURSE 6:10 plus, April, 1975.

"Morgentaler case." NATION 221:6, July 5, 1975.

"The Morgentaler case," by P. N. Coles. CANADIAN MEDICAL ASSOCIATION JOURNAL 113(3):181, August 9, 1975.

"Morgentaler case divides Supreme Court in interpretation of Criminal Code," by D. Phillipson. CANADIAN MEDICAL ASSOCIATION JOURNAL 112(8):1003-1004, April 19, 1975.

"Morgentaler vs. the Queen," by L. E. Rozovsky. DIMENSIONS IN HEALTH SERVICE 52:8-9, June, 1975.

"National committee for a human life amendment inc.: its goals and origins," by R. N. Lynch. CATHOLIC LAWYER 20:303-308, Autumn, 1974.

"New doubts about abortion," by J. Kagan. McCALLS 101:121-123, June, 1975.

"New legislation on pregnancy interruption," by I. Stegane. SYKEPLEIEN 62(6-7):267, March 20, 1975.

"A new set of rules for the abortion fight," by M. Bunson. OUR SUNDAY VISITOR 64:1 plus, August 17, 1975.

"No final solution," by M. R. Benjamin, et al. NEWSWEEK 85:30-31, March 10, 1975.

"No going back," by D. Gould. NEW STATESMAN
89:132, January 31, 1975.

"Not a fetus but a baby, jury decides in Boston." OUR
SUNDAY VISITOR 63:1, March 2, 1975.

"Not self decided abortion but liberal laws in future
Norwegian family politics," by B. Grünfeld.
NORDISK MEDICIN 90(2):44-47, February, 1975.

"Of many things; Edelin case: victims of ambiguity."
AMERICA 132: inside cover-141, March 1, 1975.

"On abortion and neonatal mortality," by M. J.
Mahoney. AMERICAN JOURNAL OF PUBLIC
HEALTH 65(7):747-748, July, 1975.

"On a constitutional amendment protecting unborn
human life." CATHOLIC MIND p. 43, October,
1974.

"On 'the right to choose abortion', an editorial," by
M. J. Mahoney. AMERICAN JOURNAL OF PUBLIC
HEALTH 65(7):748, July, 1975.

"Opposition to a constitutional amendment on abortion:
American Public Health Association revolution."
AMERICAN JOURNAL OF PUBLIC HEALTH AND
THE NATION'S HEALTH 65:203, February, 1975.

"Parental preferences and selective abortion: a commentary on Roe v. Wade (93 Sup Ct 705), Doe v. Bolton
(93 Sup Ct 739) and the shape of things to come," by R.
Delgado. WASHINGTON UNIVERSITY LAW QUARTER-
LY 1974:203-226, 1974.

"Perforation of the uterus and injuries of the internal
organs in violent interruption of pregnancy," by B.

Vekovič, et al. MEDICINSKI ARCHIV 28(6):
585–587, November–December, 1974.

"Politicizing the Catholic community," by V. Blum.
HOSPITAL PROGRESS 56:84–88, September, 1975.

"Prenatal pediatric ethics," by A. Prado-Vértiz.
BOLETIN MEDICO DEL HOSPITAL INFANTIL DE
MEXICO 31(2):183–197, March–April, 1974.

"Priests urged to pro-life leadership in new booklet;
abortion, attitudes and the law, by NCCB and Our
Sunday Visitor." OUR SUNDAY VISITOR 64:1,
August 31, 1975.

"Private hospitals not required to perform nontherapeutic
abortions," by W. A. Regan. HOSPITAL PROGRESS
56:28 plus, April, 1975.

"The problem of the medical indication for artificial
abortion," by G. Fanconi. MINERVA PEDIATRICA
27(8):455–461, March 10, 1975.

"Pro-lifers bring high hopes, food, to Washington
march," by S. Shoemaker. NATIONAL CATHOLIC
REPORTER 11:1–2, January 31, 1975.

"Prophylactic use of tetracycline for first trimester
abortions," by J. E. Hodgson, et al. OBSTETRICS
AND GYNECOLOGY 45(5):574–578, May, 1975.

"Proposed decree on abortion and nurses' role," by
S. A. Jegede. NIGERIAN NURSE 7(1):33–34,
January–March, 1975.

"Prosecution of Dr. Morgentaler," by M. Gordon, et
al. CANADIAN DIMENSION 10:9–11, June, 1975.

"Psychological sequelae of elective abortion," by B. D. Blumberg, et al. WESTERN JOURNAL OF MEDICINE 123(3):188-193, September, 1975.

"Putting the clock back on abortion," by P. Ferris. OBSERVER p. 10, February 16, 1975.

"Questions no one asked Dr. Kenneth Edelin on the witness stand: interview edited by G. Steinem," by K. C. Edelin. MS MAGAZINE 4:76-78 plus, August, 1975.

"Refusal of assistance in abortion," by A. Hollmann. DEUTSCHE MEDIZINISCHE WOCHENSCHRIFT 100(2):65-67, January 10, 1975.

"Relations of personality factors and student nurses' attitudes toward abortion," by J. M. Jones. PSYCHOLOGICAL REPORTS 35:927-931, October, 1974.

"Religion and legal abortion in Northern Ireland," by P. A. Compton, et al. JOURNAL OF BIOSOCIAL SCIENCE 6(4):493-500, October, 1974.

"Requests for abortion in general practice," by H. W. Ashworth. JOURNAL OF THE ROYAL COLLEGE OF GENERAL PRACTITIONERS 24(142):329-330, 335-339, May, 1974.

"Restricting legal abortion: some maternal and child health effects in Romania," by N. H. Wright. AMERICAN JOURNAL OF OBSTETRICS AND GYNECOLOGY 121(2):246-256, January 15, 1975.

"Reversal of abortion decisions urgent issue U. S. bishops say after series of meetings." OUR SUNDAY VISITOR 64:1, August 24, 1975.

"Review of legal challenges to Catholic hospitals," by
E. J. Schulte. HOSPITAL PROGRESS 56:10-11,
April, 1975.

"The right of privacy: what next?" by K. O'Rourke.
HOSPITAL PROGRESS 56:58-63, April, 1975.

"Right to life: time for a new strategy; symposium:
Moral credibility," by W. Carroll; "Grassroots
revolution," by R. Engel; "Conditional allegiance,"
by W. Devlin; "The best chance," by P. Fisher;
"Get tough," by T. May; "Unacceptable principle,"
by C. Rice; "Bear witness," by M. Schwartz; "The
ethical issue," by J. Willke. TRIUMPH 10:11-16,
January, 1975.

"Roma locuta, causa finita? Prevention or insensitivity?" SCHWESTERN REVUE 13(3):10, March 15,
1975.

"Rules prohibiting abortions at St. Louis city hospitals are upheld by court." HOSPITALS 49:17,
February 16, 1975.

"Second thoughts about abortions." U. S. NEWS AND
WORLD REPORT 78:78, March 3, 1975.

"Sellout on abortion," by L. Komisar. NEWSWEEK
85:11, June 9, 1975.

"Senate rejects anti-abortion amendment [key provisions,
committee action, floor action]," by E. Bowman.
CONG Q W REPT 33:814-816, April 19, 1975.

"Senate unit kills pro-life amendments," by R. Rashke.
NATIONAL CATHOLIC REPORTER 11:1 plus,
September 26, 1975.

"Setback for abortion." TIME 105:67, February 24, 1975.

"Should abortion laws be nullified? 'Yes,' by Robert E. Bauman; 'No,' by Ronald V. Dellums." AMERICAN LEGION MAGAZINE 98:32-33, April, 1975.

"Social effects of abortion." NEW ENGLAND JOURNAL OF MEDICINE 292(9):484-486, February 27, 1975.

"Social aspects of legal abortion in Yugoslavia," by N. J. Jurukovski. GODISEN ABARNIK NA MEDI-CINSKIAT FAKULTET VO SKOPJE 20:159-164, 1974.

"Sounding board. Deeper into abortion," by B. N. Nathanson. NEW ENGLAND JOURNAL OF MEDI-CINE 291(22):1188-1190, November 28, 1974.

"South Dakota's abortion experience: constitutional right or unfulfilled promise?" SOUTH DAKOTA LAW REVIEW 20:205-226, Winter, 1975.

"Statement concerning the discussion about the 'initative for descriminialisation' of abortion," by P. A. Gloor, et al. PRAXIS 63(48):1423-1429, December 3, 1974.

"Statute requiring parental consent to minor's abortion unconstitutional: Massachusetts." HOSPITAL LAW 8:6, June, 1975.

"Supreme court considers Morgentaler abortion case," by D. Phillipson. CANADIAN MEDICAL ASSOCIA-TION JOURNAL 111(8):872-873, October 19, 1974.

"Supreme court rules: commercial ads protected by First amendment," by I. W. Hill. EDITOR AND PUBLISHER--THE FOURTH ESTATE 108:11, June

21, 1975.

"Survey of Ottawa area general practitioners and obstetrician-gynecologists on abortion," by M. C. Diner. CANADIAN JOURNAL OF PUBLIC HEALTH 65(5):351-358, September-October, 1974.

"Tax-exempt, bond-financed hospital can disallow abortions," by E. J. Schulte. HOSPITAL PROGRESS 56:18, August, 1975.

"Tax-supported abortions: the legal issues," by E. Schulte. CATHOLIC LAWYER 21:1-7, Winter, 1975.

"Taxes – where the dollars go – abortions yes, private schools no," by J. Doyle. LIGUORIAN 63:7-11, September, 1975.

"Teen-age pregnancies in Denmark, 1940-71," by A. Braestrup. JOURNAL OF BIOSOCIAL SCIENCE 6(4):741-745, October, 1974.

"10 interviews about physicians and the population change. Abortion inevitable in developing countries. Is forced birth control near?" by Y. Karlsson. NORDISK MEDICIN 89(8):234-240, October, 1974.

"Termination of pregnancy," (letter), by N. A. Simmons. LANCET 2(7928):281, August 9, 1975.

"This awful silence hanging over abortion on demand," by R. Butt. TIMES p. 16, January 23, 1975.

"Trials: who is a person? conviction of K. C. Edelin for killing of fetus." NEWSWEEK 85:20, February 24, 1975.

"The unmet need for legal abortion services in the
U. S." FAMILY PLANNING PERSPECTIVES
7:224-230, September-October, 1975.

"Unwanted pregnancy and abortion," by C. W. Kok.
CANADIAN MEDICAL ASSOCIATION JOURNAL
112(4):419-420, February 22, 1975.

"Vaginal ligation in first trimester of pregnancy,"
by B. Ghosh. JOURNAL OF THE INDIAN MEDI-
CAL ASSOCIATION 62(11):380-383, June 1, 1974.

"Verdict of the Federal Constitutional Court on term
regulation," by H. J. Rieger. DEUTSCHE
MEDIZINISCHE WOCHENSCHRIFT 100(12):637-
639, March 21, 1975.

"Voluntary versus compulsory sterilization in Sweden
then and now," by H. Sjövall. LAKARTIDNINGEN
72(4):241-245, January 22, 1975.

"West German high court denies right of abortion."
OUR SUNDAY VISITOR 63:2, March 9, 1975.

"What about an abortion amendment?" by F. Lee.
AMERICA 132:166-168, March 8, 1975.

"What the abortion argument is about," by M. Muggeridge. SUNDAY TIMES p. 19, February 2, 1975.

"When is an abortion not an abortion? K. C. Edelin
case," by S. Mydans. ATLANTIC 235:71-73,
May, 1975.

"The White Bill on abortion," by M. Simms. LANCET
1(7905):523-524, March 1, 1975.

"Who is a victim?" by G. Hughes. DALHOUSIE LAW

JOURNAL 1:425-440, October, 1974.

"Will abortion go back underground?" by D. Loshak.
DAILY TELEGRAPH p. 16, February 7, 1975.

"Will the clock go back on abortion?" by M. Russell.
OBSERVER p. 26, February 2, 1975.

"Will Congress be allowed to dodge the abortion issue?"
by R. Shaw. COLUMBIA 55:38, July, 1975.

"Will medicine be strangled in law?" by H. Schwartz.
JOURNAL OF FAMILY PRACTICE 2(3):232, June,
1975.

"Women and the Supreme Court: anatomy is destiny,"
by N. S. Erickson. BROOKLYN LAW REVIEW
41:209-282, Fall, 1974.

"Women exploited unite," by J. Anderson. OUR SUNDAY
VISITOR 64:1 plus, September 21, 1975.

"Women help themselves," by A. Phillips. NEW
SOCIETY p. 267-268, January 30, 1975.

"Working of the abortion act." BRITISH MEDICAL
JOURNAL 02(5966):337, May 10, 1975.

"Working of the abortion act," by P. J. Huntingford.
BRITISH MEDICAL JOURNAL 2(5965):278, May 3,
1975.

"Would you buy an abortion from this man? the Harvey
Korman controversy," by L. C. Wohl. MS MAGA-
ZINE 4:60-64 plus, September, 1975.

LISTERIOSIS

MALE ATTITUDES

see: Sociology and Behavior

MARCH OF DIMES

MEFENAMIC ACID

MENSTRUATION
see also: Complications
Induced Abortion

"Ribonucleic acid content in the endometrium of women
suffering from habitual abortions in inadequacy of
the luteinic phase of the menstrual cycle," by E. P.
Maizel', et al. VOPROSY OKHRANY MATERINSTVA
I DETSTVA 18(5):65-71, 1973.

MENTALLY RETARDED
"Sterilization and therapeutic abortion counseling for
the mentally retarded," by C. W. Smiley. ILLINOIS
MEDICAL JOURNAL 147(3):291-292, March, 1975.

MICROBIOLOGY
see: Research

MISCARRIAGES
"Content of certain chloroganic pesticides in the blood
of pregnant women and embryos after miscarriage,"
by B. F. Mazorchuk, et al. PEDIATRIIA AKUSH-
ERSTVO I GINEKOLOGIIA (6):59-61, November-
December, 1974.

"The danger of threatened miscarriage and steps to be
taken," by K. Soiva. KATILOLEHTI 80(1):7-16,
January, 1975.

"Miscarriages among operating theatre staff," by P.
Rosenberg, et al. ACTA ANAESTHESIOLOGICA
SCANDINAVICA. SUPPLEMENT 53(0):37-42, 1973.

MISCARRIAGES

"Placental lactogenic hormone content of the blood of
women with normal pregnancies and those complicated
by late toxemia or miscarriage," by N. A. Stepanova,
et al. AKUSHERSTVO I GINEKOLOGIIA (Moscow)
(9):15-17, September, 1974.

"The prognostic value of chorionic-gonadotrophins in
the urine of miscarrying women," by H. Dyková, et
al. CESKOSLOVENSKA GYNEKOLOGIE 40(6):417-
420, July, 1975.

"Psychological problems following birth and miscarriage,"
by K. L. Trick. NURSING MIRROR AND MIDWIVES'
JOURNAL 141(2):61-62, July 10, 1975.

"Roentgenological image of the uterus after miscarriage,"
by E. P. Maizel', et al. AKUSHERSTVO I GINEKOL-
OGIIA (Moscow) (5):65-67, May, 1974.

"Role of sensitization of the body of pregnant women
with antigens of embryonal tissues and placenta in
the pathogenesis of miscarriage," by N. S. Motavkina,
et al. AKUSHERSTVO I GINEKOLOGIIA (Moscow)
0(7):30-34, July, 1974.

"Ultrasonic diagnosis of miscarriage and early preg-
nancy complications," by B. Zsolnai, et al. ACTA
CHIRURGICA ACADEMIAE SCIENTIARUM HUNGAR-
ICAE 15(4):389-407, 1974.

MORBIDITY
see also: Complications

"The effect of legalized abortion on morbidity resulting
from criminal abortion," by R. S. Kahan, et al.
AMERICAN JOURNAL OF OBSTETRICS AND GYN-
ECOLOGY 121(1):114-116, January 1, 1975.

MORBIDITY

"Morbidity in legal abortions in the Perleberg District," by J. Berg. ZENTRALBLATT FUR GYNAEKOLOGIE 96(35):1111-1115, August 30, 1974.

"Oxytocin administration, instillation-to-abortion time, and morbidity associated with saline instillation," by G. S. Berger, et al. AMERICAN JOURNAL OF OBSTETRICS AND GYNECOLOGY 121(7): 941-946, April 1, 1975.

"Prostaglandin-induced abortion: assessment of operative complications and early morbidity," by I. Z. Mackenzie, et al. BRITISH MEDICAL JOURNAL 4(5946):683-686, December 21, 1974.

"Studies of morbidity in anaesthetists with special reference to obstetric history," by A. A. Spence, et al. PROCEEDINGS OF THE ROYAL SOCIETY OF MEDICINE 67(10):989-990, October, 1974.

MORTALITY
see also: Complications
         Sepsis
         Septic Abortion and Septic Shock

"The effect of induced abortions on perinatal mortality," by G. Papaevangelou, et al. ACTA EUROPAEA FERTILITATIS 4(1):7-10, March, 1973.

"From the files of the KMA Maternal Mortality Study Committee," by J. W. Greene, Jr. JOURNAL OF THE KENTUCKY MEDICAL ASSOCIATION 73(1): 33, January, 1975.

"Genetic epidemiology of intra-uterine mortality. Result of an analysis in a rural population in Quebec," by P. Philippe, et al. UNION MEDICALE DU CANADA

MORTALITY

104(5):763-767, May, 1975.

"Induction of labour and perinatal mortality," by A.
Singer, et al. BRITISH MEDICAL JOURNAL
2(5961):35, April 5, 1975.

"On abortion and neonatal mortality," by M. J.
Mahoney. AMERICAN JOURNAL OF PUBLIC
HEALTH 65(7):747-748, July, 1975.

"Perinatology begins before conception," by F. Hecht,
et al. NEW ENGLAND JOURNAL OF MEDICINE
293(12):604-605, September 18, 1975.

MYCOPLASMA
"Infections with mycoplasma and bacteria in induced
midtrimester abortion and fetal loss," by D.
Sompolinsky, et al. AMERICAN JOURNAL OF
OBSTETRICS AND GYNECOLOGY 121(5):610-
616, March 1, 1975.

NAL
see: Laws and Legislation

NCCB

NAPTHALENE

NEONATAL
"Abortion, euthanasia, and care of defective newborns,"
by J. Fletcher. NEW ENGLAND JOURNAL OF MED-
ICINE 292:75-78, January 9, 1975.

"Ethical dilemmas in obstetric and newborn care,"
by T. K. Hanid. MIDWIFE AND HEALTH VISITOR
11(1(:9-11, January, 1975.

"On abortion and neonatal mortality," by M. J. Mahoney.

NEONATAL

AMERICAN JOURNAL OF PUBLIC HEALTH 65(7): 747-748, July, 1975.

NEURAMINIDASE

NURSES

"Abortion counseling; what we need to know and why," by C. Davis. JOURNAL OF PRACTICAL NURSING 25(6):16-17, 34, June, 1975.

"Abortion creates problems for nurses," by A. L. Salling. SYGEPLEJERSKEN 74(44):9, November 6, 1974.

"Abortion nursing expertise needed." NURSING UP-DATE 6:1 plus, May, 1975.

"Abortion uproar awaits returning airlift nurse." NATIONAL CATHOLIC REPORTER 11:2, April 25, 1975.

"Attitudes of senior nursing students toward the 1973 Supreme Court decision on abortion," by R. G. Elder. JOGN NURSING 4:46-54, July-August, 1975.

"Care by the public health nurse of the patient with threatened abortion," by K. Katayama, et al. JAPANESE JOURNAL FOR THE MIDWIFE 29(2): 90-95, February, 1975.

"Hygiene for a woman following surgical abortion," by S. L. Polchanova. FEL'DSHER I AKUSHERKA 40(1):43-46, January, 1975.

"Law for the nurse supervisor," by H. Creighton. SUPERVISOR NURSE 6:10-11 plus, April, 1975.

"Nurse's attitudes to termination of pregnancy."

NURSES

NURSING FORUM 2(5):6-7, November-December, 1974.

"Proposed decree on abortion and nurses' role," by S. A. Jagede. NIGERIAN NURSE 7:33-34, January-March, 1975.

"Relations of personality factors and student nurses' attitudes toward abortion," by J. M. Jones. PSYCHOLOGICAL REPORTS 35(2):927-931, October, 1974.

"Termination of pregnancy: the nurse's attitude," by A. B. Sclare, et al. NURSING MIRROR AND MID-WIVES' JOURNAL 140:59-60, January 16, 1975.

NURSING HOMES

OBSTETRICS
"Ethical dilemmas in obstetric and newborn care," by T. K. Hanid. MIDWIFE AND HEALTH VISITOR 11(1):9-11, January, 1975.

"Experience with the use of the preparation Faustan in obstetric and gynecologic practice," AKUSHERSTVO I GINEKOLOGIIA (Sofiia) 13(4):308-311, 1974.

"Importance of determining chorionic gonadotropin excretion in the obstetrical and gynecological clinic," by A. A. Galochkina. VOPROSY OKHRANY MA-TERINSTVA I DETSTVA 18(4):77-80, 1973.

"Prostaglandins in clinical obstetrics and gynaecology." ACTA OBSTETRICIA ET GYNECOLOGICA SCAN-DINAVICA. SUPPLEMENT (37):1-72, 1974.

"The prostaglandins in obstetrics and gynaecology. Are they living up to expectations?...," by A. Gillespie.

MEDICAL JOURNAL OF AUSTRALIA 1(2):38-41, January 11, 1975.

"Survey of Ottawa area general practitioners and obstetrician-gynecologists on abortion," by M. C. Diner. CANADIAN JOURNAL OF PUBLIC HEALTH 65(5):351-358, September-October, 1974.

ORCIPRENALINE

OUTPATIENT ABORTION
see: Hospitals

OXYTOCIN
"Comparison of extra-amniotic administration of PGF2alpha, 0.9 per cent saline, and 20 per cent saline followed by oxytocin for therapeutic abortion," by A. P. Lange, et al. ACTA OBSTETRICIA ET GYNECOLOGICA SCANDINAVICA (37):61-66, 1974.

"Intra-amniotic prostaglandin F 2alpha as a midtrimester abortifacient: effect of oxytocin and laminaria," by S. L. Corson, et al. JOURNAL OF REPRODUCTIVE MEDICINE 14(2):47-51, February, 1975.

"Intravenous prostaglandins and oxytocin for midtrimester abortion," by J. M. Beazley. LANCET 1(7902):335, February 8, 1975.

"Intravenous prostaglandins and oxytocin for midtrimester abortion," by T. M. Coltart, et al. LANCET 1(7899):173-174, January 18, 1975.

"Mid-trimester abortion with intra-amniotic prostaglandin F2 alpha and intravenous oxytocin infusion," by M. Salomy, et al. PROSTAGLANDINS 9(2):271-279, February, 1975.

OXYTOCIN

"Oxytocin administration, instillation-to-abortion time, and morbidity associated with saline instillation," by G. S. Berger, et al. AMERICAN JOURNAL OF OBSTETRICS AND GYNECOLOGY 121(7): 941-946, April 1, 1975.

"Prostaglandin F2alpha and oxytocin compared with hypertonic saline and oxytocin for the induction of second trimester abortion," by K. R. Nielsen, et al. ACTA OBSTETRICIA ET GYNECOLOGICA SCANDINAVICA. SUPPLEMENT (37):57-60, 1974.

"Prostaglandin F2alpha given by continuous transcervical extra-amniotic infusion combined with intravenous oxytocin infusion for therapeutic termination of mid-trimester pregnancies," by K. W. Waldron, et al. MEDICAL JOURNAL OF AUSTRALIA 1(17):525-527, April 26, 1975.

"Use of high doses of oxytocin in non-developing pregnancy," by B. L. Gurtovoi, et al. VOPROSY OKHRANY MATERINSTVA I DETSTVA 19(12):45-49, December, 1974.

"Water intoxication associated with oxytocin administration during saline-induced abortion," by N. H. Lauersen, et al. AMERICAN JOURNAL OF OBSTETRICS AND GYNECOLOGY 121(1):2-6, January 1, 1975.

PARAMEDICS

PARSLEY EXTRACT

PATIENT COUNSELING
see: Sociology and Behavior

PENTAZOCINE

PHARMACISTS

PHYSICIANS
see also: Psychology
Sociology and Behavior

"Abortion: the dangerous pressure on doctors," by
R. Butt. TIMES p. 16, January 30, 1975.

"Attitude of the physician towards abortion," by J. M.
Cantú, et al. GINECOLOGIA Y OBSTETRICIA DE
MEXICO 37(223):275-285, May, 1975.

"General practitioners and abortion." JOURNAL OF
THE ROYAL COLLEGE OF GENERAL PRACTI-
TIONERS 24(142):298, 303, May, 1974.

"MDs wary of abortion verdict implications." AMERI-
CAN MEDICAL ASSOCIATION NEWS 18:3, March 3,
1975.

"Medical cop-out? the physician's role in abortion
counseling," by H. Klaus. AMERICA 133:68-70,
August 16, 1975.

"New doctors' dilemma: late abortion," by M. Clark,
et al. NEWSWEEK 85:24-25, March 3, 1975.

"Report on abortion activities in nearly 3,000 hospitals,
clinics and private physicians' offices," by M. Clark.
NEWSWEEK 85:97, February 17, 1975.

"Survey of Ottawa area general practitioners and obstetrician-gynecologists on abortion," by M. C.
Diner. CANADIAN JOURNAL OF PUBLIC HEALTH
65(5):351-358, September-October, 1974.

POPULATION

see also: Demography

"The effect of legalization of abortion on population growth and public health," by C. Tietze. FAMILY PLANNING PERSPECTIVES 7(3):123-127, May-June, 1975.

"From Comstockery through population control: the inevitability of balancing," by E. Silverstein. NORTH CAROLINA CENTRAL LAW JOURNAL 6:8-47, Fall, 1974.

"Population and the crisis of culture," by T. Lane. HOMILETIC AND PASTORAL REVIEW 75:61-65, April, 1975.

"10 interviews about physicians and the population change. Abortion inevitable in developing countries. Is forced birth control near?" by Y. Karlsson. NORDISK MEDICIN 89(8):234-240, October, 1974.

POTASSIUM AMPICILLIN

PREGNANCY INTERRUPTION
see: Induced Abortion

PROGESTERONE
"Bleeding in early pregnancy investigated by ultrasound, plasma progesterone and oestradiol," by O. Piiroinen, et al. ANNALES CHIRURGIAE ET GYNECOLOGIAE FENNIAE 63(6):451-456, 1974.

"The effect of prostaglandin F2alpha on the placental progesterone level in midtrimester abortion," by F. A. Aleem, et al. AMERICAN JOURNAL OF OBSTETRICS AND GYNECOLOGY 123(2):202-205, September 15, 1975.

PROGESTERONE

"Importance of hormone assays and high dose HCG,
estrogen and 17-alpha-hydroxyprogesterone treatment in the prevention of threatened abortion due
to endocrine causes," by G. Cubesi, et al. ACTA
EUROPAEA FERTILITATIS 2(3):355-358, September,
1970.

"Midtrimester pregnancy interruption and the placental
progesterone levels," by F. A. Aleem, et al.
PROSTAGLANDINS 9(3):495-500, March, 1975.

"Rate of fall in plasma progesterone and time to abortion following intra-amniotic injection of prostaglandin F2alpha, with or without urea, in the second
trimester of human pregnancy," by S. M. Walker,
et al. BRITISH JOURNAL OF OBSTETRICS AND
GYNAECOLOGY 82(6):488-492, June, 1975.

"Serum levels of oestradiol and progesterone during
administration of prostaglandin F2alpha for induction of abortion and labour," by O. Widholm, et al.
ACTA OBSTETRICA ET GYNECOLOGICA SCAN-
DINAVICA 54(2):135-139, 1975.

PROSTAGLANDINS
"Abortifacient from the land of the prostaglandins," by
J. A. Owen, Jr. HOSPITAL FORMULARY MANAGE-
MENT 10:407 plus, August, 1975.

"Anti-fertility drugs; novel non-hormonal compounds
that inhibit prostaglandin metabolism," by L. J.
Lerner, et al. NATURE 256(5513):130-132, July
10, 1975.

"Artificial termination of advanced pregnancy by extra-
amniotic administration of prostaglandin F2 alpha
and 15-me-PGF2 alpha," by E. A. Ghernukha, et
al. SOVETSKAIA MEDITSINA (6):21-26, June, 1975.

"Blood coagulation tests in prostaglandin F-2alpha induced and a one-time mechanically induced therapeutic abortion," by W. D. Junge, et al. ZENTRAL-
BLATT FUER GYNAEKOLOGIE 96(35):1116-1120,
August 30, 1974.

"Cervical dilatation with prostaglandin analogues prior
to vaginal termination of first trimester pregnancy
in nulliparous patients," by S. M. Karim, et al.
PROSTAGLANDINS 9(4):631-638, April, 1975.

"Circadian aspects of prostaglandin F2alpha-induced
termination of pregnancy," by I. D. Smith, et al.
JOURNAL OF OBSTETRICS AND GYNAECOLOGY OF
THE BRITISH COMMONWEALTH 81(11):841-848,
November, 1974.

"Circadian timing, duration, dose and cost of prostaglandin F2alpha - induced termination of middle
trimester pregnancy," by I. D. Smith. CHRONO-
BIOLOGIA 1(1):41-53, January-March, 1974.

"Clinical results of therapeutic induction of abortion
by extraamniotic application of prostaglandin F2
alpha," by H. Lahmann, et al. ZEITSCHRIFT FUR
GEBURTSHILFE UND PERINATOLOGIE 178(6):423-
428, December, 1974.

"Coagulation changes during intraamniotic prosta-
glandin-induced abortion," by G. J. Kleiner, et al.
OBSTETRICS AND GYNECOLOGY 44(5):757-761,
November, 1974.

"Comparison of abortion performed with prostaglandin
F2 alpha and hysterotomy," by H. Koeffler, et al.
ANNALES CHIRURGIAE ET GYNAECOLOGIAE
GENNIAE 63(6):483-486, 1974.

"Comparison of prostaglandin F2alpha and hypertonic saline for induction of midtrimester abortion," by N. H. Lauersen, et al. AMERICAN JOURNAL OF OBSTETRICS AND GYNECOLOGY 120(7):875-879, December 1, 1974.

"A comparison of termination of pregnancies in the 2nd trimester induced by intraamniotic injection of hypertonic saline, prostaglandin F2alpha or both drugs," by E. Bostofte, et al. ACTA OBSTETRICIA ET GYNECOLOGICA SCANDINAVICA. SUPPLEMENT (37): 47-50, 1974.

"Complete molar abortion induced with prostaglandin F2 alpha," by M. Herrera, et al. REVISTA CHILENA DE OBSTETRICIA Y GINECOLOGIA 38(3):146-149, 1973.

"Complications following prostaglandin F2alpha-induced midtrimester abortion," by J. H. Duenhoelter, et al. OBSTETRICS AND GYNECOLOGY 46(3):247-250, September, 1975.

"Complications of prostaglandin-induced abortion." BRITISH MEDICAL JOURNAL 4(5941):404-405, November 16, 1974.

"Complications of prostaglandin-induced abortion," by J. J. Amy. BRITISH MEDICAL JOURNAL 4(5945): 654, December 14, 1974.

"Cyclic adenosine 3',5'-monophosphate in prostaglandin-induced abortion," by K. Raij, et al. SCANDINAVIN JOURNAL OF CLINICAL AND LABORATORY INVESTIGATION 34(4):337-342, December, 1974.

"Decrease of utero-placental blood flow during prostaglandin F2alpha induced abortion," by M. O. Pulkkinen, et al. PROSTAGLANDINS 9(1):61-66, January, 1975.

"Early mid trimester abortion - by intramuscular 15 methyl prostaglandin E2," by S. D. Sharma, et al. PROSTAGLANDINS 8(2):171-178, October 25, 1974.

"The effect of anti-prostaglandin on the hypertonic saline-induced uterine activity," by A. I. Csapo, et al. PROSTAGLANDINS 9(4):627-629, April, 1975.

"Effect of prostaglandin F2 alpha and hypertonic saline on the placental function during midtrimester abortion," by S. Sayaraman, et al. AMERICAN JOURNAL OF OBSTETRICS AND GYNECOLOGY 121(4):528-530, February 15, 1975.

"Effect of prostaglandin F2a on the contractility of the pregnant human uterus," by G. Romero-Salinas, et al. GINECOLOGIA Y OBSTETRICIA DE MEXICO 35(212):627-656, June, 1974.

"The effect of prostaglandin F2alpha on the placental progesterone level in midtrimester abortion," by F. A. Aleem, et al. AMERICAN JOURNAL OF OBSTETRICS AND GYNECOLOGY 123(2):202-205, September 15, 1975.

"Efficacy and acceptability of 15-(S)-15-methyl-prostaglandin E2-methyl ester for midtrimester pregnancy termination," by J. Bieniarz, et al. AMERICAN JOURNAL OF OBSTETRICS AND GYNECOLOGY 120(6):840-843, November 15, 1974.

"The efficacy of intramuscular 15 methyl prostaglandin E2 in second-trimester abortion. Coagulation and hormonal aspects," by T. F. Dillon, et al. AMERICAN JOURNAL OF OBSTETRICS AND GYNECOLOGY 121(5):584-589, March 1, 1975.

"Electroencephalographic changes after intra-amniotic prostaglandin F2alpha and hypertonic saline," by R. P. Shearman, et al. BRITISH JOURNAL OF OBSTETRICS AND GYNECOLOGY 82(4(:314-317, April, 1975.

"Extraovular prostaglandin F2alpha for early mid-trimester abortion," by A. G. Shapiro. AMERICAN JOURNAL OF OBSTETRICS AND GYNECOLOGY 121(3):333-336, February 1, 1975.

"Fetal thymus glands obtained from prostaglandin-induced abortions. Cellular iummune function in vitro and evidence of in vivo thymocyte activity following transplantation," by D. W. Wara, et al. TRANSPLANTATION 18(5):387-390, November, 1974.

"Hormone changes occurring during second trimester abortion induced with 15 (S)-15-methyl prostaglandin F2alpha," by S. L. Corson, et al. PROSTAGLANDINS 9(6):975-983, June, 1975.

"Induced abortion using prostaglandin E2 and F2alpha gel," by T. H. Lippert, et al. GYNAEKOLOGISCHE RUNDSCHAU 14(3):234-235, 1974.

"Induction of abortion by different prostaglandin analogues," by M. Bygdeman, et al. ACTA OBSTE-TRICIA ET GYNECOLOGICA SCANDINAVICA. SUPPLEMENT (37):67-72, 1974.

"Induction of abortion with prostaglandins: clinical and metabolic aspects," by M. Bygdeman, et al. SOUTH AFRICAN MEDICAL JOURNAL 0(0):Suppl:3-8, October 16, 1974.

"Induction of labour and abortion by intravenous prosta-

glandins in pregnancies complicated by intra-
uterine foetal death and hydatidiform mole," by
G. Roberts. CURRENT MEDICAL RESEARCH
AND OPINION 2(6):342-350, 1974.

"Interruption using prostaglandin F2alpha and E2,"
by H. Henner, et al. GYNAEKOLOGISCHE
RUNDSCHAU 14(3):236-237, 1974.

"Intra-amniotic administration of prostaglandin E2
in midtrimester abortions," (letter), by H. Neifeld.
SOUTH AFRICAN MEDICAL JOURNAL 48(63):2614,
December 28, 1974.

"Intraamniotic administration of prostaglandin F2alpha
for therapeutic abortion," by R. Nyberg. ACTA
OBSTETRICIA ET GYNECOLOGICA SCANDINAVICA
(37):41-46, 1974.

"Intra-amniotic administration of prostaglandin in
second trimester of pregnancy," by C. Galatis.
SOUTH AFRICAN MEDICAL JOURNAL 49(3):65,
January 18, 1975.

"Intra-amniotic prostaglandin F 2alpha as a midtrimester
abortifacient: effect of oxytocin and laminaria," by
S. L. Corson, et al. JOURNAL OF REPRODUCTIVE
MEDICINE 14(2):47-51, February, 1975.

"Intra-amniotic prostaglandin techniques for induction
of mid-trimester abortion and associated changes in
plasma steroid hormones," by I. Craft, et al. SOUTH
AFRICAN MEDICAL JOURNAL 0(0):Suppl:31-35,
October 16, 1974.

"Intra-amniotic urea and low-dose prostaglandin E2
for midtrimester termination," by I. Craft. LAN-
CET 1(7916):1115-1116, May 17, 1975.

"Intramuscular administration of 15-(S)-15-methyl-prostaglandin E2-methyl ester for induction of abortion," by W. E. Brenner, et al. AMERICAN JOURNAL OF OBSTETRICS AND GYNECOLOGY 120(6):833-836, November 15, 1974.

"Intramuscular administration of 15(S) 15 methyl prostaglandin E2 methyl ester for induction of abortion: a comparison of two dose schedules," by W. E. Brenner, et al. FERTILITY AND STERILITY 26(4):369-379, April, 1975.

"Intrauterine death treated with intrauterine extra-amniotic prostaglandin E2," by H. Wagman, et al. BRITISH JOURNAL OF CLINICAL PRACTICE 28(9):318, September, 1974.

"Intrauterine instillation of prostaglandin F2ALPHA IN EARLY PREGNANCY," by J. R. Jones, et al. PROSTAGLANDINS 9(6):881-892, June, 1975.

"Intravenous prostaglandins and oxytocin for mid-trimester abortion," by J. M. Beazley. LANCET 1(7902):335, February 8, 1975.

"Intravenous prostaglandins and oxytocin for mid-trimester abortion," by T. M. Coltart, et al. LANCET 1(7899):173-174, January 18, 1975.

"Management of missed abortion, intrauterine death and hydatidiform mole using prostaglandin E2," by C. P. Murray, et al. IRISH MEDICAL JOURNAL 68(6):133-135, March 22, 1975.

"Mid-trimester abortion induced by intravaginal administration of prostaglandin E2 suppositories," by N. H. Lauersen, et al. AMERICAN JOURNAL OF OBSTETRICS AND GYNECOLOGY 122(8):947-

954, August 15, 1975.

"Midtrimester abortion induced by serial intramuscular
injections of 15(S)-15-methyl-prostaglandin F2alpha,"
by N. H. Lauersen, et al. AMERICAN JOURNAL OF
OBSTETRICS AND GYNECOLOGY 121(2):273-276,
January 15, 1975.

"Midtrimester abortion induced by serial intravaginal
administration of prostaglandin E2 suppositories in
conjunction with a contraceptive diaphragm," by N.
H. Lauersen, et al. PROSTAGLANDINS 10(1):139-
150, July, 1975.

"Midtrimester abortion induced by single intra-amniotic
instillation of two dose schedules of 15(S)-15-methyl-
prostaglandin F2alpha," by N. H. Lauersen, et al.
PROSTAGLANDINS 9(4):617-625, April, 1975.

"Mid-trimester abortion with 15 (S) methyl prostaglandin
F 2 alpha," by T. Leibman, et al. PROSTAGLANDINS
7(5):443-448, September 10, 1974.

"Mid-trimester abortion with intra-amniotic prostaglan-
din F2 alpha and intravenous oxytocin infusion," by
M. Salomy, et al. PROSTAGLANDINS 9(2):271-279,
February, 1975.

"Monitoring of the induction of labour by prostaglandin
f2alpha in early pregnancy," by H. Wiechell, et al.
MUNCHENER MEDIZINISCHE WOCHENSCHRIFT
116(38):767-775, September 20, 1974.

"Opportunities for the application of the prostaglandins
in gynecology. Interruption of pregnancy in acute
leukosis. Description of a case," by P. Krieglsteiner, et al. MUNCHENER MEDIZINISCHE
WOCHENSCHRIFT 117(7):245-248, February 14, 1975.

"Preliminary experience in the clinical use of F2alpha prostaglandins in missed abortion," by M. Herrera, et al. REVISTA CHILENA DE OBSTETRICIA Y GINECOLOGIA 38(4):187-190, 1973.

"Preliminary experience with 15 (S) 15-methyl prostaglandin F2 alpha for midtrimester abortion," by B. E. Greer, et al. AMERICAN JOURNAL OF OBSTETRICS AND GYNECOLOGY 121(4):524-527, February 15, 1975.

"Prostaglandin abortions in an outpatient ward," by O. Ylikorkala, et al. DUODECIM 90(19):1308-1316, 1974.

"Prostaglandin delivery by cervical dilator," by H. Balin, et al. JOURNAL OF REPRODUCTIVE MEDICINE 13(6):208-212, December, 1974.

"Prostaglandin F alpha in amniotic fluid in man," by K. Hillier, et al. JOURNAL OF ENDOCRINOLOGY 64(1):13P, January, 1975.

"Prostaglandin F2alpha and oxytocin compared with hypertonic saline and oxytocin for the induction of second trimester abortion," by K. R. Nielsen, et al. ACTA OBSTETRICIA ET GYNECOLOGICA SCANDINAVICA. SUPPLEMENT (37):57-60, 1974.

"Prostaglandin F2alpha as a method of choice for interruption of pregnancy," by V. Zahn, et al. GEBURTSHILFE UND FRAUENHEILKUNDE 35(3): 203-210, March, 1975.

"Prostaglandin F2-alpha for induction of midterm abortion: a comparative study," by I. F. Lau, et al. FERTILITY AND STERILITY 26(1):74-79, January, 1975.

"Prostaglandin F2alpha given by continuous transcervical extra-amniotic infusion combined with
intravenous oxytocin infusion for therapeutic
termination of mid-trimester pregnancies," by
K. W. Waldron, et al. MEDICAL JOURNAL
OF AUSTRALIA 1(17):525-527, April 26, 1975.

"Prostaglandin-induced abortion and cervical incompetence," by M. P. Embrey. BRITISH MEDICAL
JOURNAL 2(5969):497, May 31, 1975.

"Prostaglandin-induced abortion: assessment of operative complications and early morbidity," by I. Z.
Mackenzie, et al. BRITISH MEDICAL JOURNAL
4(5946):683-686, December 21, 1974.

"Prostaglandin induction of midtrimester abortions:
three years' experience of 626 cases," by P. Kajanoja,
et al. ACTA OBSTETRICIA ET GYNECOLOGICA
SCANDINAVICA. SUPPLEMENT (37):51-56, 1974.

"The prostaglandins," by C. B. Clayman. JOURNAL
OF THE AMERICAN MEDICAL ASSOCIATION 233(8):
904-906, August 25, 1975.

"Prostaglandins and induction of abortion," by P.
Kopecky. HIPPOKRATES 46(1):117-119, February,
1975.

"Prostaglandins F2 alpha (Amoglandin, Dinoprost) for
induced abortion in the second trimester," by E. B.
Obel. UGESKRIFT FOR LAEGER 137(25):1417-1418,
June 16, 1975.

"Prostaglandins for termination of second trimester
pregnancy," by U. R. Krishna, et al. JOURNAL OF
POSTGRADUATE MEDICINE 20(4):176-181, October,
1974.

"The prostaglandins in obstetrics and gynaecology.
Are they living up to expectations?...," by A.
Gillespie. MEDICAL JOURNAL OF AUSTRALIA
1(2):38-41, January 11, 1975.

"Rate of fall in plasma progesterone and time to
abortion following intra-amniotic injection of
prostaglandin F2alpha, with or without urea, in the
second trimester of human pregnancy," by S. M.
Walker, et al. BRITISH JOURNAL OF OBSTE-
TRICS AND GYNAECOLOGY 82(6):488-492, June,
1975.

"Reassessment of systemic administration of prostaglandins for induction of midstrimester abortion,"
by M. Bygdeman, et al. PROSTAGLANDINS 8(2):
157-169, October 25, 1974.

"Reduction of cervical resistance by prostaglandin
suppositories prior to dilation for induced abortion," by J. R. Dingfelder, et al. AMERICAN
JOURNAL OF OBSTETRICS AND GYNECOLOGY
122(1):25-30, May 1, 1975.

"Rupture of uterus during prostaglandin-induced
abortion," by A. M. Smith. BRITISH MEDICAL
JOURNAL 1(5951):205, January 25, 1975.

"Serum levels of oestradiol and progesterone during
administration of prostaglandin F2alpha for induction of abortion and labour," by O. Widholm, et al.
ACTA OBSTETRICIA ET GYNECOLOGICA SCAN-
DINAVICA 54(2):135-139, 1975.

"Single extra-amniotic injection of prostaglandin E2
in viscous gel to induce mid-trimester abortion,"
by I. Z. Mackenzie, et al. BRITISH MEDICAL
JOURNAL 1(5952):240-242, February 1, 1975.

"The synergistic activity of intra-amniotic prostaglandin F2 alpha and urea in the midtrimester elective abortion," by T. M. King, et al. AMERICAN JOURNAL OF OBSTETRICS & GYNECOLOGY 120(5):704-718, November 1, 1974.

"Termination by prostaglandin pellets in very early pregnancy," by A. I. Csapo, et al. LANCET 2(7883): 789-790, September 28, 1974.

"Termination of second trimester pregnancy with intra-amniotic 15 (S) 15 methyl prostaglandin F-2alpha - a two dose schedule study," by S. M. M. Karim, et al. PROSTAGLANDINS 9(3):487-494, March, 1975.

"Therapeutic abortion by a single extra-amniotic instillation of prostaglandin f2alpha," by P. Fylling, et al. ARCHIV FUR GYNAEKOLOGIE 217(2):119-125, 1974.

"The use of F2 alpha prostaglandin for induction of therapeutic abortion and labor in the 2d trimester of pregnancy," by G. Scarselli, et al. MINERVA GINECOLOGICA 26(12):711-716, December, 1974.

"Use of prostaglandin E2 vaginal suppositories in intrauterine fetal death and missed abortion," by C. D. Bailey, et al. OBSTETRICS AND GYNECOLOGY 45(1):110-113, January, 1975.

"Use of prostaglandins for induced abortion," by E. A. Chernukha. FEL'DSKER I AKUSHERKA 39(7):35-37, July, 1974.

"Vaginally administered prostaglandin E2 as a first and second trimester abortifacinet," by S. L. Corson, et al. JOURNAL OF REPRODUCTIVE MEDICINE 14(2):43-46, February, 1975.

PSYCHOLOGY

see also: Sociology and Behavior

"Abortion and the techniques of neutralization," by
W. C. Brennan. JOURNAL OF HEALTH AND
SOCIAL BEHAVIOR 15(4):358-365, December,
1974.

"Abortion counseling: What we need to know and
why," by C. Davis. J PRACT NURS 25:16-17
plus, June, 1975.

"Abortion: nursing expertise needed." NURSING
UPDATE 6:1 plus, May, 1975.

"Biological and psychological consequences of the
induced abortion. Therapeutic abortion," by
C. MacGregor, et al. GACETA MEDICA DE
MEXICO 108(5):318-326, November, 1974.

"Clinical studies of psychotic disorders appearing
during pregnancy, puerperal period and following
induced abortion," by J. Ichikawa. PSYCHIATRIA
ET NEUROLOGIA JAPONICA 76(8):457-483,
August 25, 1974.

"Emotional responses of women following therapeutic
abortion," by N. E. Adler. AMERICAN JOURNAL
OF ORTHOPSYCHIATRY 45:446-454, April, 1975.

"The evil of mandatory motherhood," by G. Hardin.
PSYCHOLOGY TODAY p. 42, November, 1974.

"Mental and social stress of motherhood over 40,
with a view to psychiatric indication for interruption of pregnancy," by H. Kind, et al. SCHWEIZ-
ERISCHE MEDIZINISCHE WOCHENSCHRIFT 104(35):
1221-1224, August 31, 1974.

"No medicaid payments for abortion counseling."
MEDICAL WORLD NEWS 16:96-97, January 27,
1975.

"Psychodiagnostic factors of indication for abortion,"
by A. Blaser, et al. SCHWEIZERISCHE MEDIZIN-
ISCHE WOCHENSCHRIFT 105(14):436-438, April 5,
1975.

"Psychological antecedents to conception among abortion seekers," by W. B. Miller. WESTERN JOUR-
NAL OF MEDICINE 122:12-19, January, 1975.

"Psychological aspects of interruption," by S. Fukalová.
CESKOSLOVENSKA GYNEKOLOGIE 39(3):204-206,
April, 1974.

"Psychological factors in contraceptive failure and
abortion request." MEDICAL JOURNAL OF
AUSTRALIA 1(26):800, June 28, 1975.

"Psychological femininity and legal abortion," by L.
Jacobsson, et al. ACTA PSYCHIATRICA SCAN-
DINAVICA. SUPPLEMENT (255):291-298, 1974.

"Psychological problems following birth and miscarriage," by K. L. Trick. NURSING MIRROR AND
MIDWIVES' JOURNAL 141(2):61-62, July 10, 1975.

"The psychological sequelae of abortion performed for
a genetic indication," by B. D. Blumberg, et al.
AMERICAN JOURNAL OF OBSTETRICS AND GYNE-
COLOGY 122(7):799-808, August 1, 1975.

"Psychological sequelae of elective abortion," by B. D.
Blumberg, et al. WESTERN JOURNAL OF MEDI-
CINE 123(3):188-193, September, 1975.

PSYCHOLOGY

"Psychosexual problems connected with artificial interruption of pregnancy," by F. Kohoutek, et al. CESKOSLOVENSKA GYNEKOLOGIE 39(3):206-207, April, 1974.

"Short-term psychiatric sequelae to therapeutic termination of pregnancy," by B. Lask. BRITISH JOURNAL OF PSYCHIATRY 126:173-177, February, 1975.

"A social-psychiatric comparison of 399 women requesting abortion and 118 pregnant women intending to deliver," by L. Jacobsson, et al. ACTA PSYCHIATRICA SCANDINAVICA. SUPPLEMENT (255):279-290, 1974.

"Termination of pregnancy on psychiatric grounds," by K. Böhme, et al. DEUTSCHE MEDIZINISCHE WOCHENSCHRIFT 100(16):865-872, April 18, 1975.

"Unwanted pregnancy: background and psychological characteristics of women who choose abortion," by D. Clayson, et al. PRAXIS 63(42):1260-1264, October 22, 1974.

PUBLIC HEALTH
"The effect of legalization of abortion on population growth and public health," by C. Tietze. FAMILY PLANNING PERSPECTIVES 7(3):123-127, May-June, 1975.

"The Institute of Medicine reports on legalized abortion and the public health," by R. Lincoln. FAMILY PLANNING PERSPECTIVES 7(4):185-188, July-August, 1975.

RADIOLOGISTS
"Radiological aspects of indications for pregnancy in-

terruption." ORVOSI HETILAP 116(23):1351,
June 8, 1975.

REFERRAL AGENCIES SERVICES
see: Sociology and Behavior

REGITINE

RELIGION AND ETHICS
see also: Sociology and Behavior

"Abortion and the golden rule," by R. M. Hare. PHIL-
OSOPHY AND PUBLIC AFFAIRS 4:201-222, Spring,
1975.

"Abortion and the true believer," by J. Fletcher;
Discussion CHRISTIAN CENTURY 92:69-70,
January 22, 1975.

"Abortion, animation, and biological hominization,"
by J. Diamond. THEOLOGICAL STUDIES 36:305-
324, June, 1975.

"Abortion calls for public ahd private reparation effort; Program of reparation and apology and
spiritual adoption to save the unborn baby," by C.
Lenta. OUR SUNDAY VISITOR 64:1 plus, July 20,
1975.

"Abortion decision: two years later," by R. G. Decker,
et al. COMMONWEAL 101:384-392, February 15,
1975; Discussion 102:35 plus, April 11, 1975.

"Abortion: an emotional issue rejoined." TIME
CANADA 105:6-7, April 14, 1975.

"Abortion in a predominantly Catholic community,"
by G. T. Schneider. JOURNAL OF THE LOUISIANA

STATE MEDICAL SOCIETY 126(9):323-325, September, 1974.

"Abortion: the moral status of the unborn," by R. Werner. SOCIAL THEORY AND PRACTICE 3:201-222, Fall, 1974.

"The abortion movement; reprint from Seido Foundation, Catholic Position Paper published in Japan," by C. Burke. L'OSSERVATORE ROMANO 19(371): 8-11, May 9, 1975.

"Abortion on trial: Dr. Kenneth C. Edelin." NEWS-WEEK 85:55, January 27, 1975.

"Abortion: an open letter," by B. Stephenson. CANADIAN MEDICAL ASSOCIATION JOURNAL 112(4): 492, 494, 497, February 22, 1975.

"Abortion or the unwanted child: a choice for a humanistic society," by J. W. Prescott. HUMANIST 35: 11-15, March, 1975.

"Abortion: the religious debate," by M. DeBolt. LINK p. 35, September, 1974.

"Abortion--Right? Wrong?" by N. Price. HERALD OF HOLINESS p. 12, July 31, 1974.

"Abortion under ethical indication," by H. J. Rieger. DEUTSCH MEDIZINISCHE WOCHENSCHRIFT 99(42): 2126, October 18, 1974.

"Alternatives to abortion needed," by E. M. Kennedy. HOSPITAL PROGRESS 56:11, September, 1975.

"Anti-abortion: not parochial." CHRISTIANITY TODAY 19:22, August 8, 1975.

"Antiabortionists challenge March of dimes," by B. J. Culliton. SCIENCE 190:538, November 7, 1975.

"Anti-Catholicism trades fantasy for fact in the media," by J. Anderson. OUR SUNDAY VISITOR 63:1, April 27, 1975.

"The anti-life movement cover-up; reformers using words as weapons," by A. Serb. OUR SUNDAY VISITOR 64:1 plus, August 31, 1975.

"The Biblical view of abortion," by W. Luck. PRESBY-TERIAN JOURNAL p. 9, April 23, 1975.

"Biology, abortion, and ethics," by M. Potts. LANCET 1(7912):913, April 19, 1975.

"Biology, abortion, and ethics," by M. Wilkinson. LANCET 1(7914):1029-1031, May 3, 1975.

"Bishop bars sacraments to backers of abortion." NATIONAL CATHOLIC REPORTER 11:1 plus, April 18, 1975.

"Bishop Maher stands firm against abortion advocates," by R. McMunn. OUR SUNDAY VISITOR 63:1, April 27, 1975.

"Bishops draft abortion letter." NATIONAL CATHOLIC REPORTER 11:15, January 24, 1975.

"By what authority (refuses to accept antiabortion as only Biblical position)," by A. Taylor. PRESBY-TERIAN JOURNAL p. 9, July 31, 1974.

"Can God forgive abortion?" by R. Fox. OUR SUNDAY VISITOR 63:1 plus, April 6, 1975.

"The case against abortion," by J. Humber.
THOMIST 39:65-84, January, 1975.

"Catholic Hospital Association rejects Canadian Medical Association abortion stand," by M. Beaton-Mamak. DIMENSIONS HEALTH SERVICE 52:36, April, 1975.

"Catholic Peace Fellowship statement on abortion." CATHOLIC MIND 73:7-8, February, 1975.

"Children--abortion--responsibility," by M. Lysnes. SYKEPLEIEN 62(3):96, February 5, 1975.

"Church in the world: abortion and divorce: a change in attitudes?" by J. Deedy. THEOLOGY TODAY 32:86-88, April, 1975.

"Clear answer to a political dilemma; the Church's teaching on abortion," by E. von Feldt. COLUMBIA 55:4, February, 1975.

"Compulsory pregnancy," by E. Doerr. HUMANIST 34:30-31, May, 1974.

"Declaration on abortion." CATHOLIC MIND p. 54, April, 1975.

"Declaration on abortion: a religious, not political act; interview of J. Hamer, Secretary of S. Congregation for the Doctrine of the Faith," by J. Hamer. L'OSSERVATORE ROMANO 2(354):8, January 9, 1975.

"Edelin spent $10,000 to survey prospective jurors." OUR SUNDAY VISITOR 63:2, March 16, 1975.

"Edelin trial; jury not persuaded by scientists for

the defense," by B. J. Culliton. SCIENCE 187: 814-816, March 7, 1975.

"Ethical dilemmas in obstetric and newborn care," by T. K. Hanid. MIDWIFE AND HEALTH VISITOR 11(1):9-11, January, 1975.

"Ethical issues in amniocentesis and abortion," by T. R. McCormick. TEXAS REPORTS ON BIOLOGY AND MEDICINE 32(1):299-309, Spring, 1974.

"Ethical standards for fetal experimentation," by M. M. Martin. FORDHAM LAW REVIEW 43:547-570, March, 1975.

"Ethics of selective abortion." (letter). BRITISH MEDI-CAL JOURNAL 4(5946):676, December 21, 1974.

"The game-plan of pro-life and anti-life," by E. McCormack. SOCIAL JUSTICE REVIEW 68:54-55, May, 1975.

"History of the pro-life movement in Quebec," by A. Morais. CATHOLIC HOSPITAL 3:6-9, January-February, 1975.

"Human life is sacred; pastoral letter of the archbishops and bishops of Ireland." L'OSSERVATORE ROMANO 21(373):6-8 plus, May 22, 1975; 24(376):6-8, June 12, 1975; 25(377):6-9, June 19, 1975.

"Ideal family size as an intervening variable between religion and attitudes towards abortion," by M. Rerzi. JOURNAL FOR THE SCIENTIFIC STUDY OF RELI-GION 14:23-27, March, 1975.

"Julie who walks in the sunlight," by R. DuBois. LIGUORIAN 63:26-29, July, 1975.

"Law, morals and abortion," by D. Degnan. COMMON-
WEAL p. 305, May 31, 1974.

"Legitimacy of a diverse society," by K. J. Ryan.
JOURNAL OF THE AMERICAN MEDICAL ASSOCIA-
TION 233:781, August 18, 1975.

"Let live," by M. Belton. HEALTH VISITOR 47(9):
278, September, 1974.

"Life/death decisions; interview by J. Castelli," by
R. McCormick. ST. ANTHONY MESSENGER
83:32-35, August, 1975.

"Life-saving and life-taking: a comment," by R.
McCormick. LINACRE QUARTERLY 42:110-115,
May, 1975.

"Moral issue and resolution of the time limit," by W.
Becker. MEDIZINISCHE KLINIK 69(49):2039-2040,
December 6, 1974.

"The moral message Bucharest," by D. P. Warwick.
HASTINGS CENTER REPORT 4:8-9, December,
1974.

"Morality of abortion," by G. M. Atkinson. INTER-
NATIONAL PHILOSOPHICAL QUARTERLY 14:347-
362, September, 1974.

"The morality of abortion," by D. Doherty. AMERICAN
ECCLESIASTICAL REVIEW 169:37-47, January, 1975.

"The mystery of the unborn," by P. Fazziola. BIBLE
TODAY 78:388-390, April, 1975.

"New doctors' dilemma," by M. Clark, et al. NEWS-
WEEK 85:24-25, March 3, 1975.

"Not our Nancy! (a feature)." CHRISTIAN HERALD
p. 26, February, 1975.

"Occupational disease among operating room personnel,"
by L. F. Walts, et al. ANESTHESIOLOGY 42:608-
611, May, 1975.

"On human life," by W. Reinsdorf. HOMILETIC AND
PASTORAL REVIEW 65:65-68, January, 1975.

"On life and death," by R. Sterner. VITAL CHRISTIAN-
ITY p. 15, August 25, 1974.

"On priests and abortion," by A. E. Hellegers. FAMILY
PLANNING PERSPECTIVES 6(4):194-195, Fall, 1974.

"Ontario bishops blast government on abortion." OUR
SUNDAY VISITOR 64:2, May 25, 1975.

"The pastoral care of those confronted with abortion,"
by H. McHugh. CLERGY REVIEW 60:218-223,
April, 1975.

"Pastoral counseling and abortion," by M. Pable.
PRIEST 31:15-16 plus, October, 1975.

"Population and the crisis of culture," by T. Lane.
HOMILETIC AND PASTORAL REVIEW 75:61-65,
April, 1975.

"Prenatal pediatric ethics," by A. Prado-Vértiz.
BOLETIN MEDICO DEL HOSPITAL INFANTIL DE
MEXICO 31(2):183-197, March-April, 1974.

"Priests urged to pro-life leadership in new booklet;
Abortion, attitudes and the law, by NCCB and Our
Sunday Visitor." OUR SUNDAY VISITOR 64:1,
August 31, 1975.

"Protestant women mobilize forces against abortion."
OUR SUNDAY VISITOR 64:2, September 7, 1975.

"Protestants organize to speak out on abortion; the
Christian Action Council." OUR SUNDAY VISITOR
64:1, July 20, 1975.

"Religion and legal abortion in Northern Ireland," by
P. A. Compton, et al. JOURNAL OF BIOSOCIAL
SCIENCE 6(4):493-509, October, 1974.

"Right-to-life--two crusaders," by J. B. Cumming,
Jr. NEWSWEEK 85:29, March 3, 1975.

"Russell Shaw criticizes news media." OUR SUNDAY
VISITOR 63:1, March 2, 1975.

"Saying no to NOW; restrictions placed on Catholic
members by San Diego Bishop L. T. Maher. TIME
105:75-76, April 28, 1975.

"Says support for abortion cuts Catholic from Church; a
new publication with comments on the document by
the Congregation for the Doctrine of the Faith, November 18, 1974." OUR SUNDAY VISITOR 64:2, August
31, 1975.

"Semantics can't justify abortion, Lutheran says." OUR
SUNDAY VISITOR 64:2, August 10, 1975.

"Senator Kennedy explains his position on abortion in
letter to Boston paper." OUR SUNDAY VISITOR
64:2, August 31, 1975.

"Strategy on abortion; Catholic bishops' plan." TIME
106:59, December 1, 1975.

"They fight for life - by telephone," by F. Grones.

COLUMBIA 55:6-15, July, 1975.

"Thinking straight about abortion," by N. B. Barcus. CHRISTIANITY TODAY 19:8-9 plus, January 17, 1975.

"Unwanted child wanted," by T. Francis. NATIONAL CATHOLIC REPORTER 11:14, January 24, 1975.

"What are your feelings about death and dying," by D. Popoff. NURSING 5:55-62, September, 1975.

"What is life," by R. Sterner. VITAL CHRISTIANITY p. 1, July 28, 1974.

"When does human life begin," by H. Harrod. CHRISTIAN HOME p. 16, May, 1974.

"Whose 'right to life'?" by D. W. Fisher. HOSPITAL PRACTICE 10:11-12, April, 1975.

"Why is abortion wrong?" by J. Donceel. AMERICA 133:65-67, August 16, 1975.

RESEARCH

"Abortion and research," by M. Lappe. HASTINGS CENTER REPORT 5(3):21, June, 1975.

"Advances in the diagnosis of bovine abortion," by H. W. Dunne, et al. PROCEEDING OF THE UNITED STATES ANIMAL HEALTH ASSOCIATION (77):515-523, 1973.

"Bovine abortion associated with Haemophilus somnus," by D. W. Chladek. AMERICAN JOURNAL OF VETERINARY RESEARCH 36(7):1041, July, 1975.

"Brucella abortus biotype 1 as a cuase of abortion in

a bitch," by D. J. Taylor, et al. VETERINARY RECORD 96(19):428-429, May 10, 1975.

"Characteristics of Chlamydia isolated from domestic animals," by L. N. Abramova, et al. VOPROSY VIRUSOLOGII (6):737-739, November-December, 1974.

"Comparison of antigenic structure and pathogenicity of bovine intestinal Chlamydia isolate with an agent of epizootic bovine abortion," by D. E. Reed, et al. AMERICAN JOURNAL OF VETERINARY RESEARCH 36(08):1141-1143, August, 1975.

"Dicoumarol as the cause of abortion in mink," by J. Kangas, et al. NORDISK VETERINAER MEDICIN 26(7-8):444-447, July-August, 1974.

"Enzootic (viral) abortion in sheep," by A. G. Shakhov, et al. VETERINARIIA (3):52-53, March, 1975.

"Equine herpesvirus 1: biological and biophysical comparison of two viruses from different clinical entitles," by H. C. Borgen, et al. INTERVIROLOGY 4(3):189-198, 1974.

"Fetal research," by B. J. Culliton. SCIENCE 187: 237-238 plus, January 24, 1975.

"Fetal research and antiabortion politics: holding science hostage," by D. S. Hart. FAMILY PLANNING PERSPECTIVES 7:72-82, March-April, 1975.

"Foetal cerebral leucomalcia associated with Cupressus macrocarpa abortion in cattle," (letter), by R. W. Mason. AUSTRALIAN VETERINARY JOURNAL 50(9): 419, September, 1974.

"Fungi isolated from bovine mycotic abortion and pneumonia with special reference to Mortierella wolfii," by M. E. Carter, et al. RESEARCH IN VETERINARY SCIENCE 14(2):201-206, March, 1973.

"Gonadotrophic hormone activity in female Angora goats exhibiting normal and aberrant reproductive activity," by P. S. Pretorius. JOURNAL OF THE SOUTH AFRICAN VETERINARY ASSOCIATION 43(1): 35-41, March, 1972.

"Haematological changes associated with Aspergillus fumigatus infection in experimental mycotic abortion of sheep," by C. A. Day, et al. BRITISH JOURNAL OF EXPERIMENTAL PATHOLOGY 55(4):352-362, August, 1974.

"Hormonal determinism of the embryolethality of Triton W. R. 1339 in mice," by C. Roussel, et al. COMPTES RENDUS DES SEANCES DE LA SOCIETE DE BIOLOGIE ET DE SES FOLIALES 167(12):1713-1717, 1973.

"Hydrocallantois in the bitch," (letter), by P. E. Holt, et al. VETERINARY RECORD 95(5):112, August 3, 1974.

"Immunological disruption of implantation in monkeys with antibodies to human pregnancy specific beta 1-glycoprotein (SP1)," by H. Bohn, et al. ARCHIV FUR GYNAEKOLOGIE 217(2):209-218, 1974.

"Inducing abortion in cattle." MODERN VETERINARY PRACTICE 56(9):659-661, September, 1975.

"Induction of abortion by oestrogens in animals. A review," by W. Velle. NORDISH VETERINAER MEDI-

RESEARCH

CIN 26(10):563-571, October, 1974.

"Induction of abortion in rhesus monkeys with urea,"
by B. Malvaiya, et al. INDIAN JOURNAL OF EX-
PERIMENTAL BIOLOGY 12(4):372-373, July, 1974.

"Infectious bovine rhinotracheitis virus and its role
in bovine abortion," by P. J. Durham. NEW ZEALAND
VETERINARY JOURNAL 22(10):175-180, October, 1974.

"Proceedings: intramuscular administration of a
prostaglandin analogue during pregnancy in the
goat," by P. J. Holst, et al. JOURNAL OF RE-
PRODUCTIVE FERTILITY 43(2):403-404, May,
1975.

"Intravaginal insertion of a dimethylpolysiloxane-
polyvinyl pyrrolidone-prostaglandin F2alpha tube
for midterm abortion in rabbits," by I. F. Lau, et
al. AMERICAN JOURNAL OF OBSTETRICS AND
GYNECOLOGY 120(6):837-839, November 15, 1974.

"Isolation of bacteria and viruses from aborted bovine
fetuses," by T. Sugimura, et al. NATIONAL IN-
STITUTE OF ANIMAL HEALTH QUARTERLY 14(1):
42-47, Summer, 1974.

"The isolation of Leptospira hardjo from an aborting
cow," by S. W. Michna, et al. RESEARCH IN
VETERINARY SCIENCE 17(1):133-135, July, 1974.

"Isolation of leptospira serotype pomona and brucella
suis from swines from the State of Santa Catarina,
Brazil," by C. A. Santa Rosa, et al. ARQUIVOS
DE INSTITUTO BIOLOGICO 40(1):29-32, January-
March, 1973.

"Isolation of Mycoplasma bovigenitalium from an aborted

equine foetus," by E. V. Langford. VETERINARY
RECORD 92(23):528, June 8, 1974.

"Leptospira pomona and reproductive failure in California sea lions," by A. W. Smith, et al. JOURNAL
OF THE AMERICAN VETERINARY MEDICAL ASSOCIATION 165(11):996-998, December 1, 1974.

"Listeria as a cause of abortion and neonatal mortality
in sheep," by K. L. Hughes. AUSTRALIAN VETERINARY JOURNAL 51(2):97-99, February, 1975.

"Listeria monocytogenes type 5 as a cause of abortion
in sheep," by N. S. Macleod, et al. VETERINARY
RECORD 95(16):365-367, October 19, 1974.

"Male-induced pregnancy termination in the prairie vole,
Microtus ochrogaster," by A. C. Fraser-Smith.
SCIENCE 187(4182):1211-1213, March 28, 1975.

"Maternal influence on postimplantation survival in
inbred rats," by D. V. Cramer, et al. JOURNAL
OF REPRODUCTION AND FERTILITY 44(2):317-
321, August, 1975.

"Methods for early termination of pregnancy in the
cow," by F. L. Dawson. VETERINARY RECORD
94(23):542-548, June 8, 1974.

"Methods for early termination of pregnancy in the
cow," by P. G. Millar. VETERINARY RECORD
94(26):626, June 29, 1974.

"Midterm abortion in hamsters induced by silastic-
PVP-PGE2 tubes," by I. F. Lau, et al. PROSTAGLANDINS 8(5):423-431, December 10, 1974.

"Midterm abortion with silastic-PVP implant containing

prostaglandin F2 alpha in rabbits, rats, and hamsters," by I. F. Lau, et al. FERTILITY AND STERILITY 25(10):839-844, October, 1974.

"Morphological changes in the aborted fetuses and placentae in cases of diplococcus abortions in cows," by A. K. Angelov. VETERINARO-MEDITSINSKI 11(8):72-77, 1974.

"Morphological changes in aborted fetuses in swine brucellosis," by L. Diakov, et al. VETERINARNO-MEDITSINSKI 11(6):91-97, 1974.

"Observations on abortions in cattle: a comparison of pathological, microbiological and immunological findings in aborted foetuses and foetuses collected at abattoirs," by R. B. Miller, et al. CANADIAN JOURNAL OF COMPARATIVE MEDICINE 39(3): 270-290, July, 1975.

"Occurrence of viral abortion in mares (Contribution to diagnosis)," by H. Hartmann, et al. SCHWEIZER ARCHIV FUR TIERHEILKUNDE 117(7):393-395, July, 1975.

"Outbreak of vibrio abortion in sheep in Iraq," by G. M. Al-Khatib, et al. BERLINER UND MUNCHENER TIERAERZTLICHE WOCHENSCHRIFT 88(5):86-88, March 1, 1975.

"Pathomorphological changes in guinea pigs and their aborted fetuses in experimental Neorickettsia infection," by A. Dzhurov, et al. VETERINARNO-MEDITSINSKI 10(6):57-66, 1973.

"Perinatal lamb mortality in Western Australia. 3. Congenital infections," by S. M. Dennis. AUSTRALIAN VETERINARY JOURNAL 50(11):507-510, November,

1974.

--5. Vibrionic infection," by S. M. Dennis. AUSTRALIAN VETERINARY JOURNAL 51(1):11-13, January, 1975.

--6. Listeric infection," by S. M. Dennis. AUSTRALIAN VETERINARY JOURNAL 51(2):75-79, February, 1975.

"Persistence of Salmonella abortus ovis in soil," by H. Tadjebakhche, et al. REVUE D'ELEVAGE ET DE MEDECINE VETERINAIRE DES PAYS TROPICAUX 27(1):57-59, 1974.

"Possibilities of contraception, artificial abortion and permature labor in cattle," by E. Grunert, et al. DEUTSCHE TIERAERZTLICHE WOCHENSCHRIFT 81(23):588-591, December 1, 1974.

"Prostaglandin F2 alpha implant-induced abortion: effect on progestin and luteinizing hormone concentration and its reversal by progesterone in rabbits, rats, and hamsters," by S. K. Saksena, et al. FERTILITY AND STERILITY 25(10):845-850, October, 1974.

"Prostaglandin F2alpha: modification of its abortifacient effect by depo-estradiol cypionate in rats," by S. K. Saksena, et al. FERTILITY AND STERILITY 26(2):126-130, February, 1975.

"Response of the primate fetus to intra-amniotic saline injection," by A. Comas-Urrutia, et al. AMERICAN JOURNAL OF OBSTETRICS AND GYNECOLOGY 122(5):549-554, July 1, 1975.

"Salmonella dublin abortion in cattle: incidence and epidemiology," by M. Hinton. BRITISH VETERINARY JOURNAL 131(1):94-101, January-February, 1975.

"Salmonella dublin abortion in cattle: studies on the clinical aspects of the condition," by M. Hinton. BRITISH VETERINARY JOURNAL 130(6):556-563, November-December, 1974.

"Serologic evidence for etiologic role of Akabane virus in epizootic abortion-arthrogryposis-hydranencephaly in cattle in Japan, 1972-1974," by H. Kurogi, et al. ARCHIVES OF VIROLOGY 47(1):71-83, 1975.

"Sheep placenta water-soluble proteins," by S. Georgiev. VETERINARNO-MEDITSINSKI 12(2):83-89, 1975.

"Spermatozoa in the abomasum of aborted bovine foetuses," by D. Jakovijevic. AUSTRALIAN VETERINARY JOURNAL 51(1):56, January, 1975.

"Study of allylestrenol (Turinal) in pregnancy. I. Animal experiments," by G. Gyŏry, et al. THERAPIA HUNGARICA 21(3-4):127-130, 1973.

"Termination of pregnancy in the rat by the antiserum to the beta subunit of ovine interstitial cell stimulating hormone," by M. R. Sairam, et al. PROCEEDINGS OF THE SOCIETY FOR EXPERIMENTAL BIOLOGY AND MEDICINE 147(3):823-825, December, 1974.

"Toxoplasma abortions in sheep in Switzerland," by U. Frei. SCHWEIZER ARCHIV FUR TIERHEILKUNDE 117(7):401-406, July, 1975.

"T-strain mycoplasmas and reproductive failure in monkeys," by R. B. Kundsin, et al. LABORATORY ANIMAL SCIENCE 25(2):221-227, April, 1975.

"Vaccination against Vibrio (Campylobacter) fetus infection in sheep in late pregnancy," by N. J. Gilmour, et al. VETERINARY RECORD 96(6):129-131, February 8,

RESEARCH

1975.

RESPIRATORY SYSTEM
see: Complications

RIFAMPICIN

RIVANOL

RUBELLA
see: Complications

SEPSIS

SEPTIC ABORTION AND SEPTIC SHOCK
see also: Complications
Sepsis

"Cerebral abscess following septic abortion with the
use of a Dalkon shield," by A. A. Op de Coul.
NEDERLANDS TIJDSCHRIFT VOOR GENEESKUNDE
119(12):470-472, March 22, 1975.

"Certain indicators of the oxidation-reduction processes
in patients with septic abortions," by A. S. Shakhbazov.
AKUSHERSTVO I GINEKOLOGIIA (Moscow) (5):47-51,
May, 1974.

"Characteristics of clinical course of acute post-abortion
renal insufficiency," by T. I. Gromova. VRACHEBNOE
DELO (1):86-88, January, 1975.

"Concentration of DDT and its metabolities in placental
tissue and venous blood of women with missed abortion," by B. Trebicka-Kwiatkowska, et al. POLSKI
TYGODNIK LEKARSKI 29(42):1769-1772, October 21,
1974.

"Dalkon Shield," by F. A. Clark, et al. JOURNAL OF
THE AMERICAN MEDICAL ASSOCIATION 233(3):
225-226, June 21, 1975.

"Dalkon shield and septic abortion," by M. H. Briggs.
MEDICAL JOURNAL OF AUSTRALIA 1(3):81,
January 18, 1975.

"Dalkon shield: mid-trimester septic abortion," by J.
Matthews. MEDICAL JOURNAL OF AUSTRALIA
2(23):856-857, December 7, 1974.

"Diagnosis of acute suppurative peritonitis in patients
with sepsis and acute renal insufficiency," by O. S.
Shkrob, et al. AKUSHERSTVO I GINEKOLOGIIA
(Moscow) (6):32-35, June, 1974.

"The effects of antibiotics on indices of immunity
during treatment of endomyometritis following infectious abortion," by G. S. Minasova, et al.
ANTIBIOTIKI 19(1):86-89, January, 1974.

"Hazards of IUDs," by J. W. Records. SOUTHERN
MEDICAL JOURNAL 68(9):1061-1062, September,
1975.

"Heparin therapy for septic abortion," by U. Stosiek.
GEBURTSHILFE UND FRAUENHEILKUNDE 34(12):
1045-1046, December, 1974.

"Infective complications of the IUD," MEDICAL
JOURNAL OF AUSTRALIA 2(7):241-242, August
16, 1975.

"Management of septic abortion," by R. H. Bartlett.
NEW ENGLAND JOURNAL OF MEDICINE 293(3):
152-153, July 17, 1975.

"Management of septic chemical abortion with renal failure. Use of a conservative regimen," by D. F. Hawkins, et al. NEW ENGLAND JOURNAL OF MEDICINE 292(14):722-725, April 3, 1975.

"Post-abortum acute renal insufficiency," by A. Amerio, et al. MINERVA NEFROLOGICA 21(2): 95-103, March-April, 1974.

"Second trimester septic abortion and the Dalkon shield," by J. Vujcich, et al. MEDICAL JOURNAL OF AUSTRALIA 2(7):249-252, August 16, 1975.

"Septic abortion and IUD," (letter), by K. A. Carey-Smith. NEW ZELAND MEDICAL JOURNAL 80(523): 225, September 11, 1974.

"Septic abortion and IUD," (letter), by R. W. Jones. NEW ZEALAND MEDICAL JOURNAL 80(522): 186, August 28, 1974.

"Septic abortion, excluding that produced by Bacillus perfringens," by M. Herrera, et al. REVISTA CHILENA DE OBSTETRICIA Y GINECOLOGIA 38(4):176-186, 1973.

"Septic conditions following gynecologic interventions in pregnancy," by G. Bodor, et al. ORVOSI HETILAP 116(1):14-17, January 5, 1975.

"Some indices of the blood coagulation system in postnatal and postabortion septic diseases," by T. S. Dramplan, et al. ZHURNAL EKSPERIMENTAL' NOI I KLINICHESKOI MEDITSINY 14(3):92-95, 1974.

"State of the infectious foci after spontaneous abortion," by A. P. Egorova, et al. VOPROSY OKHRANY MATERINSTVA I DETSTVA 19(5):63-66, May, 1974.

"Unusual protraction of oliguria in a patient with acute
renal insufficiency following a medical abortion,"
by S. A. Glants, et al. UROLOGIIA I NEFROLOGIIA
(2):54, March-April, 1974.

SOCIOLOGY AND BEHAVIOR
see also: Family Planning
Religion and Ethics

"Abortion and family planning in the Soviet Union:
public policies and private behaviour," by H. P.
David. JOURNAL OF BIOSOCIAL SCIENCE 6(4):
417-426, October, 1974.

"Abortion and promiscuity," by L. F. Eickhoff.
BRITISH MEDICAL JOURNAL 3(5975):99-100,
July 12, 1975.

"Abortion and promiscuity," by R. G. Wilkins.
BRITISH MEDICAL JOURNAL 3(5977):233, July
26, 1975.

"Abortion and the public good," by M. Pogonowska.
AMERICAN JOURNAL OF PUBLIC HEALTH 65(7):
748, July, 1975.

"Abortion bothers young males." NATIONAL CATHOLIC
REPORTER 11:4, July 4, 1975.

"Abortion information: a guidance viewpoint," by P. L.
Wolleat. SCHOOL COUNSELOR 22(5):338-341,
May, 1975.

"Abortion, obtained and denied: research approaches,"
by S. H. Newman, et al. STUDIES IN FAMILY
PLANNING (53):1-8, May, 1970.

"Abortion--on the social scene," by R. Sterner. VITAL

CHRISTIANITY p. 12, August 11, 1974.

"Abortion, personal freedom, and public policy," by
R. J. Adamek. FAMILY COORDINATOR 23(4):411–
418, October, 1974.

"Abortion--a personal testimony," by M. Potts.
JAMAICAN NURSE 14:6 plus, August, 1974.

"Can you change people's minds on abortion?" by S.
Lockwood. LIGUORIAN 63:13-16, February, 1975.

"Children born to women denied abortion," by Z. Dytrych,
et al. FAMILY PLANNING PERSPECTIVES 7(4):165–
171, July-August, 1975.

"Conflicting coverage given abortion attitudes survey."
OUR SUNDAY VISITOR 63:1, March 23, 1975.

"Incidence of unwanted pregnancy in Australia," by
E. L. Snyder. MEDICAL JOURNAL OF AUSTRALIA
2(6):233-234, August 9, 1975.

"Matters of life and death. The manipulative society,"
by E. H. Patey. NURSING MIRROR AND MIDWIVES'
JOURNAL 139(23):40-41, December, 1974.

"Medical and social aspects of adolescent pregnancies.
I. Adolescents applying for termination of an illegiti-
mate pregnancy," by O. Widholm, et al. ACTA
OBSTETRICIA ET GYNAECOLOGICA SCANDINAVICA
53(4):347-353, 1974.

"Medical cop-out? the physician's role in abortion
counseling," by H. Klaus. AMERICA 133:68-70,
August 16, 1975.

"No medicaid payments for abortion counseling." MEDI-

CAL WORLD NEWS 16:96-97, January 27, 1975.

"NY Times is for the birds but not for unborn babies."
OUR SUNDAY VISITOR 63:1, March 9, 1975.

"Or manslaughter?" ECONOMIST 254:61, February 22,
1975.

"Pat Goltz - pro-life feminist," by J. Anderson. OUR
SUNDAY VISITOR 64:1 plus, May 18, 1975.

"Pregnancy wastage and age of mother among the
Amish," by L. J. Resseguie. HUMAN BIOLOGY
46(4):633-639, December, 1974.

"Profile of an abortion counselor," by B. Dauber.
FAMILY PLANNING PERSPECTIVES 6(3):185-187,
Summer, 1974.

"Relations of personality factors and student nurses'
attitudes toward abortion," by J. M. Jones. PSYCHO-
LOGICAL REPORTS 35(2):927-931, October, 1974.

"Social and demographic determinants of abortion in
Poland," by D. P. Mazur. POPULATION STUDIES
29:21-35, March, 1975.

"Social aspects of legal abortion in Yugoslavia," by N. J.
Jurukovski. GODISEN ZBORNIK NA MEDICINSKIAT
FAKULTET VO SKOPJE 20:159-164, 1974.

"Social effects of abortion." NEW ENGLAND JOURNAL
OF MEDICINE 292(9):484-486, February 27, 1975.

"Stage of pregnancy is key to public approval of abortion." GALLUP OPINION INDEX p. 11-13, July,
1975.

SOCIOLOGY AND BEHAVIOR

"The unmet need for legal abortion services in the U. S."
FAMILY PLANNING PERSPECTIVES 7:224-230,
September-October, 1975.

"Unwanted pregnancy: background and psychological
characteristics of women who choose abortion," by
D. Clayson, et al. PRAXIS 63(42):1260-1264, October
22, 1974.

"What are your feelings about death and dying? Controversial
questions surrounding abortion," by D. Popoff. NURSING
5:55-62, September, 1975.

"Would you buy an abortion from this man? the Harvey
Karman controversy," by L. C. Wohl. MS MAGAZINE
4:60-64 plus, September, 1975.

SODIUM CHLORIDE

S.P.U.C.
see: Religion and Ethics

SPONTANEOUS ABORTION
see also: Threatened Abortion

"Anti-D antibodies after spontaneous abortion," by P. F.
Bolis, et al. ARCHIVIO DI OSTETRICIA E GINECOL-
OGIA 78(1-3):12-17, January-June, 1973.

"Competition between spontaneous and induced abortion,"
by R. G. Potter. DEMOGRAPHY 12(1):129-141,
February, 1975.

"Congenital-malformation rates and spontaneous-abortion rates," by W. H. James. LANCET 1(7917):1201,
May 24, 1975.

"Cytochemical changes in the endometrium of women

after spontaneous abortion," by R. K. Ryzhova.
AKUSHERSTVO I GINEKOLOGIIA (Moscow) (5):63-
65, May, 1974.

"Cytogenetic studies on spontaneous abortions," by L.
Wiśniewski, et al. GYNAEKOLOGISCHE RUND-
SCHAW 14(3):184-193, 1974.

"Cytomegalovirus endometritis: report of a case associated with spontaneous abortion," by L. P. Dehner,
et al. OBSTETRICS AND GYNECOLOGY 45(2):211-
214, February, 1975.

"Etiology and pathogenesis of spontaneous abortions
and elaboration of differentiated complex therapy,"
by E. S. Kononova, et al. VOPROSY OKHRANY
MATERINSTVA I DETSTVA 20(3):62-67, March,
1975.

"Histophysiology of human amnion in the normal state
and in spontaneous abortion at the early periods of
pregnancy," by A. V. Shurlygina, et al. AKUSH-
USTVO I GINEKOLOGIIA (Moscow) 0(7):66-67,
July, 1974.

"Induced abortion and its sequelae: prematurity and
spontaneous abortion," by L. H. Roht, et al.
AMERICAN JOURNAL OF OBSTETRICS AND
GYNECOLOGY 120(7):868-874, December 1, 1974.

"Magnesium electrophoresis by means of a sinusoid
modulated current in the treatment of spontaneous
abortion," by A. I. Liubimova, et al. AKUSHER-
STVO I GINEKOLOGIIA (Moscow) (9):45-48, September, 1974.

"Marker chromosomes in parents of spontaneous abortuses," by S. Holbek, et al. HUMANGENETIK

25(1):61-64, 1974.

"Materno-fetal ABO incompatibility as a cause of
spontaneous abortion," by J. G. Lauritsen, et al.
CLINICAL GENETICS 7(4):308-316, April, 1975.

"Morphogenetic disturbances in a spontaneous abortus
with trisomy B," by V. P. Kulazenko. HUMAN-
GENETIK 25(1):53-59, 1974.

"Pathological changes in tetrasploid abortuses after
spontaneous abortion," by V. P. Kulazhenko, et
al. AKUSHERSTVO I GINEKOLOGIIA (Moscow)
(3):32-37, March, 1974.

"Placental energy adequacy and tissue respiration in
the normal course of pregnancy and in its spontaneous
interruption," by V. V. Andrashko, et al. PEDI-
ATRIIA AKUSHERSTVO I GINEKOLOGIIA (5):41-44,
September-October, 1974.

"Previous reproductive history in mothers presenting
with spontaneous abortions," by E. Alberman, et
al. BRITISH JOURNAL OF OBSTETRICS AND
GYNECOLOGY 82(5):366-373, May, 1975.

"Recent advances in the cytogenetic study of human
spontaneous abortions," by H. D. McConnell, et
al. OBSTETRICS AND GYNECOLOGY 45(5):547-
552, May, 1975.

"Retrospective and prospective epidemiological studies
of 1500 karyotyped spontaneous human abortions,"
by J. Boué, et al. TERATOLOGY; JOURNAL OF
ABNORMAL DEVELOPMENT 12(1):11-26, August,
1975.

"Sequential aspects of spontaneous abortion: maternal

age, parity, and pregnancy compensation artifact,"
by A. F. Naylor. SOCIAL BIOLOGY 21(2):195-204,
Summer, 1974.

"Serum level of pregnancy associated alpha2-globulin
in patients with spontaneous abortions," by G. N.
Than, et al. ARCHIV FUR GYNAEKOLOGIE 218(3):
183-187, July 29, 1975.

"The significance of oral contraceptives in causing
chromosome anomalies in spontaneous abortions,"
by J. G. Lauritsen. ACTA OBSTETRICIA ET
GYNECOLOGICA SCANDINAVICA 54(3):261-264,
1975.

"Spontaneous abortion." LANCET 2(7935):591-592,
September 27, 1975.

"Spontaneous abortion and aging of human ova and
spermatozoa," by R. Guerrero, et al. NEW ENG-
LAND JOURNAL OF MEDICINE 293(12):573-575,
September 18, 1975.

"Spontaneous abortion and sensitization to elements of
the fertilised ovum," by I. N. Odarenko. AKUSHER-
STVO I GINEKOLOGIIA (Moscow) 49(4):64-65,
April, 1973.

"State of the infectious foci after spontaneous abortion,"
by A. P. Egorova, et al. VOPROSY OKHRONY
MATERINSTVA I DETSTVA 19(5):63-66, May, 1974.

"Studies on spontaneous abortions. Fluorescence analysis of abnormal karyotypes," by J. G. Lauritsen, et
al. HEREDITAS 71(1):160-163, 1972.

STATISTICS
"Abortion advocates using false statistics." OUR SUNDAY

VISITOR 63:3, April 27, 1975.

"Abortion is second-place operation: nationwide survey
finds tonsillectomy the only surgery more common."
MEDICAL WORLD NEWS 16:54, March 10, 1975.

"Abortion: 300,000 clandestine operations per year in
France." BRUXELLES-MEDICAL 54(1):26-27,
January, 1974.

"Clandestine abortion. Sketches of a numerical study,"
by R. Bourg. BRUXELLES-MEDICAL 54(1):19-25,
January, 1974.

"Clinical aspects of abortion due to genetic causes
studies in fifty-two cases," by J. Cohen, et al.
ACTA EUROPAEA FERTILITATIS 2(3):405-425,
September, 1970.

"Complications of 10,453 consecutive first-trimester
abortions: a prospective study," by J. E. Hodgson,
et al. AMERICAN JOURNAL OF OBSTETRICS AND
GYNECOLOGY 120(6):802-807, November 15, 1974.

"Congenital-malformation rates and spontaneous-abortion rates," by W. H. James. LANCET 1(7917):1201,
May 24, 1975.

"Cytogenetical studies on couples with repeated abortions,"
by K. Rani, et al. INDIAN JOURNAL OF EXPERI-
MENTAL BIOLOGY 12(1):98-99, January, 1974.

"Cytogenetic study of 30 couples having had several
spontaneous abortions," by A. Broustet, et al.
SEMAINE DES HOPITAUX DE PARIS 51(5):299-
302, January 26, 1975.

"Factors influencing conception in women seeking termination of pregnancy. A pilot study of 100 women," by Y. Lucire. MEDICAL JOURNAL OF AUSTRALIA 1(26):824-827, June 28, 1975.

"On unbiased estimation for randomized response models," by P. K. Sen. AMERICAN STATISTICAL ASSOCIATION JOURNAL 69:997-1001, December, 1974.

"Prostaglandin induction of midtrimester abortions: three years' experience of 626 cases," by P. Kajanoja, et al. ACTA OBSTETRICIA ET GYNECOLOGICA SCANDINAVICA. SUPPLEMENT (37):51-56, 1974.

"Report on abortion activities in nearly 3,000 hospitals, clinics and private physicians' offices," by M. Clark. NEWSWEEK 85:97, February 17, 1975.

"Retrospective and prospective epidemiological studies of 1500 karyotyped spontaneous human abortions," by J. Boué, et al. TERATOLOGY; JOURNAL OF ABNORMAL DEVELOPMENT 12(1):11-26, August, 1975.

"A review of 700 hysterotomies," by B. J. Nottage, et al. BRITISH JOURNAL OF OBSTETRICS AND GYNAECOLOGY 82(4):310-313, April, 1975.

"Salting out: experience in 9,000 cases," by D. H. Sherman. JOURNAL OF REPRODUCTIVE MEDICINE 14(06):241-243, June, 1975.

"Scottish abortion statistics 1973." HEALTH BULLE- TIN (Edinburgh) 32(3):121-129, May, 1974.

"Scottish abortion statistics 1974." HEALTH BULLE- TIN (Edinburgh) 33(4):167-181, July, 1975.

"A social-psychiatric comparison of 399 women requesting abortion and 118 pregnant women intending
  to deliver," by L. Jacobsson, et al. ACTA
  PSYCHIATRICA SCANDINAVICA. SUPPLEMENT
  (255):279-290, 1974.

"10 interviews about physicians and the population
  change. Abortion inevitable in developing countries.
  Is forced birth control near?" by Y. Karlsson.
  NORDISK MEDICIN 89(8):234-240, October, 1974.

"Termination of pregnancy in Wales," by B. Knight.
  NURSING MIRROR AND MIDWIVES' JOURNAL
  140(14):69-70, April 3, 1975.

"Various technics of interruption of pregnancy used
  in our statistical service. Incidents and accidents,"
  by S. Boudjemaa, et al. TUNISIE MEDICALE
  52(2):83-87, March-April, 1974.

"Volume and sodium concentration studies in 300
  saline-induced abortions," by T. D. Kerenyi, et
  al. AMERICAN JOURNAL OF OBSTETRICS AND
  GYNECOLOGY 121(5):590-596, March 1, 1975.

STERILITY
  "Fertility rates and abortion rates: simulations of
  family limitation," by C. Tietze, et al. STUDIES
  IN FAMILY PLANNING 6(5):114-120, May, 1975.

"The impact of the New York State abortion law on
  black and white fertility in Upstate New York," by
  K. J. Roghmann. INTERNATIONAL JOURNAL OF
  EPIDEMIOLOGY 4(1):45-49, March, 1975.

STERILIZATION
  "Combined laparoscopic sterilization and pregnancy
  termination: II. Further experiences with a larger

series of patients," by R. G. Cunanan, Jr., et al.
JOURNAL OF REPRODUCTIVE MEDICINE 13(5):
204-205, November, 1974.

"Outpatient laparoscopic sterilization with therapeutic
abortion versus abortion alone," by J. I. Fishburne,
et al. OBSTETRICS AND GYNECOLOGY 45(6):665-
668, June, 1975.

"Simultaneous laparoscopic sterilization and suction
curettage as an outpatient procedure," by N. Rezai.
MARYLAND STATE MEDICAL JOURNAL 24(4):35-
39, April, 1975.

"Sterilization and therapeutic abortion counseling for
the mentally retarded," by C. W. Smiley. ILLINOIS
MEDICAL JOURNAL 147:291-292, March, 1975.

"Therapeutic abortion with concurrent sterilization:
comparison of methods," by M. K. Leong, et al.
CANADIAN MEDICAL ASSOCIATION JOURNAL
111(12):1327-1329, December 21, 1974.

"Voluntary versus compulsory sterilization in Sweden
then and now," by H. Sjövall. LAKARTIDNINGEN
72(4):241-245, January 22, 1975.

STILBESTROL
"Prenatal exposure to stilboestrol." MEDICAL JOURNAL
OF AUSTRALIA 1(12):373-374, March 22, 1975.

STUDENTS
see: Youth

SURGICAL TREATMENT AND MANAGEMENT
see also: Techniques of Abortion

"Advantages and disadvantages of surgical treatment

in imminent abortions and premature delivery," by
E. Zajacová, et al. BRATISLAVSKE LEKARSKE
LISTY 63(2):189-194, February, 1975.

"The effect of abortions on the birth weight in infants,"
by O. Pohánka, et al. ORVOSI HETILAP 116(34):
1983-1989, August 24, 1975.

"Perforation of a cornual pregnancy at induced first-
trimester abortion," by B. Delson. AMERICAN
JOURNAL OF OBSTETRICS AND GYNECOLOGY
121(4):581-582, February 15, 1975.

"Preventive treatment of habitual abortion caused by
internal os incompetence," by S. Krzysztoporski.
ZENTRALBLATT FUER VETERINAERMEDIZINE
JOURNAL OF VETERINARY MEDICINE 3(4):215-218,
November, 1974.

"Septic conditions following gynecologic interventions
in pregnancy," by G. Bodor, et al. ORVOSI
HETILAP 116(1):14-17, January 5, 1975.

"Surgical treatment of isthmocervical incompetence
in pregnant women suffering from premature delivery," by L. P. Zubareva. VOPROSY OKHRONY
MATERINSTVA I DETSTVA 18(5):71-75, 1973.

SURVEYS
see: Sociology and Behavior

SYMPOSIA
"The abortion decision--two years later (relates to U. S.
Supreme Court decision)," by R. Decker, et al.
COMMONWEAL p. 384, February 14, 1975.

"Inhibition of labour. Symposium by letter," by J.
Hütter, et al. MUENCHENER MEDIZINISCHE

WOCHENSCHRIFT 116(38):689-698, September 20, 1974.

"Right to life: time for a new strategy; symposium: Moral credibility," by W. Carroll; "Grassroots revolution," by R. Engel; "Conditional allegiance," by W. Devlin; "The best chance," by P. Fisher; "Get tough," by T. May; "Unacceptable principle," by C. Rice; "Bear witness," by M. Schwartz; "The ethical issue," by J. Willke. TRIUMPH 10:11-16, January, 1975.

SYNTOCINON

TECHNIQUES OF ABORTION
see also: Induced Abortion
Surgical Treatment and Management

"Abortion cannula should not be reused,'' by W. L. Sim, et al. CANADIAN MEDICAL ASSOCIATION JOURNAL 113(2):92, July 26, 1975.

"Abortion nursing expertise needed." NURSING UP-DATE 6:1 plus, May, 1975.

"Acute hematometra with peritoneal irritation following therapeutic abortion by the Karman method of suction curettage," by G. Bastert, et al. MUENCHENER MEDIZINISCHE WOCHENSCHRIFT 116(38):780-781, September 20, 1974.

"Artificial termination of advanced pregnancy by extra-amniotic administration of prostaglandin F2 alpha and 15-me-PGF2 alpha," by E. A. Chernukha, et al. SOVETSKAIA MEDITSINA (6):21-26, June, 1975.

"Cerebral abscess following septic abortion with the use of a Dalkon shield," by A. A. Op de Coul. NEDER-

LANDS TIJDSCHRIFT VOOR GENEESKUNDE 119(12):
470-472, March 22, 1975.

"Cervicovaginal fistula complicating induced midtrimester
abortion despite laminaria tent insertion," by J. H.
Lischke, et al. AMERICAN JOURNAL OF OBSTETRICS
AND GYNECOLOGY 120(6):852-853, November 15, 1974.

"Coagulation changes during intraamniotic prostaglandin-
induced abortion," by G. J. Kleiner, et al. OBSTE-
TRICS AND GYNECOLOGY 44(5):757-761, November,
1974.

"Comparative evaluation of the methods of termination
of advanced pregnancy," by V. I. Babukhadiia, et al.
SOVETSKAIA MEDITSINA (6):97-99, June, 1975.

"Comparative studies on the new legalization of legal
abortion," by S. Schultz, et al. ZENTRALBLATT
FUR GYNAEKOLOGIE 96(39):1217-1222, September
27, 1974.

"Complications of the interruption of pregnancy by
the method of intra-amnionic administration of a
hypertonic sodium chloride solution and their prevention," by Iu. M. Bloshanskii. AKUSHERSTVO
I GINEKOLOGIIA (Moscow) (9):65-66, September,
1974.

"Dalkon Shield," by F. A. Clark, et al. JOURNAL
OF THE AMERICAN MEDICAL ASSOCIATION 233(3):
225-226, June 21, 1975.

"Dalkon shield and septic abortion," by M. H. Briggs.
MEDICAL JOURNAL OF AUSTRALIA 1(3):81,
January 18, 1975.

"Dalkon shield: mid-trimester septic abortion," by J.

Matthews. MEDICAL JOURNAL OF AUSTRALIA
2(23):856-857, December 7, 1974.

"Diagnosis of death in relation to irreversably comatose
artificially ventilated patients," by G. J. Kloosterman.
NEDERLANDS TIJDSCHRIFT VOOR GENEESKUNDE
119(21):843-844, May 24, 1975.

"Diagnosis of threatened abortion using electrohysterography," by A. I. Liubimova, et al. AKUSHERSTVO
I GINEKOLOGIIA (Moscow) 49(4):65-66, April, 1973.

"The efficacy of intramuscular 15 methyl prostaglandin
E2 in second-trimester abortion. Coagulation and
hormonal aspects," by T. F. Dillon, et al. AMERI-
CAN JOURNAL OF OBSTETRICS AND GYNECOLOGY
121(5):584-589, March 1, 1975.

"Endometrial aspiration as a means of early abortion,"
by T. C. Wong, et al. OBSTETRICS AND GYNE-
COLOGY 44(6):845-852, December, 1974.

"An evaluation of abortion: techniques and protocois,"
by I. S. Burnett, et al. HOSPITAL PRACTICE 10:
97-105, August, 1975.

"The hazards of vacuum aspiration in late first trimester abortions," by P. Moberg, et al. ACTA
OBSTETRICIA ET GINECOLOGICA SCANDINAVICA
54(2):113-118, 1975.

"Interruption of the late stages of pregnancy by means
of transcervical amniocentesis and the replacement
of the amniotic fluid," by V. I. Babukhadiia, et al.
PEDIATRIIA AKUSHERSTVO I GINEKOLOGIIA (5):
53-55, September-October, 1974.

"Interruption of pregnancy at midterm by intrauterine

application of solutions," by Y. Manabe. OBSTE-
TRICAL AND GYNECOLOGICAL SURVEY 27(10:
701-710, October, 1972.

"Interruption of pregnancy without cervic dilation,"
by L. Lázló, et al. ORVOSI HETILAP 115(50):
2967-2969, December 15, 1974.

"Intramuscular administration of 15-(S) 15 methyl
prostaglandin E2 methyl ester for induction of
abortion: a comparison of two dose schedules,"
by W. E. Brenner, et al. FERTILITY AND STER-
ILITY 26(4):369-379, April, 1975.

"Is it advisable to interrupt pregnancy by vacuum
aspiration?" by G. Janny. ORVOSI HETILAP
116(15):885-886, April 13, 1975.

"Menstrual extraction," by M. F. Atienza, et al.
AMERICAN JOURNAL OF OBSTETRICS AND
GYNECOLOGY 121(4):490-495, February 15, 1975.

"Menstrual regulation in the United States: a preliminary report," by W. E. Brenner, et al. FER-
TILITY AND STERILITY 26(3):289-295, March,
1975.

"Outpatient pregnancy termination in an NHS hospital,"
by M. G. R. Hull, et al. NURSING TIMES 70:1540-
1542, October 3, 1974.

"Perforation of the uterus and injuries of the internal
organs in violent interruption of pregnancy," by B.
Veković, et al. MEDICINSKI ARHIV 28(6):585-587,
November-December, 1974.

"Prevention of Rh haemolytic disease," by C. A. Clarke.
NURSING MIRROR AND MIDWIVES' JOURNAL 139(17):

57-59, October 24, 1974.

"Prostaglandin F2alpha as a method of choice for
interruption of pregnancy," by V. Zahn, et al.
GEBURTSHILFE UND FRAUENHEILKUNDE 35(3):
203-210, March, 1975.

"Radioreceptorassay of human chorionic gonadotropin
as an aid in miniabortion," by R. Landesman, et al.
FERTILITY AND STERILITY 25(12):1022-1029,
December, 1974.

"Rapid hCG-specific radioimmunoassay for menstrual
aspiration," by T. S. Kosasa, et al. OBSTETRICS
AND GYNECOLOGY 45(5):566-568, May, 1975.

"Reduction of cervical resistance by prostaglandin
suppositories prior to dilatation for induced abortion," by J. R. Dingfelder, et al. AMERICAN
JOURNAL OF OBSTETRICS AND GYNECOLOGY
122(1):25-30, May 1, 1975.

"Second trimester abortions. Review of four procedures," by A. Risk, et al. NEW YORK STATE
JOURNAL OF MEDICINE 75(7):1022-1027, June,
1975.

"Second trimester septic abortion and the Dalkon
shield," by J. Vujcich, et al. MEDICAL JOURNAL
OF AUSTRALIA 2(7):249-252, August 16, 1975.

"Simultaneous laparoscopic sterilization and suction
curettage as an outpatient procedure," by N. Rezai.
MARYLAND STATE MEDICAL JOURNAL 24(4):
35-39, April, 1975.

"Technics for interruption of a second-trimester pregnancy," by J. H. Ravina, et al. NOUVELLE PRESSE

MEDICALE 3(45):2733-2736, December 28, 1974.

"Techniques of pregnancy termination. Part II," by
L. S. Burnett, et al. OBSTETRICAL AND GYNE-
COLOGICAL SURVEY 29(1):6-42, January, 1974.

"Termination of mid-trimester pregnancy by transcervical extra-amniotic hypertonic saline method
without in-dwelling catheter," by S. Nummi, et al.
ANNALES CHIRURGIAE ET GYNAECOLOGIAE
FENNIAE 63(6):479-482, 1974.

"Termination of pregnancy with Utus paste: report
of a fatal case," by T. A. Thomas, et al. BRITISH
MEDICAL JOURNAL 1(5954):375-376, February 15,
1975.

"Therapeutic abortion with concurrent sterilization:
comparison of methods," by M. K. Leong, et al.
CANADIAN MEDICAL ASSOCIATION JOURNAL
111(12):1327-1329, December 21, 1974.

"Vacurette--a new disposable suction apparatus in
induced legal abortion," by O. Als, et al.
UGESKRIFT FOR LAEGER 137(8):447-450,
February 17, 1975.

"Various technics of interruption of pregnancy used
in our statistical service. Incidents and accidents,"
by S. Boudjemaa, et al. TUNISIE MEDICALE
52(2):83-87, March-April, 1974.

"Very early termination of pregnancy (menstrual
extraction)," by J. Stringer, et al. BRITISH MED-
ICAL JOURNAL 3(5974):7-9, July 5, 1975.

"Volume and sodium concentration studies in 300
saline-induced abortions," by T. D. Kerenyi, et al.

TECHNIQUES OF ABORTION

AMERICAN JOURNAL OF OBSTETRICS AND
GYNECOLOGY 121(5):590-596, March 1, 1975.

TETRACYCLINE
"Prophylactic use of tetracycline for first trimester
abortions," by J. E. Hodgson, et al. OBSTETRICS
AND GYNECOLOGY 45(5):574-578, May, 1975.

TH 1165 a
"Results of treatment of threatened abortion with
Partusisten (preparation Th 1165 A)," by A.
Dzioba, et al. WIADOMOSCI LEKARSKIE 28(14):
1193-1196, July 15, 1975.

THERAPEUTIC ABORTION
"Abortion and promiscuity," by L. F. Eickhoff.
BRITISH MEDICAL JOURNAL 3(5975):99-100,
July 12, 1975.

"Abortion and promiscuity," by R. G. Wilkins.
BRITISH MEDICAL JOURNAL 3(5977):233, July
26, 1975.

"Abortion cannula should not be reused," by W. L.
Sim, et al. CANADIAN MEDICAL ASSOCIATION
JOURNAL 113(2):92, July 26, 1975.

"Abortion: an open letter," by B. Stephenson.
CANADIAN MEDICAL ASSOCIATION JOURNAL
112:492 plus, February 22, 1975.

"Acute hematometra with peritoneal irritation following
therapeutic abortion by the Karman method of suction
curettage," by G. Bastert, et al. MUENCHENER
MEDIZINISCHE WOCHENSCHRIFT 116(38):780-781,
September 20, 1974.

"Applications for abortion at a community hospital,"

by M. E. Hunter. CANADIAN MEDICAL ASSOCIA-
TION JOURNAL 111(10):1088-1089, November 16,
1974.

"Biological and psychological consequences of the induced abortion. Therapeutic abortion," by C.
MacGregor, et al. GACETA MEDICA DE MEXICO
108(5):318-326, November, 1974.

"Blood coagulation tests in prostaglandin F-2alpha
induced and a one-time mechanically induced therapeutic abortion," by W. D. Junge, et al. ZENTRAL-
BLATT FUR GYNAEKOLOGIE 96(35):1116-1120,
August 30, 1974.

"Clinical results of therapeutic induction of abortion
by extraamniotic application of prostaglandin F2
alpha," by H. Lahmann, et al. ZEITSCHRIFT
FUR GEBURTSHILFE UND PERINATOLOGIE
178(6):423-428, December, 1974.

"Comparison of extra-amniotic administration of
PGF2alpha, 0.9 per cent saline, and 20 per cent
saline followed by oxytocin for therapeutic abortion," by A. P. Lange, et al. ACTA OBSTETRICIA
ET GYNECOLOGICA SCANDINAVICA (37):61-66,
1974.

"Contraceptive therapy following therapeutic abortion:
an analysis," by W. F. Peterson. OBSTETRICS
AND GYNECOLOGY 44(6):853-857, December, 1974.

"Dark shadow at the door." IRISH MEDICAL JOURNAL
68(6):150, 158, March 22, 1975.

"The decision-making process and the outcome of therapeutic abortion," by C. M. Friedman, et al.
AMERICAN JOURNAL OF PSYCHIATRY 131(12):

1332-1337, December, 1974.

"Effect of prostaglandin F2a on the contractility of
the pregnant human uterus," by G. Romero-Salinas,
et al. GINECOLOGIA Y OBSTETRICIA DE MEXICO
35(212):627-656, June, 1974.

"Electroencephalographic changes after intra-amniotic
prostaglandin F2alpha and hypertonic saline," by
R. P. Shearman, et al. BRITISH JOURNAL OF
OBSTETRICS AND GYNAECOLOGY 82(4):314-317,
April, 1975.

"Emotional responses of women following therapeutic
abortion," by N. E. Adler. AMERICAN JOURNAL
OF ORTHOPSYCHIATRY 45(3):446-454, April,
1975.

"Hormonal parameters following termination of
pregnancy: a guide to the management of threatened
abortion," by D. M. Saunders, et al. AMERICAN
JOURNAL OF OBSTETRICS AND GYNECOLOGY
120(8):1118-1119, December 15, 1974.

"Interruption of the late stages of pregnancy by means
of transcervical amniocentesis and the replacement
of the amniotic fluid," by V. I. Babukhadiia, et al.
PEDIATRIIA AKUSHERSTVO I GINEKOLOGIIA
(5):53-55, September-October, 1974.

"Interruption of pregnancy in Boeck's disease?" (letter),
by K. Wurm. DEUTSCH MEDIZINISCHE WOCHEN-
SCHRIFT 99(46):2374-2375, November 15, 1974.

"Intra-amniotic administration of prostaglandin E2 in
midtrimester abortions," by H. Neifeld. SOUTH
AFRICAN MEDICAL JOURNAL 48(63):2614, December 28, 1974.

"Intra-amniotic administration of prostaglandin in second trimester of pregnancy," by C. Galatis. SOUTH AFRICAN MEDICAL JOURNAL 49(3): 65, January 18, 1975.

"Intraamniotic administration of prostaglandin F2 alpha for therapeutic abortion," by R. Nyberg. ACTA OBSTETRICIA ET GYNECOLOGICA SCANDINAVICA (37):41-46, 1974.

"Mental and social stress of motherhood over 40, with a view to psychiatric indication for interruption of pregnancy," by H. Kind, et al. SCHWEIZERISCHE MEDIZINISCHE WOCHENSCHRIFT 104(35):1221-1224, August 31, 1974.

"The Morgentaler case," by P. N. Coles. CANADIAN MEDICAL ASSOCIATION JOURNAL 113(3):181, August 9, 1975.

"Morgentaler vs. The Queen," by L. E. Rozovsky. DIMENSIONS IN HEALTH SERVICE 52(6):8-9, June, 1975.

"Nurse's attitudes to termination of pregnancy." NURSING FORUM 2(5):6-7, November-December, 1974.

"Opportunities for the application of the prostaglandins in gynecology. Interruption of pregnancy in acute leukosis. Description of a case," by P. Krieglsteiner, et al. MUNCHENER MEDIZINISCHE WOCHENSCHRIFT 117(7):245-248, February 14, 1975.

"The organization and results of a pregnancy termination service in a National Health Service hospital," by M. G. Hull, et al. JOURNAL OF OBSTETRICS AND GYNECOLOGY OF THE BRITISH COMMON-

WEALTH 81(8):577-587, August, 1974.

"Our approach to interruption of pregnancy in a myomatous uterus," by I. Knejzlíková, et al. CESKOSLOVENSKA GYNEKOLOGIE 40(5):353-354, June, 1975.

"Outpatient laparoscopic sterilization with therapeutic abortion versus abortion alone," by J. I. Fishburne, et al. OBSTETRICS AND GYNECOLOGY 45(6):665-668, June, 1975.

"Predicting contraceptive use in postabortion patients," by G. M. Selstad, et al. AMERICAN JOURNAL OF PUBLIC HEALTH 65:708-713, July, 1975.

"Pregnancy interruption in cardiac patients," by A. Barrillon, et al. ARCHIVES DES MALADIES DU COEUR ET DES VAISSEAUX 67(5):555-564, May, 1974.

"Prevention of genetic diseases through prenatal diagnosis," by H. Hübner, et al. GINEKOLOGIA POLASKA 45(11):1313-1323, November, 1974.

"The problem of the medical indication for artificial abortion," by G. Fanconi. MINERVA PEDIATRICA 27(8):455-461, March 10, 1975.

"Prostaglandin F2alpha given by continuous transcervical extra-amniotic infusion combined with intravenous oxytocin infusion for therapeutic termination of mid-trimester pregnancies," by K. W. Waldron, et al. MEDICAL JOURNAL OF AUSTRALIA 1(17):525-527, April 26, 1975.

"Reassessment of systemic administration of prostaglandins for induction of midtrimester abortion,"

by M. Bygdeman, et al. PROSTAGLANDINS
8(2):157-169, October 25, 1974.

"Rh sensitization following abortion," (letter), by
E. P. Reid. CANADIAN MEDICAL ASSOCIATION
JOURNAL 111(11):1182, December 7, 1974.

"Scottish abortion statistics 1974." HEALTH
BULLETIN 33(4):167-181, July, 1975.

"Serotonin, 5-hiaa, total estrogen and pregnanediol
excretion in urine during therapeutic saline abortion," by K. Fuchs, et al. ACTA OBSTETRICIA
ET GYNECOLOGICA SCANDINAVICA 54(2):157-
160, 1975.

"Short-term psychiatric sequelae to therapeutic termination of pregnancy," by B. Lask. BRITISH
JOURNAL OF PSYCHIATRY 126:173-177, February,
1975.

"Sterilization and therapeutic abortion counseling for
the mentally retarded," by C. W. Smiley. ILLI-
NOIS MEDICAL JOURNAL 147(3):291-292, March,
1975.

"Study of reported therapeutic abortions in North Carolina," by E. M. Howell. AMERICAN JOURNAL OF
PUBLIC HEALTH AND THE NATION'S HEALTH
65:480-483, May, 1975.

"Technics for interruption of a second-trimester
pregnancy," by J. H. Ravina, et al. NOUVELLE
PRESSE MEDICALE 3(45):2733-2736, December
28, 1974.

"Termination of pregnancy on psychiatric grounds," by
K. Böhme, et al. DEUTSCHE MEDIZINISCHE WOCH-

ENSCHRIFT 100(16):865-872, April 18, 1975.

"Termination of pregnancy with Utus paste: report of a fatal case," by T. A. Thomas, et al. BRITISH MEDICAL JOURNAL 1(5954):375-376, February 15, 1975.

"Therapeutic abortion," (letter). CANADIAN MEDICAL ASSOCIATION JOURNAL 111(12):1299-1301, December 21, 1974.

"Therapeutic abortion," (letter), by H. Baunemann. CANADIAN MEDICAL ASSOCIATION JOURNAL 112(1):27, January 11, 1975.

"Therapeutic abortion," (letter), by P. G. Coffey. CANADIAN MEDICAL ASSOCIATION JOURNAL 112(3):283, February 8, 1975.

"Therapeutic abortion," (letter), by B. Gibbard. CANADIAN MEDICAL ASSOCIATION JOURNAL 112(1):25, 27, January 11, 1975.

"Therapeutic abortion," (letter), by R. Halliday. CANADIAN MEDICAL ASSOCIATION JOURNAL 113(4):276-278, August 23, 1975.

"Therapeutic abortion," (letter), by A. C. Hayes. CANADIAN MEDICAL ASSOCIATION JOURNAL 112(10):1166, May 17, 1975.

"Therapeutic abortion," (letter), by J. J. Krayenhoff. CANADIAN MEDICAL ASSOCIATION JOURNAL 112(1):25, January 11, 1975.

"Therapeutic abortion," (letter), by J. J. Krayenhoff. CANADIAN MEDICAL ASSOCIATION JOURNAL 112(12):1388, June 21, 1975.

"Therapeutic abortion," (letter), by C. A. Ringrose.
CANADIAN MEDICAL ASSOCIATION JOURNAL
112(1):22, 25, January 11, 1975.

"Therapeutic abortion," (letter), by G. Schneider.
CANADIAN MEDICAN ASSOCIATION JOURNAL
112(9):1045, May 3, 1975.

"Therapeutic abortion," (letter), by W. W. Watters.
CANADIAN MEDICAL ASSOCIATION JOURNAL
112(5):558, March 8, 1975.

"Therapeutic abortion and the minor," by R. F. Gibbs.
JOURNAL OF LEGAL MEDICINE 1(1):36-42, March-
April, 1973.

"Therapeutic abortion by a single extra-amniotic
instillation of prostaglandin f2alpha," by P. Fylling,
et al. ARCHIV FUR GYNAEKOLOGIE 217(2):119-
125, 1974.

"Therapeutic abortion in N. Z. public hospitals," by
W. A. Facer. NURSING FORUM 2(4):12-13, September-October, 1974.

"Therapeutic abortion in N. Z. public hospitals. II," by
W. A. Facer. NURSING FORUM 2(5):8-10, November-
December, 1974.

"Therapeutic abortion with concurrent sterilization: comparison of methods," by M. K. Leong, et al. CAN-
ADIAN MEDICAL ASSOCIATION JOURNAL 111(12):
1327-1329, December 21, 1974.

"The use of F2 alpha prostaglandin for induction of
therapeutic abortion and labor in the 2d trimester
of pregnancy," by G. Scarselli, et al. MINERVA
GINECOLOGICA 26(12):711-716, December, 1974.

THERAPEUTIC ABORTION

"Uneasy lies the head that wears a crown," by J. D.
Wallace. CANADIAN MEDICAL ASSOCIATION
JOURNAL 112(3):344, February 8, 1975.

"United States: therapeutic abortions, 1963 to 1968,"
by C. Tietze. STUDIES IN FAMILY PLANNING
(59):5-7, November, 1970.

"Unwanted pregnancies," by L. E. Mason. CANADIAN
MEDICAL ASSOCIATION JOURNAL 112(2):145-147,
January 25, 1975.

"Unwanted pregnancies," by G. W. Piper. CANADIAN
MEDICAL ASSOCIATION JOURNAL 112(2):145,
January 25, 1975.

"Why admit abortion patients?" (letter), by D. Kerslake.
LANCET 2(7888):1078, November 2, 1974.

THREATENED ABORTION
"Advantages and disadvantages of surgical treatment
in imminent abortions and premature delivery," by
E. Zajacová, et al. BRATISLOVSKE LEKARSKE
LISTY 63(2):189-194, February, 1975.

"Bleeding in early pregnancy investigated by ultra-
sound, plasma progesterone and oestradiol," by
O. Pilroinen, et al. ANNALES CHIRURGIAE ET
GYNAECOLOGIAE FENNIAE 63(6):451-456, 1974.

"Breast gland following artifical termination of early
pregnancy and following threatened and completed
abortion," by F. Glenc. WIADOMOSCI LEKARSKIE
28(7):549-551, April 1, 1975.

"Care by the public health nurse of the patient with
threatened abortion," by K. Katayama, et al.
JAPANESE JOURNAL FOR THE MIDWIFE 29(2):

90-95, February, 1975.

"Characteristics of the functional state of the
myometrium in threatened abortion," by E. F.
Kaplun-Kryzhanovskaia, et al. VOPROSY OKHRANY
MATERINSTVA I DETSTVA 19(11):64-66, November,
1974.

"Chorionic gonadotropin titer and anti-hormone antibodies in the blood in uterine and extrauterine
pregnancy," by Iu. G. Fedorov. AKUSHERSTVO I
GINEKOLOGIIA (Moscow) (9):53-56, September, 1974.

"Clinical use of a beta-mimetic drug in the control of
uterine dynamics," by G. Casati, et al. ANNOLI DI
OSTETRICIA GINECOLOGIA, MEDICINA PERINA-
TALE 94(9-10):587-594, September-October, 1973.

"Comparative assays on chorionic gonadotropin excretion and concentrations of some protein fractions in
cases of threatened abortion," by J. Jakowicki, et al.
GINEKOLOGIA POLASKA 46(1):17-21, January, 1975.

"Complex evaluation of recent threatened pregnancy
with special reference to placental lactogen," by J.
Lukasik, et al. GINEKOLOGIA POLSKA 46(7):777-
781, July, 1975.

"Cytological evaluation of amniotic fluid in threatened
pregnancy," by A. Cekański, et al. WIADOMOSCI
LEKARSKIE 28(16):1375-1380, August 15, 1975.

"The danger of threatened miscarriage and steps to
be taken," by K. Soiva. KATILOLEHTI 80(1):7-16,
January, 1975.

"Diagnosis of threatened abortion using electrohysterography," by A. I. Liubimova, et al. AKUSHERSTVO I

GINEKOLOGIIA (Moscow) 49(4):65-66, April, 1973.

"Diagnostic and prognostic value of bidimentional echography in threatened abortion," by N. Rodriguez. REVISTA CHILENA DE OBSTETRICIA Y GINECOLOGIA 38(5):228-239, 1973.

"Diagnositc and prognostic value of the 'spot' phenomenon and of the colpocystogram in threatened abortion," by E. B. Derankova, et al. AKUSHERSTVO I GINEKOLOGIIA (Moscow) 49(4):46-50, April, 1973.

"Epsilon-aminocaproic acid in the treatment of abortion," by R. Klimek, et al. GINEKOLOGIA POLSKA 46(7):747-750, July, 1975.

"Evaluation of the outcome of pregnancy in threatened abortion by biochemical methods," by O. Karjalainen, et al. ANNAELS CHIRURGIAE ET GYNAECOLOGIAE FENNIAE 63(6):457-464, 1974.

"Experiences with hormonal treatment of imminent abortuses and premature deliveries," by V. Kliment, et al. BRATISLOVSKE LEKARSKE LISTY 63(2):209-213, February, 1975.

"Hysterographic studies in complex treatment of pregnant women with threatened abortion," by T. A. Aivazian. VOPROSY OKHRANY MATERINSTVA I DETSTVA 19(11):67-70, November, 1974.

"Immunological problems connected with pregnancy and therapeutic deductions in case of threatened abortion," by M. Goisis, et al. MINERVA GINECOLOGICA 27(4): 319-328, April, 1975.

"Importance of determining chorionic gonadotropin excretion in the obstetrical and gynecological clinic,"

by A. A. Galochkina. VOPROSY OKHRANY
MATERINSTVA I DETSTVA 18(4):77-80, 1973.

"Importance of hormone assays and high dose HCG,
estrogen and 17-alpha-hydroxyprogesterone treatment in the prevention of threatened abortion due to
endocrine causes," by G. Cubesi, et al. ACTA
EUROPAEA FERTILITATIS 2(3):355-358, September, 1970.

"Inhibition of labour. Symposium by letter," by J.
Hütter, et al. MUENCHENER MEDIZINISCHE
WOCHENSCHRIFT 116(38):689-698, September 20,
1974.

"Isoxsuprine chlorhydrate in the treatment of threatened
abortion," by L. Ballestrin. ARCHIVIO DI OSTETRI-
CIA E GINECOLOGIA 78(1-3):53-66, January-June,
1973.

"Nursing of patients with threatened abortion who are
on forced bedrest," by F. Kuwabara, et al. JAPAN-
ESE JOURNAL FOR THE MIDWIFE 28(6/7):333-335,
June-July, 1974.

"Prediction of fetal outcome in threatened abortion by
maternal serum placental lactogen and alpha fetopro-
tein," by L. Garoff, et al. AMERICAN JOURNAL OF
OBSTETRICS AND GYNECOLOGY 121(2):257-261,
January 15, 1975.

"Prenatal exposure to stilboestrol." MEDICAL JOUR-
NAL OF AUSTRALIA 1(12):373-374, March 22, 1975.

"The prognosis in pregnancy after threatened abortion,"
by P. Jouppila, et al. ANNLES CHIRURGIAE ET
GYNAECOLOGIAE FENNIAE 63(6):439-444, 1974.

"Prognosis in threatened abortion and chorionic hormone levels in the blood," by N. Medoki, et al.
FOLIA ENDOCRINOLOGICA JAPONICA 50(2):
520, February 20, 1974.

"The prognostic value of chorionic-gonadotrophins
in the urine of miscarrying women," by H. Dyková,
et al. CESKOSLOVENSKA GYNEKOLOGIE 40(6):
417-420, July, 1975.

"The prognostic value of human placental lactogen
(HPL) levels in threatened abortion," by M. W.
Gartside, et al. BRITISH JOURNAL OF OBSTE-
TRICS AND GYNECOLOGY 82(4):303-309, April,
1975.

"Prolactin in the blood-serum during physiological and
pathological gravidity," by F. Gzaárek, et al.
CESKOSLOVENSKA GYNEKOLOGIE 40(1):39-40,
February, 1975.

"Results of HPL radioimmunoassay in normal and
pathologic early pregnancy," by G. Hör, et al.
NUCLEAR-MEDIZIN 13(4):371-378, January 31,
1975.

"Results of treatment of threatened abortion with
Partusisten (preparation Th 1165 A)," by A.
Dzioba, et al. WIADOMOSCI LEKARSKIE 28(14):
1193-1196, July 15, 1975.

"Simultaneous determination of blood and urinary HCG
and observation of its daily differences and circadian
rhythm for prevention of abortion," by Y. Abe, et
al. FOLIA ENDOCRINOLOGICA JAPONICA 50(2):
519, February 20, 1974.

"Some problems in the etiology and pathogenesis of

prematurity," by L. V. Sukhopol'skaia. PEDIATRIIA
AKUSHERSTVO I GINEKOLOGIIA (5):33-36, September-October, 1974.

"Study of allylestrenol (Turinal) in pregnancy. II. Clinical observations," by G. Györy, et al. THERAPIA
HUNGARICA 21(3-4):131-133, 1973.

"Therapeutic policies in threatened aboation," by N.
Fujita. JAPANESE JOURNAL FOR THE MIDWIFE
28(9):444-447, September, 1974.

"Ultrasonic diagnosis of miscarriage and early pregnancy complications," by B. Zsolnai, et al. ACTA
CHIRURGICA ACADEMIAE SCIENTIARUM HUNGARICAE
15(4):389-407, 1974.

"Ultrasound in management of clinically diagnosed
threatened abortion," by J. E. Drumm, et al.
BRITISH MEDICAL JOURNAL 02(5968):424, May
24, 1975.

"Urinary oestrone and chorionic gonadotrophin in
threatened abortion," by U. Jarvilehto, et al. ANNALES CHIRURGIAE ET GYNAECOLOGIAE FENNIAE
63(6):445-450, 1974.

"Use of inductothermy of the perirenal region in the
complex treatment of threatened interruption of
pregnancy," by N. M. Suvorova, et al. AKUSHERSTVO I GINEKOLOGIIA (Moscow) (9):48-51, September, 1974.

"Use of intrapelvic novocaine blocks in the overall
treatment of threatened and beginning late abortions and premature labor," by R. I. Il'ina.
VOPROSY OKHRANY MATERINSTVA I DETSTVA
19(5):73-76, May, 1974.

THREATENED ABORTION

"Vaginal adenomatesis and adenocarcinoma in young women after diethylstilbestrol treatment," by G. Vooijs. REVUE MEDICALE DE LIEGE 29(22): 682-687, November 15, 1974.

TOXOPLASMAS
see: Complications

TRANSPLACENTAL HEMORRHAGE
see: Complications

TRIPLOIDY
"Origin of triploidy in human abortuses," by J. Jonasson, et al. HEREDITAS 71(1):166-172, 1972.

"A triploid human abortus due to dispermy," by N. Niikawa, et al. HUMAGENETIK 24(3):261-264, 1974.

TURINAL
"Study of allylestrenol (Turinal) in pregnancy. II. Clinical observations," by G. Györy, et al. THEROPIA HUNGARICA 21(3-4):131-133, 1973.

VETERINARY ABORTIONS
see: Research

YOUTH
"Abortion counselling: focus on adolescent pregnancy," by C. Nadelson. PEDIATRICS 54(6):765-769, December, 1974.

"Attitudes of American teenagers toward abortion," by M. Zelnik, et al. FAMILY PLANNING PERSPECTIVES 7(2):89-91, March-April, 1975.

"Contraception, abortion and veneral disease: teenagers' knowledge and the effect of education [based on con-

ference papers]," by P. A. Reichelt, et al. FAMILY
PLANNING PERSPECTIVES 7:83-88, March-April,
1975.

"Facts about abortion for the teenager," by S. Greenhouse. SCHOOL COUNSELOR 22(5):334-336, May,
1975.

"Medical and social aspects of adolescent pregnancies.
I. Adolescents applying for termination of an illegiti-
mate pregnancy," by O. Widholm, et al. ACTA OB-
STETRICIA ET GYNAECOLOGICA SCANDINAVICA
53(4):347-353, 1974.

"Medical consequences of teenage sexuality," by A. R.
Hinman, et al. NEW YORK STATE JOURNAL OF
MEDICINE 75(9):1439-1442, August, 1975.

"Pregnancy in the single adolescent girl: the role of
cognitive functions," by W. G. Cobliner. JOURNAL
OF YOUTH AND ADOLESCENCE 3(1):17-30, March,
1974.

"A sex information program for sexually active teenagers," by P. A. Reichelt, et al. JOURNAL OF
SCHOOL HEALTH 45(2):100-107, February, 1975.

"Sexual life of young women and girls following interruption," by L. Kovácová, et al. CESKOSLOVENSKA
GYNEKOLOGIE 39(3):218-219, April, 1974.

"Teen-age pregnancies in Denmark, 1940-71," by A.
Braestrup. JOURNAL OF BIOSOCIAL SCIENCE
6(4):741-745, October, 1974.

"Therapeutic abortion and the minor," by R. F. Gibbs.
JOURNAL OF LEGAL MEDICINE 1(1):36-42, March-
April, 1973.

AUTHOR INDEX

Abe, Y., 86
Abramova, L. N., 23
Adachi, A., 54
Adamek, R. J., 13
Adler, N. E., 38
Aivazian, T. A., 47
Alberman, E., 73
Aleem, F. A., 38, 62
Al-Khatib, G. M., 67
Alpern, D. M., 6, 7
Als, O., 97
Amerio, A., 71
Amy, J. J., 29
Anderson, J., 17, 19, 68, 100
Anderson, M. F., 42
Andrashko, V. V., 70
Angelov, A. K., 64
Ashworth, H. W., 80
Atienza, M. F., 60
Atkinson, G. M., 63

Babukhadiia, V. I., 27, 51
Badyva, O. S., 48
Bailey, C. D., 96
Balin, H., 74
Ballestrin, L., 55
Barcus, N. B., 93
Barrillon, A., 71
Bartlett, R. H., 58

Bastert, G., 15
Bauman, R. E., 85
Baunemann, H., 92
Baxter, S. J., 47
Beaton-Mamak, M., 22
Beazley, J. M., 54
Becker, W., 63
Belton, M., 57
Benjamin, M. R., 64
Berg, J., 63
Berger, C. A., 36
Berger, G. S., 68
Bhakthavathsalan, A., 38
Bieniarz, J., 37
Blaser, A., 77
Bloshanskii, Iu. M., 29
Blum, M., 50
Blum, V., 70
Blumberg, B. D., 77
Bodor, G., 84
Bohm, W., 23
Bohme, K., 91
Bohn, H., 47
Bolis, P. F., 17
Bolognese, R. J., 1
Borgen, H. C., 39
Bostofte, E., 28
Boudjemaa, S., 98
Boue, A., 24
Boue, J., 81
Bourg, R., 25, 56

Bowman, E., 84
Bracken, M. B., 33
Braestrup, A., 44, 90
Brekke, B., 44
Brennan, W. C., 8, 86
Brenner, W. E., 53, 60
Briggs, M. H., 32
Brody, B. A., 1
Brosseau, B. L. P., 25
Broustet, A., 32
Brundtland, G. H., 44
Buczek, B., 78
Bunson, M., 64
Burchell, R. C., 73
Burnett, I. S., 40
Burnett, L. S., 53, 90
Butt, R., 10, 94
Bygdeman, M., 49, 50, 79

Cantu, J. M., 18
Carey-Smith, K. A., 84
Carroll, W., 82
Carter, M. E., 43
Casati, G., 26
Casey, R., 36
Castelazo, A. L., 31, 48, 97
Castelli, J., 22, 57
Cekański, A., 32
Chakravarty, B. N., 15
Chernukha, E. A., 18, 96
Chisholm, N., 80
Chladek, D. W., 21
Chowdhury, N. N., 15
Cittadini, E., 38
Clark, F. A., 32
Clark, M., 64, 80
Clark, S. W., 89

Clarke, C. A., 72
Clayman, C. B., 76
Clayson, D., 95
Cobliner, W. S., 71
Coffey, P. G., 92
Cohen, J., 25
Coles, P. N., 63
Collins, L. D., 56
Coltart, T. M., 54
Coman-Urrutia, A., 80
Compton, P. A., 79
Connon, A. F., 9
Corson, S. L., 46, 52, 97
Craft, I., 52
Craig, J. M., 69
Cramer, D. V., 58
Creighton, H., 56, 63
Csapo, A. I., 37, 90
Cubesi, G., 48
Culliton, B. J., 7, 12, 17, 36, 41
Cumming, J. B., Jr., 82
Cunanan, R. G., Jr., 26
Cushner, I. M., 10

Daling, J. R., 49
Dauber, B., 73
David, H. P., 1, 6
Davis, C., 9
Davis, C. D., 41
Dawson, F. L., 61
Day, C. A., 44
DeBolt, M., 14
Decker, R., 10
DeDanois, V., 1
Deedy, J., 24
Degnan, D., 56
Dehner, L. P., 32
Delgado, R., 68

Dellums, R. V., 85
Delson, B., 69
Denis, F., 18
Denlinger, D. L., 51
Dennis, S. M., 69
Derankova, E. B., 34
Devereux, G., 2
Devlin, W., 82
Diakov, L., 64
Diamond, J., 8, 94
DiIanni, A., 54
Dillon, T. F., 37
Diner, M. C., 89
Dingfelder, J. R., 79
Dix, C., 20
Doerr, E., 29
Doherty, D., 63
Donceel, J., 100
Doring, G. K., 44
Doyle, J., 90
Dramplan, T. S., 87
Drinan, R., 13, 75
Drumm, J. E., 95
Drut, R., 70
DuBois, R., 55
DuChesne, A., 41
Duenhoelter, J. H., 28
Dunea, G., 23
Dunn, H. P., 5
Dunne, H. W., 16
Durbin, K., 51
Durham, P. J., 50
Dykova, H., 73
Dytrych, Z., 23
Dzhurov, A., 69
Dzioba, A., 81

Eastman, L. E., 2
Edstrom, K., 25
Edwards, T. K., 99

Egorova, A. P., 88
Eickhoff, L. F., 7
Eklund, J., 81
Elder, R. G., 18
Embrey, M. P., 76
Engel, R., 82
Erickson, N. S., 100

Facer, W. A., 93
Fanconi, G., 73
Faulkner, L. C., 2
Fazziola, P., 64
Fedorov, Iu. G., 24
Ferris, P., 78
Field, B., 90
Finkbine, S., 14
Finnis, J., 2
Fishburne, J. I., 68
Fisher, D. W., 100
Fisher, P., 82
Fite, G. L., 98
Fleming, A., 2
Fletcher, J., 8, 10, 42
Floyd, M. K., 2
Fox, R., 21
Francis, T., 95
Fraser-Smith, A. C., 58
Frei, U., 94
Freire-Maia, N., 15
Fried, K., 41
Friedenberg, Z., 40
Friedman, C. M., 33
Fuchs, K., 85
Fujita, N., 93
Fukalova, S., 77
Fylling, P., 93

Gabor, T., 16
Galatis, C., 52
Gaisis, M., 47

Galochkina, A. A., 48
Gardner, R. F., 2
Garoff, L., 71
Gaslonde, S., 33
Gemming, J. S., 5
Georgiev, S., 85
Ghosh, B., 97
Gibbard, B., 92
Gibbs, C. E., 56
Gibbs, R. F., 26, 93
Gillespie, A., 76
Gilmour, N. J., 97
Gilsenan, T., 22
Glants, S. A., 95
Glenc, F., 21, 49, 85
Gloor, P. A., 88
Goldsmith, S., 35
Goodhart, C. B., 12
Goodnight, L., 14
Gordon, M., 74
Gortside, M. W., 74
Gottlieb, J., 45
Gould, D., 64, 65
Greene, J. W., Jr., 43
Greenhalf, J. O., 29
Greenhouse, S., 41
Greer, B. E., 72
Gromova, T. I., 23
Grones, F., 93
Grunert, E., 70
Grunfeld, B., 65
Guerrero, R., 87
Gurtovoi, B. L., 96
Gusdon, J. P., Jr., 28
Guttmacher, A. F., 13
Gyory, G., 88, 89
Gzaarek, F., 74

Halliday, R., 92
Hanid, T. K., 39

Hardin, G., 3, 40
Hare, R. M., 6
Harlap, S., 55
Harris, H., 3
Harris, J., 55
Harrod, H., 99
Hart, D. S., 42
Hartmann, H., 66
Hawkins, D. F., 58
Hayes, A. C., 92
Hecht, F., 69
Hellegers, A. E., 66
Hempel, V., 66
Henner, H., 52
Herrera, M., 28, 72, 84
Hill, I. W., 89
Hillier, K., 75
Hinman, A. R., 59
Hinton, M., 82, 83
Hirsh, H. L., 56
Hodgson, J. E., 29, 74
Holbek, S., 58
Hollmann, A., 79
Holst, P. J., 53
Holt, P. E., 46
Holzer, J. F., 17
Hor, G., 80
Horan, D. J., 6
Howell, E. M., 89
Hubner, H., 72
Hughes, G., 100
Hughes, K. L., 57
Hull, M. G., 67, 68
Humber, J., 21
Hume, K., 9
Hunter, M. E., 17
Huntingford, P. J., 101
Huter, J., 51

Ichikawa, J., 26

Iffy, L., 12
Il'lina, R. I., 96
Ignelfinger, F. J., 36
Introcaso, D. A., 5

Jackson, S. H., 19
Jacobsson, L., 11, 18, 77, 87
Jaggar, A., 8
Jakovljevic, D., 87
Jakowicki, J., 27
James, W. H., 29
Janerich, D. T., 70
Janny, G., 54
Jarvilehto, U., 96
Jayaraman, S., 37
Jaynes, R. V., 36
Jegede, S. A., 74
Jimenez, C. T., 48
Joling, R. J., 8
Jonasson, J., 67
Jones, J. M., 79
Jones, J. R., 53
Jones, R. W., 84
Josey, A., 10
Joshi, L., 29
Jouppila, P., 65, 73
Junge, W. D., 20
Jurukovski, N. J., 86

Kagan, J., 64
Kahan, R. S., 37
Kajanoja, P., 76
Kajii, T., 24
Kalinski, R., 23
Kangas, J., 35
Kaplun-Kryzhanovskaia, E. F., 23
Karim, S. M., 22, 62, 91
Karjalainen, O., 40

Karlsson, Y., 90
Kase, N., 20
Katayama, K., 21
Kelly, M., 19
Kennedy, E. M., 16
Kerenyi, T. D., 98
Kerslake, D., 100
Kharalanbiev, K., 47
Khudr, G., 32
Kind, H., 60
King, T. M., 89
Kirchhoff, H., 31
Kirk, J., 42
Klaus, H., 59
Kleiner, G. J., 26
Klimek, R., 39
Kliment, V., 40
Kloosterman, G. J., 34
Kluge, E. W., 3
Knejzlikova, I., 67
Knight, B., 91
Koeffler, H., 27
Kohl, M., 3
Kohoutek, F., 78
Kok, C. W., 95
Komisar, L., 83
Komlos, L., 34
Kononova, E. S., 40
Kopecky, P., 76
Korner, H., 94
Kosasa, T. S., 78
Koslin, M. G., 15
Kovacova, L., 85
Kramer, M. J., 56
Krauss, E., 26
Krayenhoff, J. J., 92
Krieglsteiner, P., 67
Krishna, U. R., 76
Krzysztoporski, S., 72
Kulazenko, V. P., 24, 64, 68

Kundsin, R. B., 94
Kurogi, H., 84
Kuwabara, F., 65

Lachance, P., 21
Lahmann, H., 26
Landesman, R., 78
Lane, T., 70
Lange, A. P., 27
Langford, E. V., 55
Lappe, M., 8
Lask, B., 85
Lau, I. F., 54, 61, 75
Lauersen, N. H., 27, 61, 62, 99
Lauritsen, J. G., 58, 86, 88
Lawrence, M., 48
Lazarevski, M., 22
Lazio, L., 52
Lee, F., 99
Leibman, T., 62
Lejeune, J., 19
LeLirzin, R., 18
Lenta, C., 9
Leong, M. K., 93
Lerner, L. J., 17
Lewin, N., 6
Liljestrom, R., 19
Lincoln, R., 26, 51
Lindsay, A., 66
Lippert, T. H., 49
Lischke, J. H., 23
Littlewood, B. M., 11
Liu, D. T., 49
Liubimova, A. I., 34, 58
Llewellyn-Jones, D., 62
Lockwood, S., 21
Loomis, D.,.9, 14, 46
Loshak, D., 100

Lowry, P. L., 79
Lucire, Y., 41
Luck, W., 19
Lukasik, J., 28
Luker, K., 3
Luscutoff, S. A., 16
Lynch, R. N., 64
Lysnes, M., 23

MacDonald, P. C., 51
Macdonald, R. R., 35
MacDonald, S., 59
MacGregor, C., 19
Macleod, N. S., 57
Mackenzie, I. Z., 76, 86
Maher, L. T., 83
Mahoney, M. J., 66
Maizel', E. P., 81, 82
Malaviya, B., 49
Manabe, Y., 51
Mandel, M. D., 31
Mankekar, K., 3
Marburger, H., 7
Martorella, L. A., 71
Marty, F., 74
Mason, L. E., 95
Mason, R. W., 42
Matthews, J., 32
Mattila, M. A., 34
Mauriceau, A. M., 3
May, T., 82
Mazorchuk, B. F., 30
Mazur, D. P., 86
McConnell, H. D., 79
McCormack, E., 43
McCormick, E. P., 3
McCormick, R., 57
McCormick, T. R., 39
McEllhenney, J. G., 3
McHugh, H., 68

McKernan, M. F., Jr., 28
McLaren, H. C., 6
McMunn, R., 20
Medoki, N., 73
Menudier, H., 18
Michna, S. W., 55
Millar, P. G., 61
Miller, R. B., 65
Miller, W. B., 77
Millet, V. G., 70
Minasova, G. S., 38
Minottur, J., 60
Mladenovic, D., 49
Moberg, P., 44
Molina, R., 41
Monreal, T., 7
Morais, A., 45
Motavkina, N. S., 82
Muggeridge, M., 99
Murray, C. P., 58
Mydans, S., 99

Nadelson, C., 9
Nathanson, B. N., 87
Naylor, A. F., 84
Neifeld, H., 52
Newman, S. H., 13
Newton, L., 46
Nielsen, J. B., 35
Nielsen, K. R., 75
Niikawa, N., 94
Nottage, B. J., 81
Novak, M., 33
Nummi, S., 91
Nyberg, R., 52

Obel, E. B., 76
Odarenko, I. N., 88
Oggioni, G., 7

O'Hare, J., 10
O'Meara, J., 10
O'Neill, P. T., 41
Op de Coul, A. A., 22
Ordóñez, B. R., 39
O'Rourke, K., 81
Orth, H. F., 80
Owen, J. A., Jr., 5

Pable, M., 68
Papaevangelou, G., 37
Pasquali, F., 24
Patey, E. H., 59
Penev, I., 97
Perkins, B. B., 3
Peterson, W. F., 31
Philippe, P., 43
Phillips, A., 100
Phillipson, D., 63, 89
Piiroinen, O., 20
Pilpel, H. F., 42
Piper, G. W., 95
Pogonowska, M., 8
Pogorelova, T. N., 16
Pohánka, O., 37, 79
Polchanova, S. L., 46
Polishuk, W. Z., 60
Popoff, D., 99
Potter, R. G., 28
Potts, M., 14, 19
Prado-Vertiz, A., 72
Prescott, J. W., 13
Pretorius, P. S., 43
Price, N., 14
Pulkkinen, M. O., 33

Raij, K., 31
Rani, K., 32
Rapp, M. S., 30
Rashke, R., 12, 79, 84

Ravina, J. H., 90
Records, J. W., 44
Reed, D. E., 27
Reeder, A., 11
Rees, K. J., 57
Regan, W. A., 73
Reichelt, P. A., 30, 85
Reid, E. P., 81
Reinmoeller-Schreck, T., 11
Reinsdorf, W., 66
Rerzi, M., 47
Ressequie, L. J., 72
Reyniak, J. V., 39
Rezal, N., 86
Rice, C., 82
Rieger, H. J., 14, **30,** 98
Riga, P., 57
Ringrose, C. A., 92
Risk, A., 83
Rivet, M., 35
Roberts, G., 50
Roberts, J. J., 99
Robertson, J. A., 60
Robinson, M., 59
Rodman, H., 14
Rodríguez, N., 34
Rogers, A. F., 23
Roghmann, K. J., 47
Roht, L. H., 49
Romero-Salinas, G., 38
Rosenberg, P., 62
Rosoff, J. I., 54
Roussel, C., 45
Rozovsky, L. E., 63
Rudinaw, J., 43
Russell, M., 100
Ryan, K. J., 57
Ryzhova, R. K., 31

Sadovsky, E., 96
Sahlin, J., 12
Saier, F., 42
Sairam, M. R., 91
Saksena, S. K., 75
Salling, A. L., 10, 46
Salomy, M., 62
Santa Rosa, C. A., 55
Sasaki, A., 89
Saunders, D. M., 45
Savi, M., 69
Scarselli, G., 96
Schneider, G. T., 11, 93
Schooyans, M., 18
Schulte, E. J., 81, 90
Schultz, S., 27, 94
Schwartz, H., 100
Schwartz, M., 82
Sclare, A. B., 91
Seager, C. P., 80
Selstad, G. M., 71
Sen, P. K., 67
Serb, A., 17
Shakhbazov, A. S., 22
Shakhov, A. G., 39
Shanklin, D. R., 55
Shapiro, A. G., 40
Sharma, S. D., 35
Shaw, R., 100
Shearman, R. P., 38
Sherain, H., 19
Sherman, D. H., 83
Sherman, F., 10
Shkrob, O. S., 34
Shoemaker, S., 74
Shorosheva, T. G., 87
Short, R., 94
Shurlygina, A. V., 45
Siefert, H., 45
Silverman, E. M., 5

Silverstein, E., 43
Sim, W. L., 9
Simmons, N. A., 91
Simms, M., 12, 61, 63, 100
Simonovits, I., 47
Singer, A., 50
Sjovall, H., 98
Sloane, B. R., 4
Smid, I., 34
Smiley, C. W., 88
Smith, A. M., 82
Smith, A. W., 57
Smith, I. D., 25
Smith, T., 54
Snyder, E. L., 48
Soiva, K., 33
Sompolinsky, D., 50
Spalding, D., 15
Spence, A. A., 88
Spiazzi, R., 73
Stampar, D., 31
Starer, H. R., 4
Stegane, I., 64
Steinhoff, P. G., 71
Steinem, G., 78
Stengel, E. B., 8
Stepanova, N. A., 70
Stephenson, B., 13
Sterner, R., 13, 66, 99
Stone, M., 40
Stone, S. V., Jr., 60
Stosiek, U., 45
Stringer, J., 98
Stubblefield, P. G., 15
Sugimura, T., 54
Sukhopol'skaia, L. V., 87
Sutermeister, H. M., 45
Suvorova, N. M., 96

Swaffield, L., 14
Swan, G. S., 13
Symes, J., 11
Szontagh, F. E., 51

Tadjebakhche, H., 70
Tarnesby, H. P., 56
Taylor, A., 21
Taylor, D. J., 21
Teo, W. D. H., 11
Than, G. N., 85
Thomas, T. A., 91
Tietze, C., 31, 37, 41, 95
Trebicka-Kwiatkowska, B., 29
Trick, K. L., 77
Truskett, I. D., 9
Tweedie, J., 68

Valenzuela, R. G., 71
Van Der Tak, 4
Van Royen, E. A., 46
Vaux, K., 16
Vekovic, B., 69
Velle, W., 49
Volk, H., 43
von Feldt, E., 25
von Koskull, H., 50
Vooijs, G., 97
Vujcich, J., 83

Wagman, H., 53
Waldron, K. W., 75
Walker, S. M., 78
Wallace, J. D., 95
Walsh, D., 59
Waltman, R., 37
Walts, L. F., 66
Wara, D. W., 42

Warwick, D. P., 63
Waterson, N., 16
Watters, W. W., 93
Wax, J., 9
Way, S., 91
Wecht, C. H., 28
Weinberg, P. C., 53
Weinstock, E., 56
Weiss, P. H., 98
Wenkart, A., 5
Wentz, A. C., 61
Werner, R., 12
Whitehouse, W. L., 97
Widholm, O., 59, 85
Wiechell, H., 62
Wiese, J., 50
Wilkins, R. G., 7
Wilkinson, M., 19
Willems, J. J., 97
Williams, S. J., 38
Willke, J., 82
Wiśniewski, L., 32
Wittmann, R., 15
Wohl, L. C., 101
Wolleat, P. L., 11
Wong, T. C., 39
Wood, C., 9
Wright, N. H., 80
Wurm, K., 52

Ylikorkala, O., 74

Zahn, V., 75
Zajacova, E., 16
Zasowska, M. A. A., 44
Zelnik, M., 18
Zsolnai, B., 94
Zubareva, L. P., 89